MAY 11 2009

|AUG 1 8 2014

Where to Find Your Arab-American or Jewish

DATE DUE		

Where to Find Your Arab-American or Jewish Genealogy Records

✦

Also: Mediterranean, Assyrian, Iranian, Greek & Armenian

Anne Hart

ASJA Press
New York Lincoln Shanghai

Where to Find Your Arab-American or Jewish Genealogy Records
Also: Mediterranean, Assyrian, Iranian, Greek & Armenian

Copyright © 2005 by Anne Hart

All rights reserved. No part of this book may be used or reproduced by any means, graphic, electronic, or mechanical, including photocopying, recording, taping or by any information storage retrieval system without the written permission of the publisher except in the case of brief quotations embodied in critical articles and reviews.

ASJA Press
an imprint of iUniverse, Inc.

iUniverse books may be ordered through booksellers or by contacting:

iUniverse
2021 Pine Lake Road, Suite 100
Lincoln, NE 68512
www.iuniverse.com
1-800-Authors (1-800-288-4677)

ISBN-13: 978-0-595-37325-3
ISBN-10: 0-595-37325-9

Printed in the United States of America

Contents

CHAPTER 1	Where to Find Your Arab-American or Jewish Genealogy Records:	1

Also: Mediterranean, Assyrian, Iranian, Greek & Armenian

CHAPTER 2	Translating Names	5
CHAPTER 3	Researching Assyrian Genealogy	8
CHAPTER 4	How to Translate and Locate without Surnames	13
CHAPTER 5	Armenian Genealogy	16
CHAPTER 6	Greek Family History	22
CHAPTER 7	Polish Jewish Genealogy	25
CHAPTER 8	Ashkenazim, Sephardim, and Mizrahim	38
CHAPTER 9	Tracing the Female and Male Lineages:	41
CHAPTER 10	Merging a Mosaic of Jewish Communities by DNA	96
CHAPTER 11	Molecular Revolution	115
CHAPTER 12	What Are Your Genes Doing In That Holding Tank?	119
CHAPTER 13	The Cohen Modal Haplotype and the Armenian Modal Haplotype	125
CHAPTER 14	DNA of the Levites	127
CHAPTER 15	Life Story Genealogy: Writing and Marketing People's Life Story Highlights	129

CHAPTER 16	Personalizing Ethnic Family History Records with DNA Testing	132
CHAPTER 17	The Phenomics Revolution: DNA-Driven Genealogy	143
CHAPTER 18	Molecular Genealogy & DNA Testing Firms	155
CHAPTER 19	What is DNA? Should Genealogists Take an Interest?	157
CHAPTER 20	How to Interview for Intergenerational Writing	160
CHAPTER 21	Oral History/Personal History	166
CHAPTER 22	Does Writing Your Life Story Affect Your Memory?	179
CHAPTER 23	Diaries and DNA Equal Family History Evidence	184
CHAPTER 24	Hidden Records & Directories	191
CHAPTER 25	Understanding your Results: Ethnic Origin	194
CHAPTER 26	Managing a Genetic Genealogy Project: Participants with Poor Documentation	198
APPENDIX A	Directory of DNA-Testing Companies	207
APPENDIX B	Ethnic Genealogy Web Sites	209
APPENDIX C	Bibliographies	215
APPENDIX D	Permissions	223
APPENDIX E	List of Book by Anne Hart	225
About the Author		231
Index		233

1

Where to Find Your Arab-American or Jewish Genealogy Records:

✦

Also: Mediterranean, Assyrian, Iranian, Greek & Armenian

Are you a Christian or Moslem person from the Eastern Mediterranean, Iran, Armenia, Turkey, Greece, Iraq, or Central Asia? Or are you or your clients Jewish from Poland, Lithuania, Latvia, Estonia, the Balkans, and/or North Africa—Ashkenazim, Sephardim, or Mizrahi? Genealogy—family history research—opens portals to the artistic, cultural, religious, social, historical, and economic environment in which a particular item was designed and brought forth, from people to their icons. Genealogy is cultural geography as well as a history and ethnography of human genes.

Finding Arab-American, Iranian, Jewish, Greek, Turkish, Mediterranean, or various Middle Eastern, Levantine, and West Asian family history records usually require navigating through hidden archives. Here's how to begin your search.

When you can't find a surname, or there are no records, or you don't know whether the birth, marriage, tax, property, immigration, or other records were in Russian, Polish, Arabic, Farsi, Greek, Turkish, Judeo-Spanish, German, Czech, Lithuanian, or Yiddish, where and how do you begin your search? If no one recorded a woman's maiden name, how do you find her on a marriage certificate, school record, or other document in archives in a country you never expected in a language you never knew she was recorded? Do you begin with military records of conscripted males or religious school documents in any of the religions of your ancestors or family history research clients?

To start your search, begin with memorabilia and photos or keepsakes and keepsake albums. Look at ethnic objects, books, letters, postcards, and diaries, along with the census or other genealogy records. Genealogy allows you to view a juxtaposition of demography with memorabilia and ethnic or religious items. Learn how to research your own group and show others about the life of the people you choose to study, their history and design.

That's why running a teen (or other age group) genealogy camp is fun, especially in researching the land of your ancestors—or any other location that you want to emphasize to study ethnic history along with genealogy. Your family history is in your genetic signature as well as in records and oral traditions.

How do you start to search and trace your Arab American, Armenian, Assyrian, Iranian, Greek, Levantine, Jewish, or eastern Mediterranean genealogy? The Family History Library (Salt Lake City, UT) has a catalog that can give you rewarding and rich research ideas. So if it's the former Ottoman Empire you want to emphasize, or how the world of antiquity blends into your relatively modern genealogy, first check the Family History Library catalog (Salt Lake City, UT) for books, microfilms, civil registration, localities and jurisdictions.

Then search the Ottoman Census and Population Registers by country named in Turkish the Nüfus Defter. Check the online library catalog at Bogaziçi University (a.k.a. the University of the Bosphorus). See http://www.geog.port.ac.uk/hist-bound/country_rep/ottoman.htm. Also check out the flyer: http://www.hanover.edu/haq_center/Bogazici-Flyer.html

Records are found in the Ottoman Census archives in Turkey pertaining to tax collection during the Ottoman rule. Moslems weren't taxed. Before 1881, each census focused on tabulating male names to find Moslem men to conscript into the military service and non-Moslem men to pay personal tax. Search records according to the religion and ethnic group. Start your search with the list of countries under the Ottomans and pick your ancestor's homeland.

Jews from Egypt, Turkey and Syria

Egypt was under the former Ottoman Empire. Therefore, if you are a Jew from Egypt (regardless of whether your family members are Ashkenazim, Sepharadim, or Mizrahi), check out The Historical Society Of Jews From Egypt. Their Web site is at: http://hsje.org/. This site is designed to gather, and provide historical and current information on the Jews From Egypt, one of the most ancient established societies in the world."

According to their Web site, "We will attempt to cover the period from Joseph Saadia el Fayoumi (Saadia Gaon) to the present day." The Web site notes that, "This organization shall be known as Historical Society of Jews from Egypt, and not of Egypt or of Egyptian Jews, but from Egypt for the purpose will be to include all our co-religionists whose lineage have sojourned in the Jewish Communities of Egypt."

Contact them if you had relatives who lived in the Jewish communities of Egypt. Some Romanian and Greek Jews also lived in the Jewish communities of Egypt and some Ashkenazim also. According to their Web site, "The aims of this society are to preserve, maintain, coordinate the implementation, and to convey our rich heritage to our children and grand children's, using all educational means at our disposal to bring into being the necessary foundations."

Referring to Romania and in particular, Bessarabia, some Romanian Jews migrated to Palestine in the Ottoman era. This migration included Ashkenazim and Sephardim. Numerous Sephardim and Mizrahi had migrated to Palestine in earlier times and a smaller number of Ashkenazim. Ethnic genealogy journals are good beginning sources. Consult a Jewish genealogy journal such as Avotaynu, usually found in university and family history libraries. The publication's Web site is at: http://www.avotaynu.com/.

According to the Jews of Egypt Web site at: http://www.us-israel.org/jsource/anti-semitism/egjews.html, "In 1979, the Egyptian Jewish community became the first in the Arab world to establish official contact with Israel. Israel now has an embassy in Cairo and a consulate general in Alexandria. At present, the few remaining Jews are free to practice Judaism without any restrictions or harassment. Shaar Hashamayim is the only functioning synagogue in Cairo. Of the many synagogues in Alexandria only the Eliahu Hanabi is open for worship.[4]" The source of this information on their Web site is listed as Jewish Communities of the World.

According to researcher, Kahlile Mehr, "For searching the Ottoman period in most countries under the former Ottoman Empire, the researcher would have to read Turkish in Arabic script. The Family History library was able to film some Christian church records in Israel during the 1980s. But for most of the populace, the commonly known genealogical sources of the West simply do not exist. The best known source is the Nufus registers."

All the articles and information on Bulgaria, Macedonia, and Croatia written by former staff writer for the Family History Library, Salt Lake City, UT, Khalile Mehr, are copyrighted by The Family History Library.

"The Family History Library filmed the Nufus registers in the Israeli State Archives for Israel, parts of Jordan and Egypt. A description of these can be found in the catalog at www.familysearch.org.

"If you're searching various ethnic groups in Bessarabia, it was not part of Romania except during the period between World War I and II. It was historically part of the Ottoman and then the Russian Empire. Today, it is Moldova."

There was a time in the late 18th century and early 19th century when Bessarabia fell out of the Ottoman Empire and became under the rule of the Russians. At that time a large immigration of German Christians and German Jews as well as Jews from Poland, Ukraine, Belarus, and surrounding areas flocked to Bessarabia. So you have a community of Protestant Germans in Bessarabia along with German and Polish Jews. The immigration took place as soon as Bessarabia fell into Russian hands and out of Ottoman hands for that period of time.

You can trace names from Poland to Romania. Names such as Herkowicz, where the spelling changes to Herkowitz and Herschkowitz. Later in some cases, the name may take on a Romanian spelling as in the surname Herkovici. The name Berkowitz may change to Berkovici as some Romanian names end in 'vici.' Countries change names. Bessarabia, once a place with its own name rather than a province in a country, then becomes an area within a country, and finally today, falling in the borders of Moldova and Romania.

2

Translating Names

The name Eshkenazi, (Ashkenazi) is usually found as a Syrian-Jewish and Turkish-Jewish name, usually as a Jewish surname from Aleppo, Syria, but sometimes also found in the Balkans, including Greece, Turkey, Bulgaria, and the former Yugoslavia (and of course, in Israel and in the USA and Canada, Latin America, and Europe in current times.) It's a Mizrahi name that may signify at one time an Ashkenazim, a Jewish person from Northern or Eastern Europe migrated to Aleppo, Syria, or Turkey. The name is found almost exclusively in Sephardic and Mizrahi Jews. Interestingly, the surname, Eshkenazi doesn't appear frequently in Ashkenazim.

When you translate names, remember not to skip generations. Each generation is a vital link in countries where thousands have the same name. Check out the Middle EastGenWeb Project at: http://www.rootsweb.com/~mdeastgw/index.html.

◆   ◆   ◆

Arab American Surnames

Some religious names are used by Moslems and Christians. Christian European names are translated into Arabic in Arabic-speaking countries. For example, in Lebanon, Peter becomes Boutros and George becomes Girgis or Abdul Messikh, meaning servant of the Messiah (Christ). Shammout (strong), Deeb (wolf), or Dib (bear). Nissim (miracles) is used by Jewish Levantines, and Adam is used by Jewish, Christian, and Moslem families.

Women had the choice of taking their husband's surnames or keeping their maiden names. Neutral names, used by Moslems, Jews, and Christians such as Ibrahim (Abraham) or Yusef (Joseph) came from the Old Testament. In Lebanon, Christians often used neutral names such as Tewfik (fortunate).

Arabic-speaking and Turkic-speaking countries didn't use surnames until after the end of the Ottoman Empire. Then in Lebanon and Syria many Christians took as their surnames European or Biblical first male names such as the Arabic versions of George, Jacob, Thomas, and Peter which were in Arabic: Girgis, Yacoub, Toumas, and Boutros. Others took popular surnames describing their occupations such as Haddad meaning 'smith.'

After 1928 in Turkey, but not in any of the other Middle Eastern nations, a modified Latin alphabet replaced Arabic script. Four years later (1932) the Turkish Linguistic Society simplified the language to unify the people. Surnames were required in 1934 and, old titles indicating professions and classes were dropped. (See "Turkey" Web site at: http://www.kusadasitravel.com/turkey.html.)

In Middle Eastern countries under the former Ottoman Empire, such as Lebanon/Syria, each child was given a first name but most people in the Middle East had no surname until 1932. Also the father's given name was given as a middle name such as Yusef Girgis, meaning Yusef (Joseph), son of George. It came in handy in the days before surnames were required. Now it's used as a middle name.

Many Syrian and Lebanese families, particularly Christians, after 1932 took similar names such as Peter Jacobs or George Thomas. The name 'Thomas' in Lebanon is spelled in translation as either Touma or Toumas. Many Assyrian males in Northern Iraq took the popular name Sargon, an ancient king.

When surnames in Lebanon became a requirement, you have very popular names such as Peter George Khoury in America being Boutros Girgis Khouri in Lebanon or Syria when translated into Arabic. In the Levant, daughters have a first name and their father's given name meaning "daughter of Yusef" "'bint' Yusef" where bint and binti means 'daughter.'

Outside the home, females would be called with the proper respect "daughter of Yusef or "Bint Yusef." Inside the home to immediate family, a female would be known by her first name, which could be Ayah. She would be registered as Ayah Yusef. She'd be known by a first name, Ayah and a surname, Yusef. Translated into English at Ellis Island, it could have become Aya Joseph.

When surnames became a requirement, many included professions or place names, especially Halaby (from Aleppo) or Antaky (from Antioch). The largest Lebanese community in America is in Dearborn, Michigan.

In Lebanon, most names were Christian prior to 1870, and the Christian names could also be European, especially Greek names like Petros (Peter) which later becomes Boutros in Arabic. If you're searching Assyrians, check out the

Assyrian Nation Communities Web site at: http://www.assyriannation.com/communities/index.php.

3

Researching Assyrian Genealogy

Assyrian Presbyterian Genealogy Records Research

According to the Public Services and Outreach division of the Presbyterian Historical Society, while the Presbyterian Church sent missionaries to the Middle East, materials at the Presbyterian Historical Society document their activities there and do not contain any information about individuals from the Middle East who immigrated to the United States. To get an idea of the types of materials at the Presbyterian Historical Society useful for genealogists, review the following sections of their website at:
http://www.history.pcusa.org/famhist/ or http://www.history.pcusa.org/collect/. This second page also provides links to their on-line finding aids, http://www.history.pcusa.org/finding/index.html, and catalog, CALVIN, http://www.history.pcusa.org/dbtw-wpd/WebOPACmenu.htm.
Search each to see what they might have for your area of interest.

Records of individual congregations are the main resource for family history research at the society. There are no centralized denominational registers of church memberships, baptisms, or marriages; nor is there a comprehensive index to the thousands of family names included in the records in our holdings.

To start a search, it is essential to know both the location (city and state) and the full and correct name of the congregation associated with the individual you are researching. They do not have lists of churches by township, city, or county, or street name cross indexes.

Research genealogy records of members of the Assyrian Presbyterian Church in the US or in Iraq and Iran. Search Assyrian colonies in various US cities for genealogy records related to the Presbyterian Church.

If you are searching Assyrian records, and your family belonged to the Presbyterian Church, check out the Presbyterian Church Historical Society at: http://history.pcusa.org/finding/phs 379.xml - scopecontent where you can find book titles and/or records such as the Assyrian and National Church History, volumes

1 and 2. Look up Isaac B. Moorhatch (1880–) Papers, 1938, Finding Aid to Record Group 379, © Presbyterian Historical Society, Philadelphia, PA 19147.

From the early 20th century, many Assyrians immigrating to the US joined the Presbyterian church. This is due to the missionaries in Persia and Iraq in the early 20th century. For example, In 1910 Isaac Moorhatch established the Assyrian Presbyterian Church of Gary, Indiana.

In 1923 he arrived in Philadelphia, where the Assyrian colony asked him to serve as their pastor. After ordination, he took charge of the Persian/Assyrian Presbyterian Mission. He served this mission until retirement in 1950.

So your first step is to find out where the Assyrian colonies were in the US. Was one of your relatives a missionary in a country then under the former Ottoman Empire?

Isaac Moorhatch was born in Urumia, Persia, the son of Presbyterian missionaries. He grew up in Iran and attended the Presbyterian college in Urumia. In 1897 he began working as an evangelical and educational missionary for the Board of Foreign Missions (PCUSA).

So search the Presbyterian colleges in various Middle Eastern countries when they were under the Ottoman Empire. In 1909 Moorhatch arrived in the United States with the intention of entering a Presbyterian seminary and returning to work among the Persian Moslems after graduation. In the end he enrolled in the Baptist Theological Seminary in Kansas City, KS in 1912.

According to the Web site of the Presbyterian Church History records at: http://history.pcusa.org/finding/phs_379.xml_-_scopecontent, "In 1910 Moorhatch established the Assyrian Presbyterian Church of Gary, IN. In 1923 he arrived in Philadelphia, where the Assyrian colony asked him to serve as their pastor. After ordination, he took charge of the Persian/Assyrian Presbyterian Mission. He served this mission until retirement in 1950."

If you research the collection of Presbyterian Church History records, you can read Moorhatch's two-volume manuscript work titled: Assyrian and National Church History: History of Iran: Rise of Islam. The work is written in Aramaic. Each volume includes a table of contents. So if you come from an Assyrian family or any other ethnic group that is able to read Aramaic, such as numerous Jews and a few groups in Syria, you can read or even translate the Aramaic to English.

If you're searching the collection of Presbyterian Church history, records less than 50 years old are restricted. Contact the archivist. The collection was processed in 1993. Your reference point would be: Finding Aid to Record Group 379, Box 1 Folder 1. Assyrian and National Church History, volumes 1 and 2. Folder 2-3.

After 1870, in Lebanon and Syria names in Christian families became Arabic rather than European due to increasing pressure by the Ottoman Empire on Christians to use Arabic instead of Greek names. After the demise of the Ottoman Empire at the close of World War I, Hellenistic names such as Kostaki (Constantine) became popular in Beirut.

The distinctly Christian Lebanese surnames Khoury (priest) or Kourban sprang up again when Lebanon became a French protectorate. Neutral, Greek, and Old Testament names also return. You see many French first names in Christian families between 1914 and 1950.

After the 1950s, Christian and French first names dwindle, and Arabic names appear. If your ancestors were Moslem, instead of a surname prior to 1932, you were known as "son of" (Ibn) as in Ibn Omar, for a male, and for a married woman with children called, "mother of" (om) as in Om Kolthum, (mother of Kolthum).

You'd be called mother of your first born son, (Om___Name of first born son) (Om Ahmed). If you had no sons, you'd be called mother of your first born daughter (Om Rania) (Om___Name of first born daughter). Single women often were called "daughter of" as in Bint Ahmed (daughter of Ahmed).

Arabic women's first names were plentiful, popular, and used at mainly at home. Examples include Samara, Zobaida, Rayana, Rania, Anissa, Dayala, Azma, Aya, or Salwa. Children had first names.

If your ancestors were Armenian living in the Levant you might have the name Ter or Der before a surname designating descent from an Armenian Apostolic priest followed by a name ending in ian or yan meaning "son of" such as Manvelian or a place name such as Halebian (from Aleppo) when translated into English. If you're Armenian searching Turkish census records, the pre-1920 border of Armenian habitation usually was south of Lake Van, near Mush (in Armenia), and Bairt and Dersim (in Turkey). Each religion had a different status under the former Ottoman Empire—Moslems first class and conscripted into the military; all other religions, not conscripted, but taxed.

Narrow the Categories

Categorize the religion—not only Catholic, but Melkite Catholic or Maronite Catholic. Antiochian Syrian Orthodox or Roman Catholic? Byzantine Catholic (Byzantic) or Greek Orthodox? Lebanese immigrant to Cairo, Egypt and Coptic Orthodox? Moslem? Jewish? Druze? Armenian Apostolic? Sephardim? Ashkenazim? Protestant? Greek Orthodox? Greek Catholic? Bulgarian or Romanian Orthodox? Serbian? Croatian?

Color-code cards or files noting the date, religion, ethnic group, and town. When did the immigrant arrive in the US from a Middle Eastern country? Was it before or after the end of the former Ottoman Empire? For example, Antioch, now in Turkey used to be in Syria before World War II. And before 1918, Syria and Lebanon was one province under the Ottoman Empire. So use old and new maps to see what country to emphasize at which dates.

National Archives in the Country of Origin

Maps of old neighborhoods show locations of houses. Start with the national archives in the country of origin. For Syria that would be the Syrian National Archives in Damascus, Aleppo, Homs, or Hama where court records are archived for the years 1517 to 1919. If the relatives lived before the end of the Ottoman Empire or before World War I, also search the census records of the former Ottoman Empire in Turkey rather than the archives in the country of origin that may not have existed before the end of the Ottoman Empire.

Records stand alone rather than in groups of catalogs. Check separate Jewish genealogy sources and synagogue documents for the Jewish records of Mizrahi and Sephardim, such as marriage ketubim, bar mitzvah records, births, deaths, rabbinical documents such as a 'Get' for a divorce or a pedigree called a Yiccus.

If you're checking Sephardic (Jewish) records of the former Ottoman Empire, there's an excellent article on Jewish genealogy published in Los Muestros magazine, a publication of Sephardic and Middle Eastern Jewish genealogy titled Resources for Sephardic Genealogy at: http://www.sefarad.org/publication/lm/010/cardoza.html. Also see the magazine, Los Muestros at: http://www.sefarad.org/publication/lm/010/som10.html for archived Sephardic genealogy articles.

Another excellent publication of Jewish genealogy, Avotaynu maintains a Web site at: http://www.avotaynu.com/. If you're looking for Jewish records in the Middle East, also check the Sephardic associations, for example, Sephardim.com at http://www.sephardim.com/. Look for memorabilia, diaries, house keys, and maps of neighborhoods.

For Sephardic genealogy in the former Ottoman Empire, contact the Foundation for the Advancement of Sephardic Studies and Culture Web site at: http://www.sephardicstudies.org/cal2.html to learn how to interpret calendars and how to read birth certificates. You'll learn how to decipher the handwritten entries using Arabic script. Regardless of the religion of the individual, this site shows you how to read the certificates written with certain types of scripts.

The site also shows the dialects spoken in the various areas of the Ottoman Empire. Also there is information on how to read the Arabic script but Turkish language writing on gravestones, especially in Turkish cemeteries. The site shows you how to read the alphabet encountered in genealogical research in the former Ottoman Empire. Emphasis is on interpreting Sephardic birth certificates.

4

How to Translate and Locate without Surnames

What's in the census? Ottoman census records for the period 1831–1872 were compilations of male names and addresses for fiscal and military purposes. Instead of population counts, the Ottoman records contain the name of the head of household, male family members, ages, occupation, and property.

You won't find surnames in old records. Most Middle Eastern countries didn't require surnames until after the fall of the Ottoman Empire. If you're searching Middle Eastern genealogy before 1924, begin by familiarizing yourself with the record keeping and social history of the Ottoman Empire.

Turkish language written in Arabic script is the key to searching genealogy records in European and Middle Eastern areas formerly ruled by the Ottomans. You'll need an Arabic-English dictionary or instruction guide that at least gives you the basic Arabic script alphabet.

You'll also need the same type of phrase book with alphabet translation for modern Turkish written using Latin letters. You can put the both together to figure out phrases.

Find in your town a graduate student or teacher from abroad who reads Arabic script and modern Turkish. Hire the student or teacher to copy the records you want when overseas. Barter services. Or contact the Middle East history and area studies, archaeology, or languages departments of numerous colleges.

Who teaches courses in both Turkish and Arabic? Contact private language schools such as Language School International, Inc. at: http://www.languageschoolsguide.com/listingsp3.cfm/listing/4092.

What Religious Group Will You Search?

Social history is the key to genealogy. Records that existed under the Ottoman Empire listed names of the head of household and parents, residence, dates and places of birth and baptism, marriage, death and burial. Records also have entries for ages for marriage and death.

Baptisms included names of the godparents. Deaths sometimes included the cause of death. For Christians, entries sometimes identified residence for those not of the parish. Check the state archives in the country of your ancestors and also in Turkey. Then check the court, notary, and property records.

Contact the parish churches to look at parish registers and synagogues to look at the Jewish registers. If you're checking Bulgaria, Macedonia, or Greece, numerous pre-1872 registers are located in Greece. "The Bulgarian Orthodox Church was subordinate to the Patriarchate in Greece before 1872," notes researcher, Khalile Mehr. Find out whether a country had its state church subordinate to another country's church with records archived in a different language.

Check Business, School Alumni, Medical, Military, Marriage, and Property Records

Research wills and marriage records in order to track down property records. Search medical and dental records, hospitals, orphanages, prisons, asylums, midwives' records, marriage certificates, business licenses, work permits, migration papers, passports, military pensions, notaries, sales records of homes or businesses, or any other court, military, or official transaction that might have occurred.

Other sites: For the Balkans, look at the Center for Democracy and Reconciliation in Southeast Europe's Web site at: http://www.cdsee.org/teaching_packs_belgrade_bio.html.

Search the 'Annual' Census and the Population Registers

Check recorded births and deaths in the first Ottoman census of 1831. Each census focused on tabulating male names to find Moslem men to conscript into the military service known as "The Army." Before 1881, the annual census registered only the male population. Search the names of committee members.

Committees were set up each year to register the males in order to keep tabs on migrations in and out of each district. When the census wasn't taken, the Population Register of Moslem males kept careful records of migrations.

Find out in which local district or 'kaza' your ancestor lived. Ottomans called their annual census the sicil-i nüfus after 1881 or the nüfus between 1831–1850. You can research the Ottoman Census and Population Registers named in Turkish the Nüfus Defter. Ottoman population demographics and statistics adjusted to satisfy tax desires, since the non-Moslem population was taxed but not conscripted into military service.

The annual census didn't cover every year. Check the Ottoman census for the years 1881–1883, and 1903–1906. Family historians can search each census as well as separate registers to view supplemental registration of births, marriages, divorces, and deaths.

After 1881, the census takers counted all individuals (not only Moslem males) in the census and in the population registers. Sometimes people who thought all genealogy records were destroyed in fires in their native country are surprised to learn that census records may be archived far away in Turkey. If you need text or a Web site translated into numerous languages, check out the Systran Web site at: http://www.systranbox.com/systran/box. You can translate free an entire Web site or 150 words of text.

5

Armenian Genealogy

Check out these resources on the Web: The Armenian Research List is an on-line posting of Armenian genealogy and family history questions and answers at: http://feefhs.org/am/frg-amgs.html. Go to the Armenia Genealogy Forum. Check out this small group of dedicated Armenian-Americans that are actively engaged in seeking out Armenian records for preservation through microfilming and in assisting the formation of the first Armenian Family History Center (in-country) at Yeravan. If you want to research resources about Jews in medieval Armenia, check out the Web site at: http://www.khazaria.com/armenia/armenian-jews.html.

Then go to the Armenian Research List at: http://feefhs.org/am/amrl.html. The Armenian Research List is an on-line posting of Armenian genealogy and family history questions and answers. If you have Armenian ancestry, you are encouraged to submit your own summary genealogy and your questions. Go to the Armenian surnames as well as given male and female names at: http://feefhs.org/am/frg-amgs.html.

Search the Armenian Apostolic Church Parish Records. Then click on the online Armenia Genealogy Forum at: http://genforum.genealogy.com/armenia/. You can also search Armenian genealogy resources at http://www.distantcousin.com/. Check out genforum.genealogy.com/Armenia/and also http://www.distantcousin.com/Links/Ethnic/Armenia/.

An Armenian genealogy Web site also is at: http://www.geocities.com/Paris/Palais/2230/index2.html. Search Armenian genealogy at: genealogy.freewebsitehosting.com/links/armeniangenealogy. And links to Armenian genealogy resources Web sites are at: www.rootsweb.com/~armwgw/links.html. Then go to the Genealogy Register: Armenia at: http://genealogyregister.com/Asia/Armenia/. You'll find there these wonderful links to resources for searching Armenian genealogy such as the following: Family trees, the Armenia Genealogy Forum. It's a list of postings where Armenians having lost their relatives during the deportations and the genocide search members of their families and their descendants. The site features also a chat room.

The <u>Armenia Research List</u> contains postings by individuals who search information about lost family members during the genocide. There is also an archive. Click on <u>Armeniagenweb</u> at: <u>http://www.rootsweb.com/~armwgw/</u>. It has links to Armenian mailing lists and surname pages. You'll also find at the <u>Armenian Genealogical Society</u>. an Armenian research list and lists of Armenian names and surnames.

For passenger lists of ships transporting immigrations, check out the <u>Armenian Genealogical Web Page</u>. It also has a bibliography, and presents the book of a genealogist, cemetery data, maps, genocide survivor stories, information about Armenian legionnaires during World War I.

The <u>Distant Cousins: Armenian Genealogy Resources</u> Features an Armenian surname search engine, a list of web resources and mailing lists, links for Armenian family historians including books and personal homepages. You can also read the <u>Family Questionnaire</u>. It's provided by the Armenian Historical Association of Rhode Island. The questionnaire is intended for determining the contribution of Armenians to the history of Rhode Island.

You need various personal and family data to answer the questionnaire. There's also a link to a genealogist specializing in Armenian research. All these informational links are at the Genealogy Register at: <u>http://genealogyregister.com/Asia/Armenia/</u>. There are surname lists and a home page.

Check it out. I highly rate and recommend this Web site for Armenian genealogy resources research. Click on the link to the Armenia Genealogy Forum at: http://genealogyregister.com/Asia/Armenia/. It has a list of postings where relatives may search for the descendants of lost and deported family members' names. If you're Armenian, also check out the Turkish Armenian Reconciliation Commission (TARC) at: <u>http://www.asbarez.com/TARC/Tarc.html</u>.

◆   ◆   ◆

Web Resources and Books on Former Ottoman Empire Genealogy Web Sites

Albanian Research List: http://feefhs.org/al/alrl.html

Armenian Genealogical Society: http://feefhs.org/am/frg-amgs.html

Egyptian Genealogy: http://www.daddezio.com/egypgen.html

Egyptian Genealogy—Kindred Trails (tm) : http://www.kindredtrails.com/egypt.html

Egyptian Royal Genealogy: http://www.geocities.com/christopherjbennett/

Historical Society of Jews from Egypt: http://www.hsje.org/homepage.htm

Iranian: Persian Watch Center: Iranian-American AntiDiscrimination Council

http://www.antidiscrimination.org/

The Iranian: http://www.iranian.com/Features/2002/December/LA2/index.html

Iran: Payvand's Iran News: http://www.payvand.com/news/00/aug/1054.html

Also see: Iranian American Jewish Federation and also the Council of Iranian American Jewish Organizations: P.O.BOX 3074, Beverly Hills, CA. 90212. See news article at Payvand's Iran News at: http://www.payvand.com/news/00/feb/1014.html

Excellent Genealogy and Related Books on Iran: Also see: http://payvand.com/books/

Another Sea, Another Shore: Stories of Iranian Migration

by Shouleh Vatanabadi, et all (2003)

Funny in Farsi: A Memoir of Growing Up Iranian in America

by Firoozeh Dumas (2003)

Wedding Song: Memoirs of an Iranian Jewish Woman

by Farideh Goldin (2003)

Exiled Memories: Stories of the Iranian Diaspora

by Zohreh Sullivan (2001)

<u>Journey from the Land of No : A Girlhood Caught in Revolutionary Iran</u>
by Roya Hakakian (2004)

<u>Inside Iran: Women's Lives</u>
by Jane Mary Howard (2002)

The National Iranian American Council: www.niacouncil.org

Jewish Genealogy: http://www.jewishgen.org/infofiles/

Lebanon Genealogy: http://genforum.genealogy.com/lebanon

http://www.mit.edu:8001/activities/lebanon/map.html

Lebanese Descendants of the Bourjaily Family (Abou R'Jaily): http://www.abourjeily.com/Family/index.htm

Descendants of Atallah Abou Rjeily, born about 1712

Lebanese Club of New York City:

http://nyc.lebaneseclub.org/

http://www.rootsweb.com/~lbnwgw/lebclubnyc/index.htm

Lebanese Genealogy: http://www.rootsweb.com/~lbnwgw/

Middle East Genealogy: http://www.rootsweb.com/~mdeastgw/index.html

Middle East Genealogy by country: http://www.rootsweb.com/~mdeastgw/index.html#country

Polish Genealogical Society of America: http://feefhs.org/pol/frg-pgsa.html

Sephardim.com: http://www.sephardim.com/

Syrian and Lebanese Genealogy: http://www.genealogytoday.com/family/syrian/

Syria Genealogy: http://www.rootsweb.com/~syrwgw/

Syrian/Lebanese/Jewish/Farhi Genealogy Site (Flowers of the Orient):

http://www.farhi.org

Turkish Genealogy Discussion Group: http://www.turkey.com/forums/forumdisplay.php3?forumid=18

Turkish Telephone Directories Information: Türk Telekomünikasyon (Telecommunication) http://ttrehber.gov.tr/rehber_webtech/index.asp

Croatia Genealogy Cross Index: http://feefhs.org/cro/indexcro.html

Eastern Europe: http://www.cyndislist.com/easteuro.htm

Eastern European Genealogical Society, Inc.: http://feefhs.org/ca/frg-eegs.html

Eastern Europe Index: http://feefhs.org/ethnic.html

India Royalty: http://freepages.genealogy.rootsweb.com/~royalty/india/persons.html

Romanian American Heritage Center: http://feefhs.org/ro/frg-rahc.html

Slavs, South: Cultural Society: http://feefhs.org/frg-csss.html

Ukrainian Genealogical and Historical Society of Canada: http://feefhs.org/ca/frgughsc.html

Rom (Gypsies): http://www.cyndislist.com/peoples.htm#Gypsies

See: **McGowan, Bruce William, 1933–** Defter-i mufassal-i liva-i Sirem : an Ottoman revenue survey dating from the reign of Selim II./Bruce William McGowan.

Ann Arbor, Mich.: University Microfilms, 1967.

See: Bogaziçi University Library Web sites:

http://seyhan.library.boun.edu.tr/search/wN{232}ufus+Defter/
wN{232}ufus+Defter/1,29,29,B/frameset&FF=wN{232}ufus+Defter&9,9,

or http://seyhan.library.boun.edu.tr/search/dTaxation+—+Turkey.
/dtaxation+turkey/-5,-1,0,B/exact&FF=dtaxation+turkey&1,57,

Jurisdictions and Localities in Bulgaria:

Michev N. and P. Koledarov. *Rechnik na selishchata i selishchnite imena v Bulgariia, 1878–1987* (Dictionary of villages and village names in Bulgaria, 1878–1987), Sofia: Nauka i izkustvo, 1989 (FHL book 949.77 E5m).

6
Greek Family History

Greek Genealogy Web sites offer links to information on videos, publications, and rich oral history. Everybody becomes Greek for a day at Greek music and food festivals. At one Greek genealogy Web site at: http://www.daddezio.com/catalog/grkndx20.html, you'll learn that name days instead of birthdays are celebrated in Greece according to "fairly rigid conventions."

The Internet has numerous Greek genealogy Web sites, some helping to reunite numerous adoptees with their original families through genealogy research. To start your Greek genealogy search, I highly recommend the book titled, A History of the Greeks in the Americas 1453–1938. You can find it online at Amazon.com at the Web site: http://www.amazon.com/exec/obidos/ASIN/1882792157/. You'll find an excellent publication on Greek genealogy titled: Greek Genealogy Publications by Lica H. Catsakis at the Web site: http://www.feefhs.org/misc/pub-lhc.html.

Also I highly recommend these books on Greek genealogy:

The Greeks in America
http://www.amazon.com/exec/obidos/ASIN/0822510103/

The Family in Greek History
http://www.amazon.com/exec/obidos/ASIN/0674292707/

Check out these Greek genealogy Web sites:

goGreece.com: Genealogy
http://gogreece.com/society_culture/genealogy.html

Hellenes-Diaspora Greek Genealogy
http://www.geocities.com/SouthBeach/Cove/4537/Main1.html

- Begin your genealogy search with maps of your ancestor's town, city, and neighborhood. For example, you'll find an excellent source with Greek Genealogy Research, 2nd Edition (1993), 82 pages, with assistance from Dan Schlyter, and Greek Gazetteer, Volume 1 (1997), 120 pages, by Lica Catsakis.

It's easier to find information on searching Greek genealogy than in some of the other countries of Eastern Europe and the Middle East that formerly were under the Ottoman Empire, except where fire destroyed records as it did in parts of Crete. At the Web site titled "Greece.com Society and Culture" at http://gogreece.com/society_culture/genealogy.html, you'll find "an extensive collection of links to web sites relevant to genealogical research, as well as, mailing lists, and articles relevant to Greek culture."

What's great about this Web site is that contains a description and list of the Greek genealogy sites. Also try the message board at: GreekFamilies.com at: http://www.greekfamilies.com/pages/138257/index.htm . Look at the Hellenic Genealogy Web site at: http://www.geocities.com/SouthBeach/Cove/4537/. Also, you'll find excellent Web sites on Greek (Hellenic) genealogy at Dimitri's Surname Database at: http://www.dimitri.8m.com/surnames.html. You can search many Greek surnames there and their ancestral origins. For example, the Greek surname, Fotiadis comes from Thessalonikis in Macedonia. So to look up the origins note that the variant spellings of Photiadis and Fotiadis are variations of the same name and search in both the "F" and the "P" files. On this surname database, it's listed under "F."

If you're ancestors are Greek, chances are you've kept in contact with other Greek family members, unless you're an adoptee or come from a family that has intermarried several generations back. Then here's your chance to get in touch again. Go to the Greek Roots Center at: http://www.butterbox.gr/. Roots Research Center is a non-profit, voluntary, non governmental organization, helping adults adoptees with Greek roots to discover their origins.

The Roots Research Center has information on orphanages in Greece. Write to them at: Roots Research Center, P.O Box 71514, Vyron, 16210, Athens,Greece. They cooperate with all Founding houses of Greece, Red Cross reunion section, International Social Service Greek section, Hellenes Diasporas and every other willing Organization and offer "an independent mediation service where prospective adoptive parts, birth relatives can be helped to make cooperative arrangements about contact."

There are many Greek children who were adopted by families in many different countries, including the USA. Some of them don't have written records or adoption files. If you want to meet your birth family or find out more about your Greek roots, you should know that some Greek families who want to find descendants of adopted children can't find missing members because they can't afford to pay for research in other nations. If this is your genealogy research project, feel free to contact the Roots Research Center at: 56 PANEPISTIMIOU STR 104 31, in Athens, or at their Confidential Address, P.O Box 71514, 16210 Gr.

7
Polish Jewish Genealogy

Poland

A mailing list of surnames for anyone researching genealogy in the former historical borders of Poland including Estonia, Latvia, Lithuania, East Prussia and other Eastern European areas is called PolandBorderSurnames-L. To subscribe to this list, click on their surnames link above and type the word subscribe in the message box or email: polandbordersurnames-l-request@rootsweb.com. Archived records may be in Russian or German rather than in Latvian, Estonian, or Lithuanian.

The Polish Genealogical Society of America's site is at: http://www.feefhs.org/POL/frg-pgsa.html. The site contains maps, ethnic and religious databases, a Polish cross-index, and a link to the Federation of East European Family History Societies.

The Polish-Jewish genealogy Web site is at: http://polishjews.org/. More than 3 million Jews lived in Poland in 1939. One of the provinces with a large Jewish population in Poland was Bialystock, and for genealogy research, an excellent travelogue, cultural, and genealogical history book, *Jewish Bialystok*, by Tomasz Wisniewski (see http://www.zchor.org/BIALISTO.HTM) lists surnames from tombstone rubbings and walking guides. Also, general Polish genealogy sources are at Distant Cousin.com at: http://distantcousin.com/Links/Polish.html. Also see the Web site titled New Poland Genealogy at: http://www.newpoland.com/genealogy.htm.

Jewish Communities in Poland Today

View the Web site, Jewish Life in Poland Today at: http://www.diapozytyw.pl/en/site/zycie/po_1989/. The Ronald S. Lauder Foundation runs several cultural centers in Poland. They are located in Warsaw, Krakow, Lodz and Gdansk, and serve as centers for individuals interested in becoming acquainted with Jewish culture and religion.

According to the Web site, Poland today has two Jewish schools funded by the Lauder Foundation in Wroclaw and Warsaw. In Krakow, the first Jewish religious school, the Pardes Lauder Yeshiva, is open.

Three publications for the Jewish audience are published: *Dos Yidishe Vort/ Slowo zydowskie*, a bilingual, Polish-Jewish magazine published under the auspices of the Jewish Social and Cultural Association; the cultural and literary magazine *Midrasz*, and *Szterndlech*, which is for young children. There's also the Festival of Jewish culture, organized yearly in Kraków. It includes lectures and concerts, as well as courses in Yiddish and dance, and workshops on calligraphy and traditional paper cutouts.

Check out the Immigration and Ships' Passenger Lists Research Guide at: http://home.att.net/~arnielang/ship05.html - search. Also click on the link to the National Archives if your relatives arrived in New York. The National Archives has passenger arrival records for the port of New York dating from 1820 to 1957. When there are no more written records, perhaps you can find a long-lost descendant of cousins or great grandparents by learning to interpret your DNA-driven genealogy report or DNA test for ancestry.

Polish DNA-Driven Genealogy

Learn to interpret the results of your own DNA test and expand your historical research ability to trace your ancestry. "An interesting idea was expressed by a colleague from Canada, Dr. Charles Scriver," explains geneticist, Dr. Batsheva Bonné-Temir. "At a meeting which I organized here in Israel on Genetic Diversity Among Jews in 1990, Dr. Scriver gave a paper on 'What Are Genes Like that Doing in a Place Like This? Human History and Molecular Prosopography.' Dr. Charles Scriver is founder of the DeBelle Laboratory of Biochemical Genetics in Canada.

He also established screening programs in Montreal for thalassaemia and Tay Sachs Disease. He claimed that "a biological trait has two histories, a biological component and a cultural component."

Most biologists would call DNA a biological component and consciousness of a core identity a trait. The conscious trait of the whole person rather than the molecular level DNA would be the cultural component. A cultural trait would be the environmental familiarity of the whole person's relation to his or her family and community.

According to Bonné-Tamir, at the 1990 meeting in Israel on Genetic Diversity Among Jews, Dr. Charles Scriver stated, "When the event clusters and an important cause of it is biological, the cultural history also is likely to be important because it may explain why the persons carrying the gene are in the particular place at the time."

The term, "when the event clusters" refers to an event when genes cluster together in a DNA test because the genes are similar in origin, that is, they have a common ancestral origin in a particular area, a common ancestor.

"When I look at my own papers throughout the years," says Bonné-Tamir. "I find that I have been quite a pioneer in realizing the significance of combining the history of individuals or of populations with their biological attributes. This is now a leading undertaking in many studies which use, for example, mutations to estimate time to the most recent ancestors and alike."

What lines of inquiry are used in genetics? Dr. Charles R. Scriver wrote a chapter in Batsheva Bonné-Temir's book, titled *What are genes like that doing in a place like this? Human History and Molecular Prosopography*. The book title is: *Genetic Diversity Among Jews: Diseases and Markers at the DNA Level*. Bonné-Tamir, B. and Adam, A. Oxford University Press. 1992. With permission, an excerpt is reprinted below from page 319:

"When a disease clusters in a particular community, two lines of inquiry follow:

1. Is the clustering caused by shared environmental exposure? Or is it explained by host susceptibility accountable to biological and/or cultural inheritance?

2. If the explanation is biological, how are the determinants inherited? These lines of inquiry imply that a disease has two different histories, one biological, the other cultural. One involves genes (heredity), pathways of development (ontogeny), and constitutional factors; the other, demography, migration and cultural practice.

Neither history is mutually exclusive. Such thinking shifts the focus of inquiry from sick populations and incidence of disease to sick individuals and the cause of their particular disease. The person with the disease becomes the object of concern which is not the same as the disease the person has." (Page. 319).

After hearing from Dr. Scriver by email, I then emailed Stanley M. Diamond. He contacted writer, Barbara Khait, and got permission for me to reprint in this book some of what she wrote about Diamond's project. It's the chapter, "**Genetics Study Identifies At-risk Relatives**" from *Celebrating the Family* published by Ancestry.com Publishing. Check out the Web site at: http://shops.ancestry.com/product.asp?productid=2625&shopid=128.

Here's the reprinted article. Persons interested may go to the Web site for more information. I found out about Stanley M. Diamond from Dr. Scriver, since he mentioned Stanley M. Diamond's project in the book chapter Scriver wrote for Batsheva Bonné-Temir's book, *Genetic Diversity Among Jews: Diseases and Markers at the DNA Level*. Barbara Khait's chapter follows.

◆ ◆ ◆

"In 1977, Stanley Diamond of Montreal learned he carried the betathalassemia genetic trait. Though common among people of Mediterranean, Middle Eastern, Southeast Asian and African descent, the trait is rare among descendants of eastern European Jews like Stan. His doctor made a full study of the family and identified Stanley's father as the source.

"Stan was spurred to action by a letter his brother received in 1991 from a previously unknown first cousin. Stan asked the cousin, "Do you carry the beta-thalassemia trait?" Though the answer was no, Stan began his journey to find out what other members of his family might be unsuspecting carriers.

"Later that year, Stan found a relative from his paternal grandmother's family, the Widelitz family. Again he asked, "Is there any incidence of anemia in your family?"His newfound cousin answered, "Oh, you mean beta-thalassemia? It's all over the family!"

"There was no question now that the trait could now be traced to Stan's grandmother, Masha Widelitz Diamond and that Masha's older brother Aaron also had to have been a carrier. Stan's next question: who passed the trait onto Masha and Aaron? Was it their mother, Sura Nowes, or their father, Jankiel Widelec?

"At the 1992 annual summer seminar on Jewish genealogy in New York City, Stan conferred with Or. Robert Desnick, who suggested that Stan's first step should be to determine whether the trait was related to a known mutation or a gene unique to his family.He advised Stan to seek out another Montrealer, Dr. Charles Scriver of McGill University-Montreal Children's Hospital. With the help of a grant, Dr. Scriver undertook the necessary DNA screening with the goal of determining the beta-thalassemia mutation.

"During this time, Stan began to research his family's history in earnest and identified their nineteenth century home town of Ostrow Mazowiecka in Poland. With the help of birth, marriage, and death records for the Jewish population of Ostrow Mazowiecka filmed by The Church of Jesus Christ of Latter-day Saints (LOS), Stan was able to construct his family tree.

"Late in 1993, Dr. Scriver faxed the news that the mutation had been identified and that it was, in fact, a novel mutation. Independently, Dr. Ariella Oppenheim at Jerusalem's Hebrew University-Hadassah Hospital made a similar discovery about a woman who had recently emigrated from the former Soviet Union.

""The likelihood that we were witnessing a DNA region 'identical by descent' in the two families was impressive. We had apparently discovered a familial relationship between Stanley and the woman in Jerusalem, previously unknown to either family," says Dr. Scriver.

"It wasn't very long ago when children born with thalassemia major seldom made it past the age of ten. Recent advances have increased life span but, to stay alive, these children must undergo blood transfusions every two to four weeks. And every night, they must receive painful transfusions of a special drug for up to twelve hours.

"The repeated blood transfusions lead to a buildup of iron in the body that can damage the heart, liver, and other organs. That's why, when the disease is misdiagnosed as mild chronic anemia, the prescription of additional iron is even more harmful. Right now, no cure exists for the disease, though medical experts say experimental bone-marrow transplants and gene-therapy procedures may one day lead to one.

"Stan's primary concern is that carriers of thalassemia trait may marry, often unaware that their mild chronic anemia may be something else. To aid in his search for carriers of his family's gene mutation of the beta-thalassemia trait, he founded and coordinates an initiative known as **Jewish Records Indexing-Poland**, an award-winning **Internet-based index of Jewish vital records in Poland**, with more than one million references. This database is helping Jewish families, particularly those at increased risk for hereditary conditions and diseases, trace their medical histories, as well as geneticists."

Says Dr. Robert Burk, professor of epidemiology at the Albert Einstein College of Medicine at Yeshiva University, and principal investigator for the Cancer Longevity, Ancestry and Lifestyle (CLAL) study in the Jewish population (currently focusing on prostate cancer), "Through the establishment of a searchable database from **Poland**, careful analysis of the relationship between individuals will be possible at both the familial and the molecular level.

"This will afford us the opportunity to learn not only more about the Creator's great work, but will also allow (us) researchers new opportunities to dissect the cause of many diseases in large established pedigrees."

Several other medical institutions, including Yale University's Cancer Genetics Program, the Epidemiology-Genetics Program at the Johns Hopkins School of Medicine, and Mount Sinai Hospital's School of Medicine have recognized Diamond's work as an outstanding application of knowing one's family history and as a guide to others who may be trying to trace their medical histories, particularly those at increased risk for hereditary conditions and diseases.

In February 1998, in a breakthrough effort, Stanley discovered another member of his family who carried the trait. He found the descendants of Jankiel's niece and nephew—first cousins who married—David Lustig and his wife, Fanny Bengelsdorf. This was no ordinary find—he located the graves by using a map of the Ostrow Mazowiecka section of Chicago's Waldheim Cemetery and contacted the person listed as the one paying for perpetual care, David and Fanny's grandson, Alex.

"It turned out Alex, too, had been diagnosed as a beta-thalassemia carrier by his personal physician fifteen years earlier. The discovery that David and Fanny's descendants were carriers of the beta-thalassemia trait convinced Stan, Dr. Scriver, and Dr.Oppenheim that Hersz Widelec, born in 1785, must be the source of the family's novel mutation.

"'This groundbreaking work helps geneticists all over the world understand the trait and its effects on one family,' says Dr. Oppenheim. "A most important contribution of Stanley Diamond's work is increasing the awareness among his relatives and others to the possibility that they carry a genetic trait which with proper measures, can be prevented in future generations. In addition, the work has demonstrated the power of modern genetics in identifying distant relatives, and helps to clarify how genetic diseases are being spread throughout the world."

For more information about thalassemia, contact Cooley's Anemia Foundation (129–09 26th Avenue. Flushing,New York, 11354; by phone 800-522-7222; or online at www.cooleysanemia.org). For more about Stanley Diamond's research. visit his Web site (www.diamondgen.org). Thalassemia is not only carried by people living today in Mediterranean lands. **The first Polish (not Jewish) carrier of Beta-Thal** was discovered in the last few years in Bialystok, Poland. Stanley Diamond met with the Director of the Hematology Institute in Warsaw in November 2002, and the Director of the Hematology Institute in Warsaw indicated that they now have identified 52 carriers. Check out these Web sites listed below if the subject intrigues you.

"Genealogy with an extra reason"...Beta-Thalassemia Research Project.
http://www.diamondgen.org/
JTA genetic disorder and Polish Jewish history

http://www.jta.org/page_view_story.asp?intarticleid=11608&intcategoryid=5

IAJGS Lifetime Achievement Award
http://www.jewishgen.org/ajgs/awards.html
Jewish Records Indexing—Poland
http://www.jri-poland.org/

For more Polish genealogy links, try the Polish Genealogy Links site at: http://www.geocities.com/SiliconValley/Haven/1538/Polishpg.html. The Polish Genealogical Society of America's (PGSA) Web site is at: http://www.pgsa.org/. As of May 2, 2005 there were 878,700 surnames in PGSA's databases. If you're searching Polish genealogy, attend some of the Polish genealogical conferences.

Digital Library of Wielkopolska Web site with 3971 publications at the time this book went to press is at: http://www.wbc.poznan.pl/ gives you access to the oldest Polish writing relicts. The Web site is in English. According to the site, "You also can read scientific scripts and monographies and see exhibitions with unique resources from various Wielkopolska libraries." Also at the upper right hand corner of the site, click on the flag of language you want—English or Polish.

Also try The Association of Professional Genealogists at: http://www.apgen.org/directory/index.php to find someone who specializes in your particular town or surname research. American military sources links are at the Military Links and Record Sources Web site at: http://www.pgsa.org/MilitaryRec.htm.

The article, Genealogy and Poland—a Guide, is at: http://www.polishroots.com/genpoland/index.htm.

The excellent *Guide* at the Web site notes that, "Millions of people all around the world trace their roots to the territory of present-day Poland. Their ancestors might have been of Polish, German, Jewish, Ruthenian or other ethnic backgrounds and they might have belonged to the Roman Catholic, Greek Catholic, Lutheran, Orthodox, Calvinist or Mennonite Churches, or professed Judaism."

What's great about this site is that has a link to Polish directories at: and answers frequently asked questions with links such as the following questions and links to the answers: For example, the site called: *How to Start my Search for Ancestors* is at http://www.polishroots.org/genpoland/start.htm. It contains information you need for the compilation of data. The next question on How to locate my ancestors' place of origin site is at: http://www.polishroots.org/genpoland/where.htm, and contains the names of localities in Poland and the history of administrative divisions. Many cities in Western Poland retained their German names until 1945.

The link titled, My ancestors were Germans (Jews, Russians etc.) Why should I look for them in Poland? is at: http://www.polishroots.org/genpoland/polhistory.htm and contains a map of central Europe in 1772 and a 200 year brief history.

The Web site's article explains that during the second half of the 18th century the Kingdom of Poland included all of what we now call Lithuania, Belarus and half of contemporary Ukraine. Nearly half of the contemporary area of Poland then belonged to Prussia (Germany). Historic Prussia on an old map is found in Eastern Germany.

The boundary changes section on what 19th century provinces now belong to Poland is at: http://www.polishroots.org/genpoland/changes.htm.

See the link on What kind of records are available in Poland for my ancestors? Where can I find them?, Investigative research site is at: http://www.polishroots.org/genpoland/records.htm. Note that you can find records of births, deaths, and marriages in parishes.

The site notes that, the Civil Codex of Napoleon Bonaparte required religious clergy of all religions to make duplicates of their registers and to deliver them to the local authorities (the district courts).

All of the countries formerly governing the present territory of Poland had to deliver the registers. According to the Web site, "After the fall of Napoleon this practice continued." The Civil Registration Offices (*Standesämter*) in Prussia, established on Oct 1, 1874, controlled the registers. Therefore, registrations of births, marriages and deaths for all religions after 1874 were filed in the Civil Registration offices.

Also, check out the link answering the frequently-asked question of How to obtain a birth/marriage/death certificate from Poland. at: http://www.polishroots.org/genpoland/certif.htm. The link shows you how to deal with archivists, officials, and pastors.

If you're looking for meanings of names, click on the site titled, What does my surname mean? It's at http://www.polishroots.org/genpoland/surnames.htm. You'll find helpful hints on etymology.

Lithuanian Jewish Genealogy

Although Jewish records are in synagogues and Jewish schools, records also are kept in government archives, with some physicians' records, and hospitals or any other institutions, usually in the Russian language for records from the 19th century and from the time surnames were recorded by the government for birth, marriage, death, tax, census, or military purposes.

Look at the **Jewish Baltic & E. European Communities**: Shtetl Finder: Jewish Communities in the 19th and Early 20th Centuries in the Pale of Settlement of Russia and Poland, and in Lithuania, Latvia, Galicia, and Bukovina with Names of Residents: Heritage Books, Bowie, Maryland, USA 1989.

The Lithuanian Global Genealogical Society is at: http://www.lithuaniangenealogy.org/databases/. There are vital records for most states and Lithuanian Parishes of the Roman Catholic Diocese in America at: http://www.lithuaniangenealogy.org/databases/churches/lt_churches-us.html. The Lithuania Genealogy Forum of Genealogy.com is at: http://genforum.genealogy.com/lithuania/.

Also check out the Lithuanian Research site at: http://www.maxpages.com/poland/Lithuanian_Research. You can contact Chicago's Balzekas Museum of Lithuanian Culture, Immigration History & Genealogy Department, 6500 South Pulaski Road, Chicago, IL 60629. The Global Resources for Lithuania Web site is at: http://www.angelfire.com/ut/Luthuanian/index.html. The Lithuanian Global Genealogical Society at: http://www.lithuaniangenealogy.org/organizations/index.html - poland lists the address of the **Poland-Lithuanian Community, as the following:** Chairperson: Juozas Sigitas Paransevièius, ul.Mickiewicza 23, 16-515 Punsk,woj.Suwalki, Poland.

The Web site discussion forum called *'About'* has a Lithuanian Genealogy site of article and resources at: http://genealogy.about.com/od/lithuania/. The site reports that, "The largest Lithuanian resource center outside Lithuania, the Chicago museum offers searches of major Lithuanian-American genealogy sources, as well as an on-staff genealogist of Lithuanian ancestry. Home to the Lithuanian Americal Genealogy Society."

Check out the archives of the museum. To find ancestors in Lithuania, there's a site from 'About' called How to Find Relatives in Lithuania at: http://genealogy.about.com/gi/dynamic/offsite.

htm?zi=1/XJ&sdn=genealogy&zu=http://www.lfcc.lt/howfind.html. Some addresses recommended for inquiry include the following:

1. **Lithuanian National Historical Archive:**
   Lietuvos valstybinis istorijos archyvas
   Gerosios Vilties g. 10
   2015 Vilnius, Lithuania

   Registry department of Lithuanian National Historical Archive:
   Lietuvos valstybinis istorijos archyvas, Metriku skyrius
   K.Kalinausko g. 21, 2000 Vilnius, LITHUANIA

2. Write a **letter of inquiry** to:
   Bureau of Addresses
   Adresu Biuras
   Vivulskio g. 4a, 2009 Vilnius, LITHUANIA

Phone numbers are included on the Web site. I've left them out in this book because phone numbers could change by the time the book went to press. So check first by writing. Contact each institution at the level of local administration, that is the municipality of each district in Lithuania that you want to search, and direct your questions to the archives department.

There's a link to Lithuanian organizations collected from a variety of countries. The site is at: http://genealogy.about.com/gi/dynamic/offsite.htm?zi=1/XJ&sdn=genealogy&zu=http://www.lfcc.lt/howfind.html. Click on the Lithuanian Folk Center at: http://genealogy.about.com/gi/dynamic/offsite.htm?zi=1/XJ&sdn=genealogy&zu=http://www.lfcc.lt/howfind.html. Or check out the mirrored link at the Lithuanian Global Genealogical Society at: http://genealogy.about.com/gi/dynamic/offsite.htm?zi=1/XJ&sdn=genealogy&zu=http://www.lfcc.lt/howfind.html.

◆ ◆ ◆

Genealogy Research Archives
Estonia

Central Family Registry Office

Pikk 61

15065 Tallinn
Ph (0) 612 5164
Executive Svetlana Toots, *svetlana.toots@mail.ee*
Main specialist Piret Põldmäe
Specialist Mare Verma, *mare.verma@mail.ee*

Tallinn City family registry office

Pärnu mnt 67
10135 Tallinn
(0) 646 3364, *prksa@tallinnlv.ee*
Reception Mon-Fri 9–17

Latvia
Latvian Archives

Central State History Archives
Centralais Valsts vestures arhivs
Slokas iela 16
Riga, LV 226007

Central State Archives
Centralais Valsts vestures arhivs
Bezdeligu iela 1
Riga, LV 226007

Central State Cine-Phono-Photo Document Archives
Centralais Valsts Kino-Foto-Fono-Dokumentu arhivs
Skuna iela 11
Riga, LV 226007

Lutheran Church
Latvijas ev. lut. baznicas konsitorija
Lacplesa iela 4-4
Riga, LV 226010

Catholic Church
Katolu baznicas metropolijas Kurija
M. Pils iela 2a
Riga, LV 226047

Orthodox Church
Krievu pareizticiga baznicas parijas parvalde
M. Pils iela 2a
Riga, LV 226047

Published Latvian, Lithuanian, and Polish Genealogy & Related Information

Latvijas Ideja Amerika by Osvalds Akmentins. Boston, Massachusetts, USA c 1969.

Lielas Liesmas Atblazma by Margers Stepermanis. Riga 1971.

Jewish Baltic & E. European Communities: Shtetl Finder: Jewish Communities in the 19th and Early 20th Centuries in the Pale of Settlement of Russia and Poland, and in Lithuania, Latvia, Galicia, and Bukovina with Names of Residents: Heritage Books, Bowie, Maryland, USA 1989.

Latvian language Web sites:

http://www.sil.org/ethnologue/families/Indo-European.html

The Latvian alphabet

Uldis Balodis' t Web page on the Latvian language is at: http://www.goodnet.com/~vanags/valoda.html.

Latvia, Dundaga—Church Records on Microfiche and Microfilm

Seuberlich, Erich.
Kurland: Auszug aus dem Kirchenbuch : Dondangen, 1710–1870.—
|EUROPE |
Salt Lake City : Gefilmt durch The Genealogical Society of
|FILM AREA |
Utah, 1992.—auf 1 Mikrofilmrolle ; 35 mm.

Mikrofilm aufgenommen von Manuskripten in der Zentralstelle für Genealogie, Leipzig. Extracts of parish registers (marriages, deaths) from the Protestant community of Dondangen, Courland, Russia; now Dundaga, Latvia. Text in German.

Heiraten 1711–1836

———————————1858061
Taufen 1710–1839
item 5.
Konfirmanden 1718–1838
Tote 1712–1844
Kommunikanten 1751–1839
Vereidigungen 1819–1870

8

Ashkenazim, Sephardim, and Mizrahim

Ashkenazim and Sephardim separated about 1,000–1,500 years ago. What happened genetically to each branch since that time? This book is about researching the possible origins of Eastern European Jewish genetic markers and DNA such as mtDNA and Y-chromosomes. It's a book that addresses the questions beginners have when studying how to interpret DNA test results for family history and ancestry. The focus is on Ashkenazic/Eastern European-derived Jewish ethnic groups. And there's much of interest to Sephardi and Mizrahi. The details here also are valuable for anyone else interested in ancestry research by looking at what DNA test results can and cannot reveal about origins and migrations.

You'll learn how to start interpreting your ethnic DNA test results for family history and ancestry. Who were the mothers, the female ancestors of the Ashkenazim and their communities in Eastern and Central Europe? From where did they originate or migrate?

How does this compare to the father's, the male's points of origin? What do the details in male and female DNA and genetic markers reveal about possible origins or migrations? Or is this impossible still to discern?

Scientists comment on a merging mosaic of communities that have since homogenized and are continuing to merge. Take the name Levien. It's an old Sephardic name listed from the book, *The Jews of Jamaica*, by Richard D. Barnett and Philip Wright. The book, *Jews of Jamaica* contains tombstone inscriptions and dates of death from 1663–1880. Only names that appeared as Sephardic are included in *Jews of Jamaica*. See the Web site at: http://www.sephardim.com/, a research tool for Sephardic Genealogy/Jewish Genealogy. There also are alternative spellings, including derivatives of Levy and the name, Lewin. There are also names such as Levit and Levita.

Also see: "Sangre Judia" ("Jewish Blood") by Pere Bonnin. A list of 3,500 Jewish names as created and defined by the Holy Office (la Santo Oficio) of Spain. The list comes from a census of Jewish communities of Spain by the Catholic Church. Names listed are those of Jewish origin.

Note that Levien, Levin, Levine and other spellings also are used by Ashkenazim and once were used and are still used by some Prussian non-Jews, the French using the spelling, LaVigne, as well as Spanish and Portuguese. Did the Ashkenazim take the name, Levine/Levin from the Sephardim or from the Prussian non-Jews? The name Levim also appears in the book, *History of the Jews in Aragon*, by Regne. Essentially a series of royal decrees by the House of Aragon, it contains Sephardic names recorded during the period 1213–1327. You're looking at 800-year old names that existed with the Sephardim and later—after the 18th century—also with the Ashkenazim in Eastern Europe. Levine existed in university records in Austria in 1598 and in Prussia in 1635 on Christian baptismal records, but is listed as a Sephardic name in the 13th century listings of Jewish names in Spain and Portugal. The pronunciation was more important than alternative spellings.

When and if you take a DNA test, you'll find that what's tested is your mtDNA or your Y-chromosome. It's affordable and easy to test that part of your non-recombining DNA for ancestry than the expensive route of trying to test your nuclear DNA that recombines. So only the non-recombining portions of your DNA are tested. Sometimes this part of your DNA is referred to as junk DNA. Note that your mtDNA or Y-chromosome only shows about 2% or 3% of your ancestry. The rest of your genes recombine and are much more difficult and expensive to test at this time.

What your mtDNA or Y-chromosome doesn't show is the rich tapestry of all your ancestors' origins. It just gives you the origin of your deep female ancestor when the mutations you have first originated. You're testing the matrilineal line—the mtDNA if you're female. For a male, he can test the mtDNA—his matrilineal line and also his patrilineal line. A male can test the DNA of his Y-chromosome to look at male ancestry possible origins. Women do not carry or pass on Y-chromosomes. What can a name tell you?

If you have a name that has a Prussian origin such as Levine, note that it also could have a Sephardic origin as Levien or other alternative spellings. Also, there were Sephardic migrations after the inquisition and sometimes before into Germanic-speaking lands, and the names could go back and forth. There is no such thing as a Sephardic gene, an Ashkenazic gene, or a Jewish gene. Jews from Poland have one of the most diverse genetic pools.

These genes or DNA existed before there was such a thing as organized religion or countries with boundaries. You almost always have a common ancestor who was another religion or ethnic group at one time or another in the past due to Paleolithic and Neolithic migrations and expansions.

If you're interested in an explanation of the DNA process with an emphasis on Ashkenazi genetic origins research, I highly recommend an excellent audio tape on DNA by Dr. Vivien Moses of University College, London, UK Microbiology Department, who with Dr. Neil Bradman, the geneticist, has focused on research with Ashkenazi DNA to see how diverse the Eastern European Jewish population is. The title of the audio tape is: DNA and Our Ancestors: Are We All Jacob's Children by Prof. Vivan Moses. It was recorded 9/8/1999 at 19th Annual Conference On Jewish Genealogy. You can purchase the tape at the Web site: http://www.audiotapes.com/.

9

Tracing the Female and Male Lineages:

With whom in the world do you share a common ancestry? With whom do you share a common ancestry and history? Looking at DNA to study ancestry or to study medical issues is all about tracing patterns—from patterns in the genes to patterns in the migrations. Where do the women—the founding mothers—of the Eastern European Jewish communities—the Ashkenazim—originate? How do their origins compare with the origins of the founding fathers, the patrilineal lines? I asked genetic scientist, Dr. Mark Thomas, Department of Biology, University College London what his latest research findings were on Ashkenazi women as I had read his recent study. *The article referred to in his letter is titled, *"Founding Mothers of Jewish Communities: Geographically Separated Jewish Groups Were Independently Founded by Very Few Female Ancestors,"* American Journal of Human Genetics. 70:1411–1420, 2002. The study was researched by Dr. Mark G. Thomas, Martin Richards, Michael E. Weale, Antonio Toroni, David B. Goldstein, et al. Here is his reply.

Dear Anne:

Our study did not conclude that they are not related to one another and not related to anyone in the Middle East. Neither did it conclude that they are wholly Slavic.

Our study presented evidence for strong independent female founding events in most Jewish communities. This evidence was not as strong for Ashkenazi Jews and we proposed that Ashkenazi Jews were made up of a mosaic of different, independently founded communities that has since homogenised.

Because of the evidence for strong independent female founding events, assigning an origin to those founding mothers becomes a very difficult, if not impossible task. There was some suggestion in two communities, Indian Jews and Ethiopian Jews, of a local rather than a Middle Eastern origin for the founding mothers.

I have enclosed a pdf version of our paper.

I hope this helps.

Best wishes

Mark

Dr Mark Thomas
Department of Biology
University College London
Web: www.ucl.ac.uk/tcga/

*1 The article referred to in his letter is titled, "*Founding Mothers of Jewish Communities: Geographically Separated Jewish Groups Were Independently Founded by Very Few Female Ancestors,*" American Journal of Human Genetics. 70:1411-1420, 2002. The study was researched by Dr. Mark G. Thomas, Martin Richards, Michael E. Weale, Antonio Toroni, David B. Goldstein, et al.

Many Middle Eastern peoples have a percentage of African genes, sometimes around 12%, but this amount varies. Who has the most genetic variation of all the world's peoples? Africans who have ancestors living south of the Sahara. What's the pattern of variation in your ancestry? Variation decreases the further you travel from Africa—that is with people dwelling farther in distance from Africa. Long ago there was a bottleneck in Africa with only a few people surviving outside of Africa to migrate to the rest of the world over a long span of time.

So the more you have historic bottlenecks in an area which reduces the population to only a few, the less variation you'll see in descendants. Different researchers such as geneticists and oral historians, archaeologists and anthropologists study very different areas of the human genome. They study different markers for a variety of reasons, focusing on different areas or loci.

When different people study different markers for different reasons, all this information gets published in different journals, databases, and other sources of

Tracing the Female and Male Lineages: 43

information. How do the archaeologists know what the geneticists are already researched which markers for what purpose? Yet science must compare populations to learn more about the history of how genetic markers traveled with migrations of people thousands of years ago and at the present time.

With all the findings scattered in a variety of publications that are not read by everyone, how do researchers learn from one another? The forensic scientists publish in forensic journals. The anthropologists have their own journals.

The medical geneticists may be publishing and reading different publications than the oral historians, and the archaeologists may not be cross-referencing all those articles in one huge database. Take the Human Genome Diversity Project....It's great with coordination of multiple markers. You need to look at the whole world's population to find where you fit in. You need a database or data set. You can search populations at the data base called ALFRED. It's at the Kidd Lab Web site at: http://alfred.med.yale.edu/alfred/index.asp. For example, if you're European or Middle Eastern, you can do a general search or search at the Web site for populations such as the following—selected from a large list of many other ethnicities:

Cypriot, Greek	Samaritans	Spaniards
Cypriot, Turkish	Sicilian, Agrigento	
Cyprus	Sicilian, Caltanissetta	
Danes	Sicilian, Catania	You can search other Asian and Central Asian populations such as:
Druze	Sicilian, Enna	
Italians	Sicilian, Messina	
Jews, Ashkenazi	Sicilian, Palermo	
Jews, Mixed	Sicilian, Ragusa	
Jews, Sephardic	Sicilian, Siracusa	Ankara Turkey
Jews, Yemenite	Sicilian, Trapani	Armenian
Azerbaijani	Indian, Overall Nontribal	Tanti
Bagdi	Indian, Overall Tribal	Tharu
Bahraini	Indian, Southern Castes	Thoti
Bihar	Indian, Southern Nontribal	Tipperah
Chuvash	Indian, Southern Tribal	Toto

Delhi	Indian, Southern overall	Turkish
Dhimers	Indian, Western Castes	United Arab Emirates
Gaud	Indian, Western Nontribal	West Bengal
Georgians	Indian, Western Overall	
Gond	Indian, Western Tribal	or some African populations, for example, selected from a much larger list of ethnicities from Africa and many other areas such as:
Gujarat	Irula	
Himachal Pradesh	Jordanian	
Ho	Pakistani	
Indian, Central Tribal	Parsi	
Indian, Eastern Castes	Pashtun	
Indian, Eastern Nontribal	Punjab	
Indian, Eastern Overall	Rajput	Algerians
Indian, Eastern Tribal	Relli	Arabs (Mauritania)
Indian, Mixed	Santal	Bambara
Indian, Northern Castes	Sikkim	Bamileke
Indian, Northern overall	Sinhalese	Egyptians
Indian, Nothern Nontribal	Tajik	Jews, Ethiopian
Indian, Overall	Tamil	Tunisian
Indian, Overall Castes	Tamil Nadu	Or search the "Unplaced."

Where will your ancestors be found among which living populations today? You'll be surprised if you think you're ancestors are from one place and the matrilineal or patrilineal lines turn up in another area, showing deep ancestral origins before your ancestors migrated to where they were for the past few hundred years.

If you're wondering whether your DNA found in Bulgaria means you are related to the Chuvash, it might be possible. The Chuvash language is the closest to the medieval Khazar language, and the Chuvash are descendants of the medieval Bulgars living in the Middle Volga region whose homeland was in the North Caucus. See the publication:—Shnirelman VA. *"Who Gets the Past? Competition for Ancestors among Non-Russian Intellectuals in Russia"*. Washington: The Woodrow Wilson Center Press (1996).

If you look at non-Ashkenazi mtDNA, you'll find that studies by Dr. David Goldstein, Dr. Mark Thomas and Dr. Neil Bradman of University College in London et al. show that the women in nine Jewish communities studied show different genetic histories than the men. Their communities had a small number of founding mothers with little exchange after the community was founded with the host country. Their genetic signatures are not always related to one another or to those of the non-Jewish host populations of Middle Eastern countries.

That's not always the case with Ashkenazi women's mtDNA. If Jewish men had kept marrying local women over the centuries, the MtDNA diversity would increase among Jewish women. You have a bottleneck effect with the mtDNA of Ashkenazi women. When you look at the mtDNA Ashkenazi men inherited from their mothers you're seeing their mother's mtDNA. Yet 27% to 32% of Ashkenazi mtDNA is of the haplogroup K, and 9% of it is the same as the Cambridge Reference Sequence (CRS), which is haplogroup H, the most common haplogroup in Europe regardless of anyone's religion.

So where and when did the Ashkenazi mothers originate? Why do Ashkenazi women resemble their host populations slightly more than non-Ashkenazi women? How many of the non-Ashkenazi women were local women from the host country compared to Ashkenazi women? Scientists say that the early Ashkenazi mothers came from a mosaic of Jewish communities that homogenized and merged. Tradition says they fled oppressed lands to other lands that invited them. What do the genes say as scientists look at the details? Did traveling Jewish traders begin the early communities? From where did they seek their brides?

In the study by Dr. David Goldstein, Dr. Mark Thomas, you see in a table that 9.3% of Iranian Jewish women in that sample have mtDNA markers with mutations at 183C, 189, and 249. This shows up in 1.5 of Yemenite Jews but not in any Ashkenazim or in any non-Jews in that sample. In what direction does this type of information guide you? Perhaps you first look at the size of the sample.

For years the origin of Ashkenazim or those practicing the Ashkenazi rite and living in northern, north central, and north Eastern Europe had been a subject of many explanations. Some say male Radhanites, merchants left Baghdad and Persia to peddle wares, mint coins, or trade and travel, coming to Poland in the eighth and ninth centuries. Others say Jewish communities under oppression in the eleventh century moved East, formed communities, and intermarried with Jews arriving from Italy, France, the Rhineland, Spain, and the Byzantine Empire. Molecular remains (proteins and lipids) on stone tools and pots can tell us something about what our ancestors were hunting and eating.

The DNA tells us what groups of people were intermarrying with our family groups, and history may tell us why they came to join our settlements. Jews whose ancestors came from Poland are very diverse genetically. People came from many countries to Poland in medieval times, and in the 18th century migrated from Poland to other lands such as Rumania, where they found Byzantine Jews from Constantinople living there, some refugees from the Spanish Inquisition of the 15th century. There also was a Jewish migration from Lithuania into the area around Bialystock, Poland around 1495. See the Web site on the history of Polish Jews at: http://members.core.com/~mikerose/history.html.

History tells us that in the third and fourth centuries, Jews fleeing oppression in the Middle East settled in Southern Italy from where they moved to Northern Italy and then into the Rhineland and then further east into what is the eastern part of Germany and then into Poland.

Still others claim that Jews living in the eastern parts of Germany intermarried with Sorbs, Wends, and Lusatians, all members of the westernmost branch of Slavs living in eastern Germany and Western Poland, developed the Yiddish language combining German words that replaced most of the Slavic ones, and finally intermarried with other Jewish communities moving into the same general area. The point is Ashkenazi DNA is a mosaic of the Jewish communities it has shared for hundreds of years, but where is its point of origin—West Asia, Europe, or the Middle East—or all three?

Studies of the male Y chromosome such as the one by DM Behar and K Skorecki, Technion, Haifa Israel researched 18 binary and 10 STR polymorphic genetic sites from eight Ashkenazi Jewish communities and compared them to non-Jewish populations from Europe in order to see what relative contributions of common ancestry, founder effects, admixture and genetic drift shaped the men's patterns and variations on the non-recombining (NRY) region of the Y-chromosome. The analysis stronger supports a "striking homogeneity among all Ashkenazi communities with extensive inter-population male migration. The studies revealed "very low rates of admixture with non-Jewish European populations, and a founder effect for at least three out of the six major non-recombining (NRY) haplogroups."

I recommend reading the article, "Jewish and Middle Eastern non-Jewish Populations Share a Common Pool of Y-Chromosome Biallelic Haplotypes," Procedures of the National Academy of Sciences, USA, Vol. 97, Issue 12, 6769–6774, June 6, 2000. Then compare this article to those researching mtDNA and y-chromosomes for later years and see what new information comes in. Keep updated on the latest research.

New research seems to tie in findings with practical applications from molecular genetics to phonemics to looking at the entire genome to how this information may be used by oral historians and genealogists, by physicians, linguists, and by researchers in many fields. See the recommended bibliography at the back of this book and in other genetics or genealogy publications you find in libraries. Also you might find of interest linguistics professor, Dr. Paul Wexler's book, *Two-tiered relexification in Yiddish: Jews, Sorbs, Khazars and the Kiev-Polessian dialect*, Berlin-NY 2002: Mouton de Gruyter Press, or the book by Jeff Malka, M.D., F.A.C.S., F.A.A.O.S, author *of Sephardic Genealogy: Discovering your Sephardic Ancestors and their World*, Avotaynu, 2002. Dr. Malka was recipient of the *Reference Book of the Year Award* for 2002 by the Association of Jewish Libraries. Avotaynu, a publisher of books and a journal of Jewish genealogy has a Web site at: http://www.avotaynu.com/

What about the women? What do their genes show as to origin? The key is extensive inter-population male migration. Ashkenazim spent two thousand years moving from the Middle East to Eastern Europe. Along the way, the Jewish communities that lived in Eastern Europe until recent times had varying degrees of admixture and gene flow with their neighboring populations in which countries they dwelled.

Mostly, the admixture was between mobile Jewish communities. As the Jewish population left the Levant after 70 CE, they set up villages at intermediate locations along the way from the Mediterranean to North Eastern Europe. After traveling through the Levant, Anatolia, and Greece, they sailed to Italy. At that time (70 CE) Rome had a large Jewish population and some Romans and Greeks converted to Judaism, especially those living among Jewish communities or living in Roman colonies and villas in Palestine during the time of Roman rule.

Greeks in Alexandria may have converted to Judaism if they had close contact with the large Jewish community there in classical times. As the centuries past and Rome fell, the population of Rome decreased from a large, highly populated city with a large Jewish component to merely 25,000 people during the early dark ages after the fall of Rome when its Empire moved east to Byzantium. Some Jews moved to Anatolia to join the bustling cities of Byzantine Jews there. Some Jews kept moving north in Italy, although the Southern Italian peninsula provided a first destination for communities of Jews.

By the fourth century CE, Jews that were to become the Ashkenazi population moved north, settling in Northern Italy and living there until around the 10th century, when they formed communities farther north in the Rhineland. By the 10th century, Jews set up communities in the Rhineland (Germany) around the

Rhine valley. This became the cultural center of the northern European Jews, the Ashkenazim as they kept moving north and east, expanding after the 11th century. As they settled in Eastern Germany and Poland, this shifting community gave rise to the largest Jewish Diaspora community to live in Europe before World War II.

Scientists have studied the heterozygote advantage versus the theory of genetic drift. Healthcare professionals have researched the recessive disease genes in the Jewish communities. Paternal lineages have been studied. What about the maternal lines? Where did they come from? Science looks at mutation rates and most of all, patterns. Research looks at genetic markers. Along come family historians to look at oral history or family traditions of who's a Cohen and who's a Levite and other information. Who contributed what genes to shape patterns?

Researchers study "polymorphic sites" to look at genetic contributions. The goal is to find common ancestry or study variability—diversity or lack of it and to look for founder effects, admixture, or genetic drift. So we know there is homogeneity among all Ashkenazi communities. We know the males traveled within the various Jewish populations, and we know the rate of admixture with non-Jewish populations is low. How much is admixture, and how much is genetic drift?

What about the women? Did the males take their women with them from the Middle East or marry local women in Italy, France, Germany, Poland, or Russia? Or did they travel the length of the Jewish communities from Spain and N. Africa to the northern most reaches of Germany, Poland, or Russia to find a "nice Jewish girl"? Did they marry local Non-Jewish women, mesmerized by the tall blondes and redheads of the German forests or marry "Viking" or Finno-Ugric-speaking women of medieval Kiev or of the Ural mountains? Who were the brides of the earliest Jewish communities in Northern Europe?

It has been said that American Jews constitute about 27 to 30 percent of any group whose distinguishing characteristic is intelligence. Scientists reveal that the mean Jewish IQ is about one standard deviation above that of other Europeans. Does this show anything genetically? You can play with unrelated statistics—about 27 percent to 30 percent of Ashkenazim have mtDNA—matrilineal lineages with the K haplogroup. But does this mean anything other than random statistics?

What you have to do is look at reality checks from what the genes actually say. You can do tissue typing, look at white blood cells—leukocytes and look at ethnic origins. It's done by anthropologists trying to find out what ethnic groups from which geographic locations match—for tissue typing reasons to help people get the correct transplant or marrow match. In the case of mtDNA looked at across three thousand years, there's a lot to research. Too often when the word "Ashkenazi" is mentioned, the question is asked whether they have absorbed the Khazars that converted to Judaism in early medieval times and then disappeared shortly after their country was conquered by the Kievan princes. Did they flee to Poland, the Ukraine, and Romania? Or did they disperse and merge with the mosaic of Jewish communities across Europe?

What happened to the medieval Jewish community of Armenia? Who else contributed to the Ashkenazi population? Who converted to Judaism in the regions near the medieval Jewish settlements? The story begins as Jews are pushed out of Western Europe and flee to the East as oppression and the bubonic plague decimates Europe. Few migration routes of Jews lead from East (Khazaria) to the West. Most routes run West to East and from Lithuania to Poland or from the Crimea to the northern Russia, from Byzantium to the Ukraine.

Immigration to Poland/Lithuania before 1600 was largely coming from Germany and Central Europe. Migrations from Hungary went east towards Russia. Polish princes invited Jewish and non-Jewish settlers from Germany right after the Mongol invasion decimated the Poles followed by the bubonic plague of the mid-1300s. The situation in Western Europe was so bad for Jews in the 1340s and 1350s, the years of the bubonic plague and Mongol invasions in the East that Poland known in Hebrew as Polin, (Poylin in Yiddish) land of rest, looked like an open invitation to great farmland and forests. The Ashkenazim moved east.

The Khazars didn't as one huge community of 500,000 people suddenly move West into Poland in the 10th to 12th centuries at the rate that the German, French, Central European, and Italian Jews moved East to escape oppression in Germany and/or N. France and the bubonic plague. Geneticists are not finding traces of Khazari genetics unless they are testing for medieval Khazari genes.

What shows up in some Ashkenazi males—possibly—are genes found in some Slavic peoples, such as the Eu 19 chromosome that appears in 56 percent of Polish men and 60 percent of Hungarians. But Eu 19 shows up in 10 percent of Syrians. The marker comes from the Gravettian wave of Paleolithic hunters who came to Eastern Europe from Western Asia and Central Asia 20,000–40,000 years ago. Western European males have Eu 18 in larger amounts. Eu 19 is a marker for Eastern European males. However, what also shows up in some Ashkenazi males also is the CMH, the Cohen Modal Haplotype. Some men carry these markers and some don't in the Ashkenazi population whose ancestors came from Eastern Europe. You have to look at where they were before they arrived in Eastern Europe.

What Eastern Europe was to Jews in medieval times was a refugium from oppression they found in Western Europe from Spain to England and especially during the crusades, the plagues, and before that, the fall of Rome that had a huge Jewish population. Southern Italy was the first route out of the Middle East into Europe, then northern Italy and onto the Rhineland valleys and France. When life in Western Europe became unbearable for Jews, they looked for lands that invited them. The princes of Poland invited them.

Poland has the most diverse Jewish genetic patterns in Europe. You find Sephardic Jews coming into Poland in small numbers, families with Spanish names such as Rangel and Angel. Rappaportes from Portugal and N. Italy. You have people coming from Lithuania and from Germany. Jews in Bialystock are diverse. Some still have ancestral features very similar to Assyrians or other peoples from N. Iraq. Only a look at the DNA will show to whom they are related the closest. You have to look at the genes before you accept at face value reports online that claim that Polish and Russian Jews are descended from Khazars.

Keep in mind that Ashkenazim are a mosaic of many Jewish communities migrating and merging, coming together to form a pattern. You have people from Persia and Spain in Poland intermarrying with people from Prague or Germany, France or the Ukraine, Romania or the Byzantine Empire. Marriage usually took place within Jewish communities, and travel was wide, especially by males from one Jewish community to another, especially for trade. Polish Jews traveled to Odessa in the Ukraine to find spouses, and Jews from Romania married Jews from N. Poland. So diversity exists, even as the mtDNA haplogroups go through a bottleneck.

Today you're told to marry outside your own Diaspora to keep genes mixing and the diversity growing. What about languages spoken by Ashkenazim? Yiddish was spoken in Eastern Europe, Ladino after the 15th century and/or Greek before, in the Byzantine Empire. Romaniots in Greece still speak Greek. These Jews have been in Greece since antiquity, later joined by Jewish refugees from Spain. Polish Jews migrated to Rumania in the 18th century and found Jews living there who came to Rumania from Constantinople in the 15th century. In medieval times, Jewish communities were founded quickly. Did the women come with the men and families? Or did the young men set out alone and find a local bride?

What will tell the story is genetics. You keep looking at the women's mtDNA and comparing it to Y-chromosomes of men until you see patterns that shape the migrations that tell a kind of oral history written in the genes. So even though most women's maiden names were not recorded (not many had last names until the 18th century), their genes identify them. They existed and have a core identity that lives on in their descendants. They were faithfully 'frum.' By 1600 nearly 20,000 to 30,000 Jews lived in 60 European communities of Eastern Europe.

Sometimes looking at the history of a language can give a clue to how the genes landed in a particular container. That answers the long pondered question of how Jewish genes landed in the most northern and eastern parts of Europe and on other continents. Yiddish has had an ancestor language it came from before it was Yiddish. So has Hebrew. You have Slavic, German and Hebrew words in Yiddish. You have a few ancient Egyptian words in Hebrew, such as Moses (from the water) in Egyptian.

What words does Yiddish have that are Khazari other than "davenin" for praying and perhaps yarmulke for kippot or skull cap? Linguists suggest some Khazar names such as alp for brave, but did the name Alpert or Halpern come from the Khazari Alp for brave or from the Germanic Heilbrun or Halpern or the Slavic Halperin? Did Kaplan, the common Ashkenazi name, come from Kaplan, a Khazari word for tiger or from another language? The people speaking the language most closely related to the Turkic dialect of the Khazars today are Christians living in Chuvashia.

You be the judge and do your research at the linguistic and Khazari history sites on the Internet. Then check out secondary and primary sources for historical research. Were the Khazari Jewish names originally Slavic? Is it important whether one or two people converted to Judaism from a Khazar, Turkic ancestry or from a Sorb/Wend/Lusatian/Slavic Polish-German ancestry? Or from a Middle Eastern ancestry?

After all, 20 to 26 percent of the population of non-Jewish Europe came to introduce agriculture in Neolithic times from the Levant/Anatolia/Syria about 8,500 years ago and carried the J mtNA haplogroup. When they arrived, they met the Paleolithic European hunters. So 20–26 percent of Europeans have the similar Middle Eastern genes to what the arriving Jews are supposed to have.

It's true that Khazars living where the Volga meets the Caspian had royal families who converted to Judaism. However, after the destruction of Khazaria, the people living under the Khazars' rule were Slavs and Armenians, and for a time, Georgians. If these Slavic people also converted, they would tend to marry into the communities of Byzantine Jews living in their lands as well as in later centuries with the Jews moving east from Germany and Central Europe.

Whatever the DNA would show would be a mosaic, a rich tapestry of mixtures of Jews of Iraq, Persia, medieval Armenia, Germany, France, Italy, Greece, Turkey, and the rest of Eastern and Central Europe. Yet even the Sorbs of Eastern Germany and Poland have had an origin in Western Asia as well as Europe. So what can the DNA tell other than that after the communities of Jews were formed from the mosaic, they remained relatively isolated and intermarried within their group?

A bottleneck of mtDNA, of the female line resulted with few women, few founding mothers in the Ashkenazi communities. Today, you have the Himyar communities of Yemen, a Jewish group marrying with Polish Jews, Moroccan Jews marrying Lithuanian, and so on, especially in Israel. In the past, dozens of studies already have shown the common genetic origin of Jewish communities by studies of molecular markers, and studies also have shown the admixture between Jewish communities and their neighbors (Mourant et al 1978; Livshits et al. 1991.

Bonné-Temir et al. 1992). You can read these scientific articles and decide for yourself about the high level of paternally inherited Y chromosomes that reveal Ashkenazi and Sephardic Jews all have high frequencies of haplogroup J as pertaining to the Y chromosome, the male or patrilineal ancestry, and that both Ashkenazi and Sephardic males are similar in their Y chromosome haplotype J with Lebanese non-Jews. The populations of Central Europe don't have this pattern.

The Cohen modal haplotype (CMH) is a microsatellite haplotype within haplotype J in the Y chromosome that links Jews—both Ashkenazi and Sephardic to a common ancestor with other non-Jewish men from the Middle East. The CMH is a type of genetic signature of the ancient Jewish priests, perhaps of the ancient Hebrew people.

Yet not all Jews have the CMH. For the ones that have the CMH, it doesn't matter whether they lived in Northern or Eastern Europe or in Spain or in the Middle East. On the other hand, in the early medieval past, conversions were common. The point is the communities mixed, intermarried, and took their religion seriously regardless of their common language or difference in language. They all had Hebrew in common as their written and sacred language.

What the studies didn't do is to decide which geographical origins brought forth the founding female mothers—the founding mtDNAs within the various Jewish groups. What studies did find out that the mtDNA of Ashkenazi women went through a bottleneck. And with the non-Ashkenazi women, the founder effects were so severe that they show a great difference from non-Jewish populations. This means there were very few female founders—at least eight—in the non-Ashkenazi population. However, in the Ashkenazi populations there were more female founders, still less than in the non-Jewish populations.

The non-CRS modal haplotypes in Jewish populations are rare in non-Jewish populations when you look at the women, the founding mothers. You can't assume that there were few female founders in the Ashkenazi communities, although there definitely was an mtDNA bottleneck in Ashkenazi shtetls or villages.

When you look at the genes, the DNA of Jewish women of Eastern Europe and Northern Europe who say they belong to ancestors who dwelled in Ashkenazi communities, spoke Yiddish, and practiced the Ashkenazi rite, you find that the Ashkenazi population has a modal haplotype with a frequency similar to the non-Jewish area in which it dwelled—that is the host population. The study found 9.0% compared to 6.9%.

This revealed that there wasn't a strong founder event for the Ashkenazi women. So if there wasn't a strong founder event for Ashkenazi Jewish mothers, from where did they come? The answer is that all these women formed a mosaic, a pattern quilt, a salad bowl, a melting pot of a few independent shtetls or villages or if not communities, than founding events only on the maternal side.

Does this mean that the Radhanites from Persia and Baghdad arrived in North Central or North East Europe and married local women? To find out, you'd have to test the mtDNA of Ashkenazi women and compare them to Jewish women in the Middle Eastern communities. Most of the women tested were not related to one another.

Some were not related to sequences found today in the Middle East and some were. So what you find is that mosaic, that salad bowl of isolated communities. With Europeans, if you want to see a bottleneck, you normally look at the extinctions that occurred during the Last Glacial Maximum ice age.

What many studies are finding about Jewish mtDNA is that 27% to 32% of Ashkenazim show mtDNA of K haplogroup, whereas only 2.6% of Ashkenazim have mtDNA U3. Compare that to 17% of non-Ashkenazi mtDNA in Iraqi Jews who have U3 mtDNA. What this shows is that the two Jewish groups have different founding mothers in those cases. Ashkenazi Jews also have mtDNA H and other types in different percentages.

You can compare that with Russians who have mtDNA T haplogroup in 22% of the cases. One way to find out the origin of people today is to compare people's mtDNA for women and Y chromosomes for men. These are the ancestry markers, at least some of them.

You can also do racial percentages tests, but they won't reveal the origin as far as geography in ancient or medieval times. People move around and intermarry as well as create communities where they can remain isolated. For example,

51.4% of the Georgian Jewish women had a transition at mtDNA site 355, a particular mutation, when compared to the CRS, that standard Cambridge Reference Sequence against which mtDNA is compared to see mutations and differences from mtDNA that makes up about 46% of Europe and 6% of the Middle East. (I use Near East and Middle East interchangeably here). West Asia is not the Middle East. It's the Urals and N.W. Asia, including Turkey.

The Middle East is the Levant, Fertile Crescent, and Iran. North of the Middle East you have Western Asia, the steppes, the Urals. Beyond that is Central Asia. You'll find H mtDNA spread as a pan-European mtDNA haplogroup from Iceland to Bashkortostan. If you want to find the origins of Ashkenazi women, you can also go back further in time and read, "Tracing European Founder Lineages in the Near Eastern mtDNA Pool," Martin Richards, et al, *American Journal of Human Genetics*, 67: 1251–1276, 2000. If you're looking for the mother of all Europeans and Middle Eastern people, this article's for you.

What you'll find is that we ultimately all descend from the same single woman, and that lines are traced from the Near East to Europe and from Central Asia to Europe, but to get to Central Asia, you had to come either from the Middle East or back-migrate from Pakistan to Central Asia and across the steppes to Eastern Europe. Or you migrated from Southwestern Europe (Spain or S.W France) straight to North East Europe. The two peoples there met and intermarried, had children, and again, we come to the mosaic communities and melting pots.

Look further back at the genetic split occurring when people migrated from Africa to the Middle East and to Europe. The study found that Georgian Jewish women had very few founders. A late Paleolithic expansion took people from southwestern to northeastern Europe. See the article, "mtDNA Analysis Reveals a Major Late Paleolithic Population Expansion from Southwestern to Northeastern Europe," American Journal of Human Genetics 62:1137–1152, 1998.

You're trying to find out the history and geography of your Ashkenazi Jewish DNA, especially the mtDNA or matrilineal side—the mother's side. The mtDNA is how your ancestry is passed from one generation of daughters to the next. If you are male, you'll want to also look at the origins and migrations, the diversity in your Y chromosome. Women don't inherit a male Y chromosome, so for women, you'll be looking at your mtDNA, your matrilineal side and any other markers you are able to have tested. Perhaps you want to contemplate your most recent common ancestor or most ancient, long ago before nations had borders and places had religions with which we are familiar today.

What do the scientists tell us about the founders or origins of the Ashkenazi Jewish communities—especially about the sometimes nameless women in ancient or early medieval times and right up to the present? Research studies on the founding mothers of the Eastern European Jewish communities look at the mtDNA and report that the genetic patterns called the "modal haplotype" in Ashkenazi Jews has a frequency **similar to that of its host population** (9.0% vs.6.9%), according to page 1418 of the article, "Founding Mothers of Jewish Communities: Geographically Separated Jewish Groups Were Independently Founded by Very Few Female Ancestors," American Journal of Human Genetics. 70:1411–1420, 2002. The study was researched by Dr. Mark G. Thomas, Martin Richards, Michael E. Weale, Antonio Toroni, David B. Goldstein, et al—the rest of the team. Read the entire article for a scientific explanation.

For those with little science background, the point is for the non-Ashkenazi women the study recommended above found that there is a high frequency of particular mtDNA haplotypes in the Jewish populations, at least according to those people sampled. What that means is that a high number of Ashkenazi Jewish women have the same haplotype. They belong to the same mtDNA haplogroup in large numbers. In particular women of certain Jewish groups such as the Georgians, Moroccan Jews, and Bene Israel of India have high modal frequencies. This means that there were very few founding mothers.

When you compare male Y-chromosome and female mtDNA patterns, you see a striking contrast between the maternal and paternal genetic heritage of Jewish people. If you look at the Y chromosome, the study didn't find a consistent pattern of lower diversity in Jewish communities compared to non-Jewish host populations—the countries in which they lived for hundreds of years.

This study contrasts with older studies showing many males having a Y chromosome relationship in 70 to 80 percent of the samples close to Lebanese and Syrian non-Jews and in other cases, a Y chromosome showing Eu 19, representative of 56 percent of Polish men and 60 percent of Hungarian men. What does this mean? Ten percent of Syrian men also have the Eu19 marker in their DNA.

With Jewish women, the pattern in the mtDNA is different than in the Jewish men. When you look at all Jewish communities, you see a significant lower mtDNA diversity than in any population with which the Jewish community is paired with other women's mtDNA markers. The finding shows that mistakes in associating any non Jewish population with any Jewish population would not influence the results of the latest study.

So what does this have to do with northern and Eastern European Jewish women, particularly those from northeastern Europe? When you look at female

Israeli military recruits and see the Moroccan Jewish females with a cholesterol level of 128, and then compare them to the same age Eastern or Central European Jewish women with a cholesterol level of 162, eating similar foods, you wonder what is it in the mtDNA of the North African Jewish women that is keeping their cholesterol to such a low level and what health benefits will it bestow in later life? Were these women prepared for a tropical climate whereas the North East European Jewish women had bodies set up to withstand the famine and rigors of a cold Ice Age climate? Both live now in Israel, but their ancestors came from different areas. Are these women related genetically at some time in the past three thousand years or not?

Among the nine Jewish groups studied by Thomas's team, there are eight different mtDNA types that are modal with a very high frequency. What this means is that their mtDNA, their matrilineal ancestry by genetics was compared to the standard Cambridge Reference Sequence (CRS). A part of the DNA was looked at called the HVS-1 CRS, occurring which occurs at 46% in Europe and 6% in the Near East (Richards et al. 2000). What the study found was that all of the seven European and Near Eastern non-Jewish populations have the CRS as their modal haplotype. Moroccan Jews had 27% of their mtDNA following the CRS. Ashkenazim had 9% of their mtDNA following the CRS.

Only two of the nine Jewish populations studied have the CRS as their modal haplotype. What this means in non-science language is that of the nine groups of Jewish women, eight of those groups have different mtDNA types "that are modal" with a very high frequency. Another study showed a high level of K mtDNA in an Ashkenazim sample.

The modal haplotype is simply the most frequently occurring haplotype in a set of haplotypes. If you want to get mathematical, scientists often speak of the Cohen Modal Haplotype for Jews and most other Middle Eastern or Southern European peoples who carry the Cohen Modal Haplotype. Historians call the Cohen Modal Haplotype the "signature of the ancient Hebrew people". Historians call the Atlantic Modal Haplotype the signature of the Western European people.

Geneticists and mathematicians use the word 'modal' to describe the most often occurring value or set of values in a given distribution of values or set of values. It's a mathematical term from statistics. And genetics is the most statistical of the biosciences, especially the field of molecular genetics.

Compare the modal value to the median value which has half of the distribution above it and half below it. The average or mean value is the sum of the values divided by the number of values. The average can be seriously skewed by a few very large or very small values. So, to simplify, once again, the modal haplotype is the most frequently occurring haplotype in a set of haplotypes.

If you're now wondering what all this talk about Cohen Modal Haplotypes and Atlantic Modal Haplotypes in a man's Y chromosome (the chromosome that determines his gender) has to do with one's right to be a "real Jew" it's about as philosophical as asking who has the right to be a Christian, Moslem, Hindu or Buddhist. A "real Jew" is someone who takes Judaism seriously and practices it. The orthodox rabbis say a real Jew is a Jew who either has a mother who practices Judaism or a grandmother who practices Judaism or who converts to Judaism.

It doesn't matter whether your hair is blonde or black or whether you look like you just stepped out of Babylon wearing the mask of King Sargon, whether you have a honey complexion, melanin deposits, wavy dark hair, Mediterranean features, or whether you look like a freckled, silver-eyed, russet-tressed Sorb milk maid from medieval East Germany or Poland. Sorbs, the most Western of Slavs, have an ancient origin perhaps in West Asia or Europe. Slavs lived in Central Europe before the 6th century CE.

When they migrated south and east, there were Iranic-speaking people living there in ancient times. Don't let anyone call you intimidating names such as "a self-styled Jew." Some people like to label others with names to make them feel that they don't have a right to practice their religion or have a country of their own. If the tiny two percent of Y chromosome genes that make up your enriched tapestry of inheritance happen to be close to the Sorbs of Germany and Poland or anybody else, it shouldn't matter when you practice your religion or seek your core identity. These names get labeled on Ashkenazi Jews. Don't let anyone take away your core identity. No one in the world would call someone a self-styled Christian or any other religion.

How often do you find non-Jews calling the Ethiopian or Indian Jews self-styled? Not much. And these two groups have genes that differ from most Jewish groups outside their geographic areas. The fact is that the genes of most Jews cluster together when the Y chromosomes of the males are studied for ancestry, and most of these sequences also occur among non-Jewish males in the Middle East. However, the matrilineal lineages—the mtDNA of the Ashkenazi females often shows they are not related to one another and often not related to anyone in the Middle East.

Some of these women were descended from local women in communities founded independently who then merged together forming a mosaic. You can't say that they are all Slavs because they are not related to one another. If these women are not related to anyone in the Middle East, then to what geographic area are they related? It depends on their individual sequences. Until you look at the sequences of individuals, you won't know whether that person is related to sequences found in the Middle East.

The answer is a community that merged together from different origins has become a mosaic of diversity, and out of that diversity has come one people. Not as diverse as the United States, but nobody calls an American a self-styled American because of a diverse genetic ancestry. Still, looking at the women's lineages, you find a bottleneck in the past and today figures among Ashkenazi female lineages of 27 percent to 32 percent having K mtDNA. Georgian Jewish female lineages show very few female founders. The whole idea is to do detailed genetic analysis to find out how useful population-based gene mapping is in tracing the founding mothers of various Jewish communities.

The plethora of hate groups direct their diatribes to Jews who look the most like northern Europeans with labels like "Khazar warrior." Genetics so far has not compared the genes of "Khazar warriors" to the genes of Ashkenazim. What would they find? Two percent traces? Or would they more likely find a rich tapestry of diversity? Or certain groups within Ashkenazim such as Ashkenazi Levite males whose Y chromosomes are found in some cases to be close to modern Sorbs of East Germany and Western Poland?

Real Jews come in all colors and hair types. The fear factor is played upon when some group gets on the Internet and announces you don't have the right to be a Jew because you come from Northern Europe instead of Iraq, that your European blood marks you as a self-styled Jew. Don't listen to that hogwash. There are no such things as self-styled Jews any more than there are self-styled Christians or any other religion. It's like saying you don't look Catholic because you aren't dressed like a Roman and speaking Latin so you must be part of the "barbaricum."

The argument comes from those who say that if you're Ashkenazi and have one drop of blood from a northern European, you have no right to call yourself a "real Jew" (and come to pray or live in Israel.) Your answer would be, show me that Palestinians or other Middle Eastern persons don't have one drop of Greek or Roman blood, as European as you can get, and therefore they become "self-styled Arabs" whose real language is Aramaic, reflecting the Greek, Roman, and Arab genes in their admixture.

The point is we are all mixed mosaics of time, and the mixture often occurred long before there were any organized boundaries or religions. Back migration from Europe to the Middle East in prehistoric times is about 15% for all populations in that area. You are what you take seriously.

Tracing the Female and Male Lineages: 59

In the book, *Genetic Diversity Among Jews* by Batsheva Bonné-Temir and Avinoam Adam, Oxford University Press, 1992, chapter 4 is titled "Types of Mitochondrial DNA among Jews." Thirty-four different mtDNA types were found in their sample studied. The sample consisted of Ashkenazi Jews from Central and Eastern Europe, and Jews from Turkey, Iraq, Yemen, Habban, Morocco, and Ethiopia. The mtDNA was studied for heterogeneity, that is, genetic diversity. Researchers calculated the degree of heterogeneity.

Researchers look for patterns in several enzymes. Each pattern is given a different number. So a series of five numbers represents the gene fragment patterns that show up after the DNA sample is "digested" with the five enzymes, and this is what makes up one's mtDNA type. Then the researchers look at how the mtDNA types are distributed. Scientists then draw up tables to look at the degree of diversity each of the Jewish communities reveals.

Researchers look at the number of people, the number of each person's mtDNA type. Then they look at how frequently each type appears. So the purpose is to study heterogeneity—that is diversity—and arrives at values of diversity for each Jewish community. The study of mtDNA is based on looking at the fragment patterns of the enzymes studied. In the chapter, five enzymes were studied based on their fragment patterns and presented in a table.

The researchers used five restriction enzymes, and 34 different mtDNA types were looked at from women from seven Jewish communities—Turkey, Ashkenazi (Central and East Europe), Iraq, Yemen, Habban, Morocco, and Ethiopia. Nine of the mtDNA types showed up in several of the Jewish communities—six in single communities and 19 were found in single individuals. The most common mtDNA type was found in 160 individuals out of 268 studied. The second most common type was found in four communities. These were 31 women from Ashkenazi, Iraqi, Yemenite, and Moroccan communities. The third cost common type was found only among the 12 Ethiopians studied.

Scientists looked for variability—diversity—heterogeneity. The overall variability of mtDNA types of these women was smaller among Jews than among the Caucasian population as a whole, Asians, Australians, or Africans. Variability is highest in Africans, lower in Jews. But some populations have mtDNA heterogeneity values even lower than Jews, such as Native Americans (Amerindians) or Finnish women.

The study found that the largest number of different mtDNA types (14 different types) were in Ashkenazi Jews. Ethiopian Jews were different from all the other Jewish groups. So there might have been an African contribution to the Ethiopian Jewish mtDNA pool. Ashkenazi mtDNA is close to Moroccan Jewish mtDNA. This was found in the study went another set of "six restriction enzymes was used." If you want to read further about the closeness of Moroccan Jewish mtDNA and Ashkenazi mtDNA, see the article "Mitochondrial DNA polymorphism in two communities of Jews," Tikochinski Y, Ritte U, Gross SR, Prager EM, Wilson, AC. (1991) American Journal of Human Genetics 48:129–136.

It's only by reading these articles in the various human genetics journals that you can follow the studies for a decade and see how new inroads are opening to finding out more about the founding mothers, the mtDNA of Ashkenazi women or other groups in which you are interested so you can perhaps get a handle on your own origins from any of these communities.

The question is how many mtDNA types in Ashkenazi or other groups of Jewish women are derived from or exclusive to one single Jewish community and how many are possibly derived from non-Jewish ancestries? What geneticists aren't able to estimate to the degree that most people want is the extent of admixture by looking at the markers. When the total human genome becomes affordable, individuals can see their own total genetic profiles and decide for themselves how rich their genetic heritage is from so many migrations, expansions and mixing or isolation.

Right now the extent of admixture can't be determined because scientists as well as science journalists like me cannot assume the lineage is or isn't the way it is due to extinctions of mtDNA in each community or due to admixture. All we know is that there are differences between communities. We don't know whether the differences are due to extinctions of lineages. So we can't estimate the extent of admixture...yet.

We do know that mtDNA in Ashkenazi women went through a bottleneck. We know that there is a striking high frequency of particular mtDNA haplotypes in Jewish populations, such as K mtDNA haplogroup showing up in 27%-32% of Ashkenazim. But when we look at K, it did come in Paleolithic times from the Middle East to Europe. mtDNA K is a clade of mtDNA U. That is, it is a branch off of U mtDNA and rather like its sister group.

Keep in mind that 17% of Iraqi Jewish mtDNA is U3. U mtDNA haplogroup has many branches such as U6 in northern Africa, U2 in Europe and in India, U7 in the Middle East, U5 in Europe, U4 in Europe and Armenia/Caucasus/Europe, and other branches off of U elsewhere from Iran (22% U mtDNA) and Central Asia to all over Western and Eastern Europe. H is the most frequent mtDNA haplogroup in Europe—about 46% and about 25% in the Middle East.

You have to look at the sequences and then at the tables to see where the sequences are present, more in Europe or more in the Middle East. The origin point is not where you have the highest number, but where the mtDNA sequences are the most diverse. Where you have the highest number tells you where most of the people migrated to and are living in today. Where the mtDNA sequences are the most diverse shows you where the mtDNA haplogroup originated.

Haplogroup K mtDNA springs up 17,000 years ago in Northern Italy where Venice is located today. Then it migrates to the Alps. Jewish populations have high modal frequencies of mtDNA, particularly Moroccan Jews, the Bene Israel of India, and Georgian Jews.

In "Founding Mothers of Jewish Communities: Geographically Separated Jewish Groups Were Independently Founded by Very Few Female Ancestors," Mark G. Thomas et al, *American Journal of Human Genetics*, 70:1411–1420, 2002, the findings were that most Jewish communities were founded by relatively few women.

So we know that the founding process was independent for different geographic areas. We know that genetic input from the host country population was limited on the female side. You go back far enough and find out there was a major late Paleolithic population expansion from southwestern to northeastern Europe. Read the article, *"Genetic Affinities of Jewish Populations,"* Livshits G, Sokal RR, Kobyliansky E (1991) American Journal of Human Genetics, 49:131–146.

The mtDNA is inherited maternally and is gender-specific. Mothers pass it on to their daughters without much change for thousands of years. It's a way of looking back at ancestry, but it mutates over time, but slowly over thousands of years.

Each mtDNA haplogroup originates from a single female founder who lived thousands of years ago, sometimes as long ago as 50,000 or 20,000 years. When scientists look at the Y chromosome of males in Jewish communities, the Y chromosome shows diversity similar to that of neighboring populations, and shows no evidence of founder effects according to the article, *"Founding Mothers of Jewish Communities: Geographically Separated Jewish Groups Were Independently Founded by Very Few Female Ancestors,"* Mark G. Thomas, et al, American Journal of Human Genetics 70:1411–1420, 2002.

The mtDNA is a female gender-specific X-chromosome microsatellite. The article also showed that the Georgian Jews have a female-specific founder that appears to have resulted in "elevated levels of linkage disequilibrium." What this all means is that when you compare Y chromosome and mtDNA diversity patterns you see a contrast between the male and female genetic heritage of the particular Jewish populations studied.

Only with the Ashkenazi populations studied, the mtDNA diversity is more like the host country population. Also compare this with the studies of Y-chromosomes done by comparing different Jewish communities and comparing Jewish and non-Jewish Middle Eastern populations (Hammer et al 2000; Nebel et al 2000).

That means that males who have the Cohen Modal Haplotype will share a common ancestor with other males who have had ancestors in the Middle East in prehistoric times, possibly a common ancestor about 7,800 years ago. It also means the males descend from a common ancestor who lived about 3,000 years ago in the Middle East who could have been Aaron, the brother of Moses, and that the 3,000 year-old CMH existed in ancient Israel and is the signature of the ancient Hebrews. The CMH also is found in some Arabs. So the CMH had an ancestor still further back in time that Jews, Arabs, and other Middle Eastern men shared 7,800 years ago. Genes have coalescence points, a time of origins that are thousands of years old.

What geneticists are not finding yet is an uncut umbilical cord going from ancient Israel to modern Jewish communities anywhere in the world. (de Lange 1984, p. 15; Encyclopedia Judaica 1972). The mobility of early Jewish communities is remarkable (Beinart 1992). You have conversions common in pre-Christian Rome and its empire.

You have the Khazars and the Himyars adopting Judaism in ancient or medieval times. Jewishness is defined my maternal descent (Encyclopedia Judaica 1972.) So what happens when a Jewish man from the Middle East travels on trade business to Northern Europe and marries a local pagan woman? He converts her. By Jewish custom, when someone converts, the person is obliged to forget past the former religion, which usually was pagan in ancient and early medieval times.

From then on, the children are reared as Jews. Only one question: When a Jewish woman marries a Sorb man, if that's the case (as in Sorb Y chromosomes being close to some (not all) Ashkenazi male **Levite** Y chromosome genes), does he convert, and for emphasis, become not only a Jew, but a Levite, a servant, reader, or temple musician, of the Cohanim in the medieval synagogue? Historically, Levites were the tribe who lived in Egypt before the Exodus and who assisted the Cohens in the temple in ancient times. They came from the same family or tribe as the Cohens.

So, if the Khazars had their own Levites and Cohens, did the medieval Sorbs—at least the ones who may have converted? And did they merge later when the Jews were expelled from Germany into Poland in 1349? The main waves of migration into cities with large Jewish populations show that Jews migrated from Germany in 1012 CE to Poland near Bialystock and Grodno. By 1495 Lithuanian Jews also migrated to Bialystock Poland. But the founding families of Lithuania by tradition are said to have come from Babylonia in early medieval times.

You have the plague in 1347 followed by a 1348 migration of Jews gong from Eastern Germany to Lemberg and Temopol, and Hungarian Jews from 1349–1360 migrating to Temopol also. Earlier you have 1096–1192 migrations of Jews from North Eastern Germany going to Grodno, Poland, to Kalisz and Lodz in 1248, to central Poland and Krakow in 1159. Seems every time a plague broke out, the Jews were thrown out of some German town and went into Poland. You have Jews going from Austria to Temopol in 1421. Most of the movements are from Germany to lands East and North.

Then you have the Lithuanian migration of 1445 due Southeast to the Crimea. And you have a 1016 migration of Jews from the eastern cost of the Black Sea near the Crimea in the Feodosiya area going to Kharkov. Interestingly both Byzantine Jews from this area as well as the Judaic Khazars who lived there might have gone to Khakov going from southeast to the north in Russia. At the same time the Jews of Kiev, a mixture of Byzantine, W. European, possibly a trace of Khazars and other Jewish communities living in Kiev moved into the Crimea in 1350. All this movement of communities focused around 1350, just after the plague receded.

You have to look not only at DNA but at rabbinic family histories, court Jews of medieval times and court Jews in the 16th century in the Germanic countries. In the Ashkenazi world, you have rabbinical dynasties as well as in the Sephardic or Mizrahi environment. Sometimes court Jews were members of rabbinical dynasties. According to an article that I highly recommend which you can find on the Web at: http://www.jewishgen.org/Rabbinic/journal/ashkenazic.htm titled, "Ashkenazi Rabbinic Families," by Dr. Neil Rosenstein, One Ashkenazi court Jew and member of a rabbinical dynasty was R. Samuel Oppenheimer. He also served as a military contractor and banker to Leopold I of Austria.

An Ashkenazi aristocratic dynasty held sway from medieval times to the end of the 16th century, especially in Austria and Germany. In Syria, the Spanish-surnamed "Signoreem" moved next to the Judeo-Arabic surnamed Mizrahi of

Aleppo and Damascus who had been living in Syria, Alexandria, Anatolia, Mesopotamia and Greece for more than two thousand years.

In the north of Europe, court Jews married the children of other court Jews. In Syria, the Signoreem with Spanish names such as Blanco and Lofez (Lopez) or the Jewish immigrants from Venice from renowned families with surnames such as Laniado or De Sola (meaning from David) intermarried with Mizrahi—Syrian Jews with Hebrew names such as Mizrahi, Levi, and Cohen or Tawil, Dwek, Gindi, Gemal, Elwi (Elway) and Mansour, among other popular Judeo-Syrian surnames. In northern Europe, according to Dr. Rosenstein's article, "Any Ashkenazi Jew living today has at least one in fifty chance of tracing back to a rabbinical dynastic lineage."

Poland also had its Jewish scholarly aristocrats, especially in Bialystock. A long line of authors, musicians, physicians, and artists came from the Levin and Levine families of Bialystock. Some Polish Jews still have their 13th century Judeo-Spanish Sephardic names, for example, the surname, Rangel, or names like Rapaporte, a surname with an origin in medieval Venice.

According to Rosenstein's article, "Ashkenazi Rabbinic Families," back in 16th century Austria, R. Samuel Oppenheimer's generation used the term "Judenkaiser." Aristocratic Jews lived also in Switzerland and the Alpine areas. In Germany, there was Leffmann Behrens, Court Jew of Hanover. Another cousin was Behrend Lehmann, Court Jew of Halberstadt. A nephew of Oppenheimer was Samson Wertheimer, said to be the wealthiest Jew of his 16th century era and Court Jew of Vienna.

Where are the descendants today? What if their descendant's DNA matches yours? After three hundred years, you could have a yichus, a pedigree. Would it matter or be important to you? Descendants carried the title, "Edler von Wertheimstein." Another fascinating surname includes that of artist, Belle Weitzmann, born in 1861 in Poland.

According to Dr. Rosenstein's article, if you track the female side by mtDNA, Leffmann Behrens' wife was the sister of Haim Hameln. His wife was a famous author of the book, Memoirs, written by Glueckel of Hameln. Her sister married the Court Jew Mordecai Gumpel of Cleves. He also was purveyor of Brandenburg and his son was Elias Cleve (Gomperz) who founded a banking house. That banking house became the largest in Prussia.

Other court Jews had last names such as Margolis, Jaffe and Schlesinger; one was military purveyor to the Austrian Court in Vienna. Then the 1670 expulsion arrived. Margolis-Jaffe-Schlesinger was the great grandson of R. Mordecai Jaffe, author of the book called the Levush. You look to their descendants in the 18th

century and come up with R. Akiva Eger (1761–1837). He was famous for his Yeshiva. His son-in-law was Moses Sofer. Was something else in the DNA? Interestingly, he was the ancestor of dozens of scholars, prominent scientists, and creative writers.

You get a lot of writers related to these people. If you look at the DNA together with the history and genealogy you get the 17th century Issachar Berish (Behrend Levi) Court Jew of Brandenburg, son of R. Levi Joshua, a writer. There is the famous author of Pnei Aryey. He was the son of R. Jacob Joshua, author of Pnei Yehoshua. His son R. Samuel Berenstein in the 18th and early 19th century preached sermons in Dutch in Amsterdam's Ashkenazic community. So it wasn't only the Sephardim in Amsterdam that had a history of family names prior to the 18th century.

You can read a lot more about these prominent individuals in Dr. Neil Rosenstein's article, "Ashkenazi Rabbinical Families," in the Rabbinic Genealogy Special Interest Group, Online Journal at the Web site: http://www.jewishgen.org/Rabbinic/journal/ashkenazic.htm. Of special interest are the genealogical chart and the section of the article on the influence of book printing. Surnames and names of individuals are in the article in the online journal at the Web site. I highly recommend this outstanding article and site. The footnotes and bibliography introduce you to the biographies of several key persons in Ashkenazi history. Most people aren't familiar with the Jewish aristocracy that arose in the Ashkenazi communities of Europe from medieval times and beyond.

In the article's section on book printing, you realize the profound influence it had since the 15th century on scholarship in the Jewish communities. In other resources on Jewish genealogy and history you see patterns linking book printing or scroll copying, family history, and genetics or DNA. That bridge is oral history, diaries, and family history journals.

When families talk about "the curse" from generation to generation, they may be referring to an inheritable disease or genetic event. For example, one Jewish family spoke in oral tradition of the "curse" on their family passed from father to son which turned out to be diabetes and glaucoma, inherited among several generations.

Tracing Jewish DNA is like investigating a mystery with many clues that may be found in records of journals and books from the time book printing began to influence the world of Jewish scholarship, writing, and study. The rabbinic world was where writing was taking place in the past centuries. Families tended to form particular cliques or groups within some Jewish communities to ensure certain positions for their heirs.

So tracing the DNA of your most recent common ancestor 250 years ago could point to something fascinating in your background possibly linked to involvement of Jews with book printing in Europe or elsewhere. Before book printing there was scroll copying with ink and quiver. You have to go back further to look at DNA and Jewish migrations, back to the 14th century.

The years 1347–1350 meant huge migrations from West to Eastern lands for Jews. It also coincided with the bubonic plague. Jews were expelled because the people didn't know the plague came from fleas piggybacking on rats. Many blamed Jews for poisoning the wells. Large migrations or expansions of Jews were coming out of Germany, Hungary, Lithuania, and Central Europe moved east into Poland and parts of Russia.

About one third of the Jewish population was said to have succumbed to the bubonic plague. There were also massacres, problems with the crusaders, and most communities were on the move. Jews from the West went east and those from the east went northeast. Nobody was going West from Russia or Poland back into Germany between the 11th century and the 15th, at least by the looks of the arrows on the migration map of Jewish waves of migration, and these were only the main waves of migration to cities with large Jewish communities.

So we know that the mtDNA of Ashkenazi women is more like the host country population as far as diversity. However, we can't assume it's because of admixture because the bottleneck in the past that occurred from possibly extinctions could have created the situation of a lesser number of mtDNA types in the founding mothers of the Ashkenazi European Jewish communities. What we can assume right now until other evidence comes forth is that the communities were made up of a mosaic of different communities of Jews from different geographic areas that eventually merged somewhat.

We can't assume that just because Sephardic and Ashkenazi Jews spoke different languages and had different prayer rituals that they didn't marry. They did. Sephardic Jews settled in Germany, Holland, and other European countries. Some married only with other Sephardim and a few married with Ashkenazim.

After the end of the Spanish Inquisition, many Sephardic Jews migrated to Livorno, Italy, and from there, sailed to Aleppo, Syria where two groups emerged, the Signoreem from Spain and Italy and the Mustarabim, living in Syria for thousands of years. Ashkenazim moved to Turkey, Bulgaria, Serbia, Romania as well as Polish Jews moved in the 18th century to Romania where both Ashkenazim and Sephardim lived in the same country. The extent to which they communicated with one another varies from country to country.

Even in medieval times, Sephardic travelers from Spain visited Russia, and the Balkans were under the Ottoman Turks for hundreds of years, then under the Russians. Jews moved around. Radhanites peddled their wares in the Middle East and in Poland in medieval times.

You have groups such as the Bene Israel of India whose mtDNA is similar to Hindu people of India. Yet the men they married could have come from the persecutions of Epiphanus in 175 BCE. The Bene Israel tribe has a local tradition that claims they are descendants of refugees from Antoichus Epiphanus. Over two thousand years, they might have taken local wives from that area of India where they live.

You'd have to test the Y chromosomes to see whether the males are linked to ancient Israelis or at least link to other Jewish communities. The Beta Israel (Ethiopian Jews) show mtDNA related to other non-Jewish Ethiopians. Again, you'd have to test their husbands or fathers to see how they relate in the scheme of genes. The point is anyone can become Jewish at any point in time. Jews come in all colors and mtDNA haplogroups or Y-chromosomes. What you're looking for is heterogeneity when you look at Jewish genes. You're looking for diversity, variability in the various communities. Ethiopian Jewish tradition says they are descended from Jewish noblemen who came with Menelik on his journey from Israel/Judea in the early years of the first millennium BCE.

So far few if any have compared ancient Israelite bones to any particular group of Jews living today, but Iraqi Jews are said to be closest to ancient Israelites in both mtDNA and Y chromosomes. There are Jews in Persia who are a branch of Iraqi Jews. Then you have Persian Jews who joined the community of Bukharan Jews in the third to seventh century of the Common Era. Jews of Central Asia, Persian Jews, and Iraqi Jews all have slightly different mtDNA sequences. Georgian Jews have mtDNA types that show they may have come from very few local women. For example, a Jewish community thrived in Tbilisi in the 4th century CE.

What's missing from articles in English in various genetic journals are studies that compare the mtDNA or Y chromosomes in the bones or teeth from Khazari burial sites in Russia or Daghestan with Ashkenazi Jews, with modern non-Jews today in various communities nearby what was once Khazaria, and with Jews from non-Ashkenazi communities.

Since so much literature abounds trying to related millions of Polish and Russian Jews to descendants of Khazar warriors, a Turkic tribe from Central Asia whose homeland actually was in what today is Daghestan—and also those lands where the Volga meets the Caspian. Cossacks presently occupy the lands that were in medieval times inhabited by Khazars (Khazari, Kosarin).

Operas have been written about Khazar princes in love with Russian maidens. There is a Viking-like aura about the Khazar warrior whose nobles, perhaps about 4000 convert to Judaism in early medieval times. The Khazar Empire ruled Slavic peoples who may or may have not converted to Judaism. Today, the language of Chuvashia is most closely related to the medieval Khazari language. Chuvashia is a country of mainly Christian peoples (Eastern Orthodox) called the Chuvash, a Turkic-derived Christian population.

Since Ashkenazim speak Yiddish, looking to the roots of Yiddish we find Sorbian (not Serbian) also known as Lusatian and called Wendish by the Germans (their word for Slavs) at the root of 13th century-derived Yiddish. The Sorbs lived in Prussia and in the areas in Eastern Germany near Poland and in Western Poland. In Yiddish, German words quickly replace the Slavic words spoken by Sorbs. They are the most Western and most little known Slavic peoples living in a country called Lusatia. According to the Columbia Electronic Encyclopedia, at http://www.factmonster.com/ce6/world/A0830646.html Sandy and forested or hilly and agricultural Lusatia is located in a region of East Germany and Southwest Poland. Jews lived in Germany and Poland, but did they live among the Sorbs?

The question for geneticists and historians is whether the Ashkenazim lived in medieval times in small communities in the vicinity of Lusatia, land of the Western Slavic Sorbs? The area in question extends north from the Lusatian Mts., at the Czech border, and west from the Oder River. Did Jews live in the sandy northern or hilly, agricultural southern Lusatia?

The particular area in question is where the Lusatian Neisse separates E Germany and SW Poland. The Sorbs were farmers and foresters, mostly raising livestock. Did the Jews come there to work the lignite mines, textile mills, and glass-making factories in medieval times? The towns in question would be Bautzen, Cottbus, Görlitz, Zagan, and Zittau—the primary Sorb towns. The Lusatians are descended from the Slavic Wends. Wendish is still spoken in the Spree Forest. Traditional Wendish traditional dress and customs are preserved. The word Wendish is what the Germans called the medieval Sorbs.

The Ashkenazi communities left Southern Italy in the 4th century and by the eighth century migrated to France and the Rhineland. Did they take Sorb/Wend brides? Did the Sorb men convert to Judaism? Was it the Sorb men, not the Khazars who mixed more into the Ashkenazi population? Or is all this legend? By the 10th century, German and some Polish Jewish communities were becoming known for their rabbinical scholarship. We know Jewish communities existed in the Rhineland and France by names such as Speyer/Shapiro, Luria for the Loire valley, and other Ashkenazic rabbinic families in the areas. When the Jews may have first met the Sorbs, the Sorbs were not yet Christianized by the Germans. Did the Jews taken pagan brides and convert them? Or did the pagan men convert to Judaism before the Germans colonized the areas of these Western Slavs and converted the remaining pagan inhabitants to Christianity?

The Sorb/Lusatian/Wend region was colonized by the Germans beginning in the 10th century. German rules constituted the area into the margraviates of Upper and Lower Lusatia. Both margraviates changed hands frequently among Saxony, Bohemia, and Brandenburg. In 1346 several towns of the region formed the Lusatian League and preserved considerable independence. By 1349, Jews migrated in large numbers eastward to found the shtetls and villages of their communities in Poland.

Back in Lusatia, Under the Treaty of Prague (1635) all of Lusatia passed to Saxony. The Congress of Vienna awarded (1815) Lower Lusatia and a large part of Upper Lusatia to Prussia. After World War II the Lusatian Wends (or Sorbs, as they are also called) sought unsuccessfully to obtain national recognition. Since Sorbs spoke a language somehow related to Yiddish, are the two peoples linked genetically?

See the article, *"The Origins Of Ashkenazic Levites: Many Ashkenazic Levites Probably Have A Paternal Descent From East Europeans Or West Asians"* Bradman, N1, Rosengarten, D and Skorecki, K21, The Centre for Genetic Anthropology, Departments of Biology and Anthropology, University College London, London, UK. And 2 Bruce Rappaport Faculty of Medicine and Research Institute, Technion, Haifa 31096, Israel and Rambam Medical Center, Haifa 31096, Israel. (See the Bradman Index at http://dna6.com/abstracts/bradman.htm which is online as part of an index to a list of abstracts and posters at http://dna6.com/abstracts/index.htm also see at: http://dna6.com/abstracts/filon.htm the article, *"An Unexpectedly High Frequency Of (-Thalassemia Carriers In Ashkenazi Jews,"* Filon, D, Jackson, N, Oron-Karni, V, Oppenheim, A and Rund, D. The Hebrew University and Hadassah Hospital, Jerusalem, Israel. Be sure to read updated and revised researcg studies that follow these types of articles periodically. New information comes in frequently.

In the article, frequencies of high resolution Y chromosome haplotypes characterised by 11 biallelic polymorphisms and six microsatellites were analyzed within the context of their genealogical relationships to investigate the paternal origins of the Ashkenazi Levites. When comparing Sephardic and Ashkenazi Levite datasets, the results of the study suggests that, "unlike the Jewish priesthood (Cohanim), there is no evidence for a shared patrilineal origin for this caste across Jewish communities."

So, are Ashkenazi Levites from Eastern Europe really sons of Sorbs? "In the research, Levite haplotype distributions were compared with distributions in Israelite Jews and candidate source populations (north Germans and two groups of Slavonic language speakers).

The Ashkenazic Levites were most similar to the Sorbians, the most westerly Slavonic speaking group," the article reports. Linguists studying the grammar of Sorbian and of Yiddish, the language of the Ashkenazim propose that on grammatical grounds, for Sorbian to have contributed to Yiddish—the language of Ashkenazic Jews. According to the article, "Comparisons of the Ashkenazic Levite dataset with the other groups studied suggest that Y chromosome haplotypes, present at high frequency in Ashkenazic Levites, are most likely to have an east European or west Asian origin and not to have originated in the Middle East."

So just when we think, well, the Levites of Eastern Europe have Y chromosomes that show male (paternal) ancestry down through the millenniums, coming from the Slavic Sorbs of East Germany and Western Poland, when did this occur? How far back in early medieval times did they convert? Was it before the Germans came to the Sorb lands to convert the pagan Slavs to Christianity? Then where geographically did the Jewish mothers originate and in what century?

In non-Ashkenazic communities, there were few female founders of Jewish communities. We know there was a bottleneck in mtDNA in the Ashkenazic communities. Yet, there is somewhat more diversity in the Ashkenazic communities in mtDNA than in the non-Ashkenazic. Only not too much diversity with 27% to 32% of Ashkenazic mtDNA being K mtDNA haplogroup and 9.0% being H haplogroup and following the CRS.

According to the Jewish Virtual Library at: http://www.us-israel.org/jsource/Judaism/Ashkenazim.html, in 1182, "Jews were expelled from France. Ashkenazi Jews continued to build communities in Germany until they faced riots and massacres in the 1200s and 1300s. Some Jews moved to Sephardi Spain while others set up Ashkenazi communities in Poland." The center of Ashkenazi Jewry shifted to Poland, Lithuania, Bohemia and Moravia in the beginning. The center of Ashkenazi Jewry shifted to Poland, Lithuania, Bohemia and Moravia in the beginning of the 16th century.

Jews were for the first time concentrated in Eastern Europe instead of Western Europe." So if your mtDNA has a center in Northern France or other areas of Western Europe, but your relatively recent ancestors came from Eastern Europe, perhaps the matrilineal line came into the Ashkenazi community when Jews lived in France in the 12th century or earlier. In the Jewish Virtual Library, it notes that, "In the 1500–1600s, Polish Jewry grew to be the largest Jewish community in the diaspora." Yet in medieval times, "Centers of rabbinic scholarship appeared in the tenth century in Mainz and Worms in the Rhineland and in Troyes and Sens in France."

As a genealogist using DNA to find matches, think about the possibility that if you're geographic center is in northeastern France, perhaps this is when you're direct matrilineal line came into the picture. For Y-chromosomes, it would signal your paternal line in men. Or perhaps it didn't. Can you really know for sure?

Technology in the future will be more precise sequence DNA than it is currently. Could the fewer mtDNA haplogroups be due to extinctions? For non-Ashkenazic communities, there were at least eight founders. How many female founders were there in Ashkenazic communities? These are questions only research will answer as more unpublished information and research becomes available.

According to another article on the high number of thassalemia (a type of severe anemia) carriers in Ashkenazic Jews, *"An Unexpectedly High Frequency Of (-Thalassemia Carriers In Ashkenazi Jews,"* Ashkenazi Jews resided for many centuries in a region in which Falciparum malaria was not prevalent. You'd think Eastern European Jews wouldn't have a significant frequency of (-thalassemia. Yet they do. So do Sephardic and Middle Eastern Jews. And also some non-Jewish Poles—so far 52 cases reported in Christian Poles.

So did the Ashkenazi Jews inherit their mutation for getting this type of anemia from their Mediterranean ancestors in ancient times, or from medieval and modern Christian Poles who are popping up with it, or at least reporting it?

Or did they get it from intermarriage with traveling Sephardic or Middle Eastern Jews, such as the Iraqi and Persian Radhanites of early medieval times who came to trade what they peddled in Poland? According to the article, "Surprisingly, a genetic study of thalassemia on a referral population of various Israeli ethnic groups suggested a high frequency of (-thalassemia in Ashkenazi Jews."

According to the article, "Two nearly identical (-globin genes, (2 and (1 are present at the tip of chromosome 16 within a duplicated region. This arrangement leads to unequal crossing over and recombination between the homologous chromosomes. The most common product is a single (-globin gene deletion of 3.7kb,-(3.7, resulting in mild microcytic anemia. This allele was found in 87% of the (-thalassemia genes of Ashkenazi Jews."

Many genetic research studies find that they negate a hypothesis rather than prove it. The article reads, "Out of 151 samples only one was found to carry the (anti3.7 allele, negating the hypothesis; b. founder effect and genetic drift; c. selective advantage against P. vivax malaria; d. non-malarial selection to a linked factor. As there are a number of developmentally important genes linked to the (-globin cluster, the last explanation is an attractive possibility."

Basically, geneticists look for attractive possibilities when they study genes. The scientific method usually starts with a hypothesis, and the research tries to find out whether the hypothesis is negated or whether an explanation is an attractive possibility. Can genes prove anything? Only that there are results in print in the scientific journals waiting until the next researcher brings in new information. What can we know about genes?

If you read the book, **Genetic Diversity Among Jews,** you'll find chapters on the major demographic trends of world Jewry, on types of mtDNA among Jews, but the book has a subtitle: "Diseases and Markers at the DNA Level." So I highly recommend this book on any books that come after it on the subject of discussing the genetic details of inheritable diseases such as the chapter, "Tay-Sachs Disease Mutations Among Moroccan Jews." It's not just an Ashkenazi mutation. Different mutations for Tay-Sachs show up in Moroccan Jews and still other mutations in the French Canadians. For example, more than one mutation underlies TSD in Moroccan Jews.

You have a population of approximately 1.5 million Ashkenazim compared to about 500,000 Moroccan Jews living in Israel. Intermarriage between Ashkenazim and Moroccan Jews is common in Israel. The studies on the book were done on people living in Israel. In Ashkenazim three mutations account for nearly al the genes that cause TSD. There's also a milder variant that strikes adults, a type of gagliosidosis.

Moroccan Jews have another TSD mutation. The Moroccan Jews came from a variety of cities—Casablanca, Marrakech, Rabat, and Res. Geneticists would have to trace their prior origins back and to relate their mutation with the geography and history of the people in their ancestral towns. It's difficult to do because the carriers come from large cities and populations that have intermarried for centuries.

So there are many other chapters such as "Genetic Complexities of Inflammataory Bowel Disease and Its Distribution among the Jewish People." Each of the chapters is by different authors. So the book is a wealth of information about not only the history and geography of Jewish genes, but mostly about the distribution of disease among Jewish populations from all over the world, but with the populations of this mosaic now living in Israel and studied there.

You find conclusions such as the less common Tay Sachs mutation could not have been kept in the Ashkenazi population by solely drift. So you may have to infer some advantage for carriers of the Tay-Sachs mutation. What was this advantage?

The field of molecular genetics is studying this. If you consider a career in this area, you would be thinking about admixture rates, population size, and a variety of selective mechanisms. The gene you pinpoint, the heterozygote advantage is part of ongoing science in looking at the whole genome. So as geneticists study these details, genealogists look at oral history and genealogy in a new way that combines DNA testing with looking at how diseases or mutations for disease are inherited. On the other hand, DNA testing can help you match your DNA to your most recent common ancestor.

If you have your DNA tested and find a match, perhaps this person shared a common ancestor with you, either male or female about 250 years ago, more or less. That's why databases used in genealogy and for DNA analysis find a common meeting point between those trained in science and those trained in family history.

So what is the conclusion here? We are a mosaic of different communities that have eventually merged. Let's take a look at the Middle Eastern Jews. Since Iraqi Jews are supposed to be the closest you can get genetically to the ancient Israelites, they have been living in Iraq since the destruction of the first temple in 586 BCE.

Since late antiquity, you have Jews living in Morocco. Not all of them came there from Spain in the 15th century. Jews from Yemen dwelled in the ancient Jewish kingdom of Himyar which is in Yemen. There were several Jewish kingdoms in ancient and medieval times—countries ruled by a Jewish king or queen. Examples include Himyar in Yemen, a Jewish Queen in northern Iraq, and Khazaria, where the Volga meets the Caspian. There were Jewish kingdoms in the Arabian Peninsula.

See the Jewish Kingdoms of Arabia (from 4th to 7th centuries) Web site at http://www.eretzyisroel.org/~jkatz/arabia.html. The second paragraph in the article "The Jewish Kingdoms of Arabia 390–626 CE" at the Web site reads: "According to Moslem tradition, conversion to Judaism started under Abu Karib Asad (ruled 390–420), who became a Jew himself and propagated his new faith among his subjects.

Arabic sources expressly state that Judaism became widely spread among Bedouin tribes of Southern Arabia and that Jewish converts also found with the Hamdan, a North Yemenite tribe. This time, many of the upper strata of society embraced the Jewish faith. The position of Judaism in Yemen reached its zenith under Dhu NuwAs."

Interestingly, the Habban (city in Yemen) Jewish community seems to have come from one single maternal origin. That means a single female actually appears in the study to be the founder of the Habban Jewish community. You can view photos of the town of Habban in Yemen at the Web site at http://www.alovelyworld.com/webyemen/htmgb/habban.htm. When the Jews of Habban left Yemen, they carried with them their special skills in working silver which had made the town famous for its silver crafts. Most of the Habbanite Jews settled in Israel.

Referring back to the book by Batsheva Bonné-Temir, et al. 1992 book, *Genetic Diversity Among Jews*, chapter four titled, "*Types of Mitochondrial DNA Among Jews*," what the mtDNA study found focused on diversity. While there was no significant difference between the *heterogeneity*—the variability—in the Moroccan Jewish community and those from the Central and East European (Ashkenazi), Iraqi, and Yemenite Jewish communities, (that is the diversity patterns were similar), there were significant differences between the Ashkenazim and the Iraqi Jews. And the differences between the Ashkenazim and the Yemenite Jews were statistically significant also. Read the chapter on "Nonisulin Dependent (Type II) Diabetes Mellitus in Jews."

I've read in popular magazines that in medieval times in Central and North Eastern Europe, Jews got diabetes and mental problems, and Christians got tuberculosis. You didn't find too many Jews with TB. Was it the custom of washing the hands three times before eating? Tuberculosis bacteria was often found in the soil in medieval times, and not too many Jews were farmers. Most were banished to small apartments in Jewish ghettos where they did close work such as copying books, minting coins, money changing, or sewing and diamond cutting.

Think about type II diabetes—possibly caused by lack of exercise and eating too many carbohydrates? Or mental illness—caused by oppression and living in tiny ghetto apartments instead of on spacious farms? When the plague broke out in 1347, Jews in the Rhineland were blamed and had to leave Germany. By 1349 they were streaming into Poland to join the small earlier communities founded by Jewish Rhadanite merchants from Persia and Byzantine Jews who came from the East at a time when Aramaic was still spoken by Jews in Baghdad.

This was at a time when the Yiddish language seemed to have developed out of Sorbian, but the Sorbians had no written language, and the Jews had Hebrew. Did the Sorbs, fleeing Germanization join up with the Jews? Only the genes will tell. Now you have DNA tests of Y chromosomes on Ashkenazic Levite males showing some of them have Y-chromosomes close to what the modern Sorbs have. What does this all mean? A richer tapestry, a mosaic quilt of communities merging? A high I.Q? Read the fascinating articles on Ashkenazim and high I.Q. titled, *"Researchers Say Intelligence and Diseases May Be Linked in Ashkenazic Genes* by Nicholas Wade, June 3, 2005, New York Times. (Science). (See the Web site: http://www.nytimes.com/2005/06/03/science/ 03gene.html?pagewanted=2&ei=5090&en=efcc603583e17b54&ex=127545120 0&partner=rssuserland&emc=rss.) Although no new principles of genetics is raised on the paper, according to a scientist interviewed in that article, genealogists looking at families throughout the generations can consider these ideas as part of family memorabilia for time capsules to hand to the next generation to research.

How do the Ashkenazim relate to the Iraqi Jewish community? Prior studies related Ashkenazic males to Iraqi Jewish males. Looking at the mtDNA of the women of Ashkenazic and Iraqi Jewish communities, you find a lot of U3 mtDNA, about 17 percent in the Iraqi Jewish mtDNA—the matrilineal lines. And you find about 27 percent to 32 percent of K mtDNA in the Ashkenazi Jewish female—matrilineal lineages.

In the study, "Types of Mitochondrial DNA Among Jews," Additionally, there were significant differences between the Iraqi Jewish community and the Yemenite Jewish community. You need to keep in mind you're looking at a sample that tested 75 Ashkenazim, 8 Turkish Jews, 26 Iraqi Jews, 65 Yemenite Jews, 17 Habbanite Jews, 22 Moroccan Jews, and 55 Ethiopian Jews. That's 268 people in the sample. The mtDNA is what was studied for diversity—heterogeneity—variability in that small sample. So you have to research how significant a small sample of 268 is before you reach a conclusion that involves a whole population.

Interestingly, past studies of Y chromosomes found only in men, showed much more similarity between the various Jewish groups. Look at the article "High-Resolution Y Chromosome Haplotypes of Israeli and Palestianian Arabs Reveal Geographic Substructure and Substantial Overlap with Haplotypes of Jews," by Almut Nebel, Ariella Oppenheim, Mark G. Thomas, et al, appearing in the publication *Human Genetics* (2000) 107:630–641. Y-chromosome variation in the Israeli and Palestinian Arabs was compared to the same in Ashkenazi and

Sephardic Jews. Then all of these Y chromosomes were compared to the Y-chromosomes of North Welsh males.

The findings: The Y chromosome distribution in the Arabs and Jews was similar—but not identical. Then the study went further to look at the haplotype level that is determined by certain markers. Haplotypes of Y chromosomes are determined by what scientists call "binary" and "microsatellite" markers. These genetic markers showed a pattern in finer detail. So when the scientists looked deeper to reveal more detailed markers, what they found was that there is a common pool for a huge portion of the Jewish and Arab Y chromosomes found only in males. This common pool suggests a recent common ancestry. By recent we are talking about several thousand years.

What the researchers saw was that the two "modal haplotypes" in the Israeli and Palestinian Arabs were closely related to the most frequent haplotype of Jews which is called the Cohen Modal Haplotype or CMH. The only problem is that not all Jews have the Cohen Modal Haplotype. And you don't have to be named Cohen to have one.

Neither do you have to be a Cohen, a direct descendant paternally of the ancient Hebrew priests of the temple to have the CMH genetic marker. Yet the CMH is said to be the genetic marker of the ancient Hebrew people as it originated around 3,000 years ago at a time when Moses's brother, Aaron become the first Cohen or high priest of Israel. The marker has a common ancestor in the Middle East that relates Jews to Arabs and other middle eastern peoples dating back to a paternal ancestor or group of ancestors who lived around 7,800 years ago.

In the article, however, the study found that the Israeli and Palestinian Arab clade that includes the two Arab modal haplotypes that makes up 32 percent of Arab chromosomes isn't found much among Jews. In fact it's found at a low frequency among Jews. So there is divergence or admixture from other communities in which the Jews lived, but how much is the question? Nevertheless, other studies show that Arabs and Jews share about 18 percent of there gene markers but not too much of the distinctive Arab clade shows up in Jews.

On the other hand, the Cohen Model Haplotype and another modal haplotype in the Israeli and Palestinian Arabs were closely related to the Cohen Modal Haplotype in the Jews. Will scientists be able to go further and show that a sizable number of Palestianian Arabs once were Jews in ancient times? We already know some Jews once were Middle Easterners before Judaism existed. Again, we see how closely people were related in ancient times and how diversity began to spread, even slightly, when people migrated to other communities.

In the article, it reads, "Based on two Y chromosome RFLP markers it was suggested that Ashkenazi and Sephardic Jews are more closely related to Arabs from Lebanon than to Czechosovakinas (Santachiara-Benerecette et al. 1993.)" Also, the article reveals that "a recent survey of 18 binary Y-specific polymorphisms showed that Y chromosome haplotypes of Middle Eastern non-Jewish populations are almost indistinguishable from those of Jews (Hammer et al. 2000)."

The study also found a significant difference between Sephardic Jews and Arabs due to a higher frequency of haplogroup 2 in the Y chromosome of Sephardic Jews. Yet there was no significant differences found between Arabs and Ashkenazi Jews nor between the communities of Sephardic and Ashkenazic Jews. Yet Arabs, Ashkenazi Jews, and Sephardic Jews all were distinguished from the Welsh samples.

The major portion of Y chromosomes of Arabs and Jews belonged to haplogroup 1. Most of the Welsh Y chromosomes belonged to haplogroup 2. Yet the frequency of haplogroup 2 chromosomes in Arabs was lower than that in Sephardic Jews and slightly, but not significantly lower than that in Ashkenazim. However, Ashkenazim were closer to the Welsh than were Ashkenazim to Arabs. Sephardim were closer to Arabs than to Welsh.

So what does this say for Ashkenazi men? Does it say they have northern European admixture or genetic drift? You can't make this assumption because two Ashkenazi individuals carried the most common Welsh haplotype, and that finding can't be based on assumptions because if two men carry the most common Welsh haplotype, it's also the most common haplotype for most other European countries such as England and Norway or Frysland, all in northern Europe.

In the study three Arab individuals from a variety of areas carried haplotype 27 which is the Cohen Modal Haplotype, the signature of the ancient Hebrew people and also found in some Arabs. None of the Welsh in the sample carried the CMH. Neither of two modal haplotypes found in Arabs showed up in the Jewish sample.

When the Romans conquered Palestine and built their villas and cities there, you get gene inflow from the Romans and some Greeks. Interestingly, in ancient times numbers of Palestinians and Jews became Christian by the fifth century of the Common Era. (Bachi 1974). Then in the first millennium of the Common Era, immigration of various Arab tribes into Palestine increased with a huge wave coming in during the seventh century CE. Some of the Christianized Jews in Palestine along with the Christian Arabs converted to Islam at that time. (Saban 1971; McGraw Donner 1981).

Then you get more people moving into Palestine in later times such as Turks and Crusaders. You get recent migrations and gene flow from Europe. So Palestinian Arabs vary genetically as well as the Jews. What Palestinians share with Jews are linguistic backgrounds as Hebrew and Arabic share common origins, and geographic origins at their roots.

Researchers are studying their genetic relationships. Okay, there are genetic affinities between Arabs and Jews. Look at articles studying mtDNA (Bonné-Temir et al 1986; Ritte et al. 1993) Bishara et al 1997. There are affinities and there are differences.

The point is Ashkenazi and Sephardic Jews are more closely related to Arabs from Lebanon than to Czechs and Y chromosome hapltoytpes of Middle Eastern non-Jews populations are almost indistinguishable from those of Jews (Hammer et al. 2000). But what about the founding mothers of the Jewish communities? What about Ashkenazi women? Are they Middle Eastern? Slavic? Germanic? Or? The answer is they form a mosaic of different communities formed from a bottleneck in ancient and medieval times.

What is known is that numerous people converted to Judaism at various times in ancient and medieval periods and in different countries varying from Southern Italy and Greece to Northern, Central and Eastern Europe. On the other hand, some people converted from Judaism to Christianity in ancient and medieval times to escape oppression and now exist in the Europe population with those same ancestral Y chromosomes or mtDNA.

Now the question remains, did more people convert to Judaism or convert to other religions in historic times? Whatever the answer is, it will show up when you compare gene markers of Jews and non-Jews in any European population or in the Middle East, considering back-migration from Europe to the Middle East taking place from prehistoric times to the present. During and right after the end of the Ice Age people in several waves back-migrated to the Middle East from Europe, which shows about 15 percent of the Middle Eastern peoples consist of individuals who migrated there from Paleolithic Europe.

Mutations are any heritable change in a DNA sequence. Polymorphisms are differences in DNA sequences among individuals that may underlie differences in ancestry or differences in health. Genetic variations occurring in more than one percent of a population would be considered useful polymorphisms for genetic linkage analysis.

To study mutations or genetic variations in DNA sequences, scientists put your DNA through a polymerase chain reaction (PCR) test. It's a method for amplifying a DNA base sequence. The researchers usually use a heat-stable polymerase and two 20-base primers, one complementary to the (+) strand at one end of the sequence to be amplified and one complementary to the (-) strand at the opposite end.

So you are copying DNA. You're synthesizing DNA strands. These newly synthesized DNA strands will serve as additional templates for the same primer sequences. You go through successive rounds of primer annealing and do things like strand elongation and dissociation. What's produced are rapid and highly specific amplification of your desired sequence of DNA. Then you can use your PCR that is your polymerase chain reaction test to detect the existence of the defined sequence in your DNA sample. Okay, now you understand what happens when DNA is tested to find certain sequences.

Polymerase DNA or RNA also refers to an enzyme that catalyzes or brings together the synthesis of nucleic acids on pre-existing nucleic acid templates. You assemble DNA from deoxyribonnucleotides and you assemble RNA from ribonucleotides. So that's how it all comes together to see the human genome or part of it.

Numerous Jewish men, including Ashkenazim are genetically indistinguishable from Arab Palestinians, and some share the Cohen Modal Haplotype (CMH). This is a subset of an insular group such as Jews, Finns, Sardinians, and Basques. The DNA tests shows up the genetic pedigrees going back around 3,000 years to the Exodus from Egypt.

Europeans in general are mixed and intermarried for thousands of years so that's it much more difficult to tell a Swede from a Russian or any one country from another in Europe. On the other hand, a study of the DNA of the Ashkenazi Male Levites revealed that some of then had Y chromosome DNA markers showing descent at least paternally, from East Europeans or West Asians.

So what can geneticists say about Levite Ashkenazi males? Are they the only Jewish males in Eastern Europe to possibly be descended from fathers who were Sorbs? What about non-Levite males? We know a percentage of the Cohens really do inherit the Cohen Modal Haplotype (CMH) that links them to the ancient Hebrews and also before there was organized religion to ancient Middle Eastern peoples and to some of the Arabs.

Let's look at what happened in the land of the Sorbs when the Jews might have lived there and picked up Yiddish from the Sorbs at a time when the Germans were trying to get Sorbs to replace their Western Slavic language with German words, words that might have shown up in Yiddish when the Jews moved to more Eastern towns in Poland.

One of Charlemagne's sons defeated the Wends and burned Bautzen in 806. Wends/Sorbs were pagan, and the Germans were moving in their territory to Christianize them. Also the area geographically had fertile farmland, forests, sand, hills and....potential brides. In the West, the Vikings were on the move also looking for trade and new lands for farming.

They sailed their long boats down the rivers to Kiev in the East, eventually to Iceland in the West. What migrations did the Jewish communities at the time begin? You have Jewish scholars and traders from Spain visiting Russia, Syrians in the land of the Norsemen as ambassadors, and Ashkenazi scholar rabbis in France and Germany speaking old French, old German, and writing in Hebrew (or Arabic in Spain and the Middle East, Judeo-Persian in the Caucasus, Persia and Central Asia).

That's the same time that Khazaria reached its golden age and the nobles converted to Judaism much further East where the Volga meets the Caspian in Khazaria. They were trading with Kiev in the Ukraine by then and had a vast empire stretching from the Black Sea across the Caucasus to the Caspian.

They inhabited parts of Georgia and Armenia, trading with the medieval Jewish population in Armenia. At the other end of Eastern Europe, here you have the defeated Sorbs. Charlemagne was Christian. The defeated Sorbs/Wends might have converted to Judaism in the 9th century just as the Khazars converted to Judaism at least in part (their nobles and some of the Slavs ruled by Khazars) around that time also. Jews from Byzantium and Persia, Anatolia, Armenia, and Baghdad moved into Khazaria.

Then as the Ashkenazic communities in the Rhineland were blooming, by the year 1100 the Wends had been subjugated. Did some of them convert to Judaism because the German Christians subjected them in the 12th century? German nobles dominated the Wendish peasants and relegated the urban Wends to homes outside the walls or to restricted sections of the city.

They could become active in society only through German institutions and the German language. The guilds were German. Mercantile activity was conducted in the German manner. Under pressure, especially in the part of Lusatia under Prussian control, many Wends adopted German names and relinquished their Slavic traditions. Only a funny thing happened.

A lot of these German names taken by Sorbs/Wends (Wend is a German word for Slav) sound Yiddish....such as Lavine/Levine. Does Levine come from the word for Levite? (Levi, Lion, Loew, Loeb, Lewin, Lewinsky, Levin, Levinson,

Levenstein)? You find the name "Levine" showing up in Austria in a university in 1598.

It's listed in genealogy records as being a Christian name with a Prussian origin in 1635. Look up Catholic baptismal records for the name "Levine" in Prussia in the 17th century. It abounds. Why did so many Jews of Bialystock, Poland and other areas in the Pale of Settlement of Eastern Europe or in Germany choose the name Levine? Were they Levites? Why did they pick this Christian, Prussian name?

Or is it merely a way of "Germanizing" Levi, according to rules in the 18th century when Jews were ordered to purchase or assume German or Slavic names in their respective countries? What happened to their secret Hebrew names? Did they remain only in the synagogue?

The Christianization of the Wends began prior to the German conquest, but it was vigorously promoted by the Germans. They also followed the Germans in the Reformation. The majority of Sorbs/Wends converted to Lutheranism in 1530 after the Council of Augsburg.

In medieval times, the pagan Sorbs/Wends did not yet have a written language. If they contributed to Yiddish as the linguists propose, the Jews who began to speak Yiddish, whether new Jews or ancient ones, used the Hebrew alphabet. In fact it wasn't until the time of Martin Luther in the 16th century that Luther emphasized using the vernacular.

The reformation and Luther encouraged the Wends to devise a written language, and in 1574 Luther's Small Catechism became the first work to be published in it. Perhaps those Wends/Sorbs/Lusatians who became Jews at a time in the medieval past before they became Christian and before they had a written language, were so happy to assume the Hebrew alphabet and to speak Yiddish, related to the medieval Sorb language in many ways.

What they have in common also is that the Germans required the Sorbs to replace what once were their Slavic words with German words—the Germanic of medieval times. Also, Yiddish has many medieval Germanic words, some Slavic ones, and Hebrew. It's almost as if the Slavic words in Yiddish had been replaced over time with German words.

That's what happened also to the Sorb language over time as Germanization of this Western Slavic community replaced some of the words. Linguists suggest that the Sorb language had some influence on Yiddish that's attributed to 13th century German. Yet the Slavic words in Yiddish show an eastern influence.

This now becomes a melting pot, a salad bowl of language so to speak. You get some words from Hebrew, some from Slavic, some from German, and one or two from ancient Egyptian and perhaps from Turkic, perhaps Khazari word for prayer similar in sound to "davenin"...for praying. .yarmulke....Or perhaps yarmulke for the Hebrew "kippot" comes from the Ukrainian feast holiday called Yarmaka?

Without DNA evidence of Khazars compared to ancient Israelites and to modern Ashkenazim compared to Slavs compared to Germanic peoples to see who carries whose genes in this mosaic of communities and migrations, no one can make a statement saying a whole community derives from another community because the details of history are carried in the DNA—the mtDNA and the Y-chromosomes, the tissue typing tests, and the tests of racial percentage. So you assume a whole group of people are descendants of another whole group of people—unless you can show it by intensive DNA analysis of the entire genome.

What you can say is that either the Y chromosomes of the majority of Ashkenazi males cluster with Sephardic and Middle Eastern Jewish males or they don't. And you have read the results of ongoing DNA research. And with the females, all you can do is see how the mtDNA fits into a pattern to shape migrations at least until the entire genome is known. You can trace female ancestry of Ashkenazi women from Eastern Europe until you arrive at the single female ancestor of each woman who lived 20,000 or 40,000 years ago in similar Ice Age refugiums in the Pyranees and/or in the Ukraine.

The clan mothers you find gave rise to almost all other Europeans. And if you reach out to that mother's ancestor, she will be found in Western Asia or in the Middle East or Africa before she reached Europe, except for V mtDNA haplogroup who possibly arose 13,000 years ago in the Pyrenees in Europe when her haplogroup split off from H mtDNA. After the Ice Age mtDNA V migrated north to Scandinavia and also is found among the Saami peoples, and a branch went south to N. Africa, found currently among the Berbers.

So you have back migration from Europe to N. Africa. Let's consider the male Levite Ashkenazim of Eastern Europe. Could they be descended partly from Sorbs? Is it this West Slavic people living in East Germany and Western Poland who contributed to the Ashkenazi gene pool and Yiddish language? Would the admixture in Ashkenazim, if any, come perhaps from Sorbs rather than Turkic Khazars? Would Yiddish have more Sorb words than Khazari Turkic words? Would some Ashkenazim even resemble Sorbs more than other Europeans? Or would they resemble more their more ancient Eastern Mediterranean ancestors?

So far no scientist has compared ancient Israelites to modern Ashkenazim and found an unbroken chain of ancestry going back until they found the Cohen Modal Haplotype that does go back—in the males to a common ancestor in the

Tracing the Female and Male Lineages: 83

Middle East thousands of years ago, perhaps 1,500–3,000 years ago—about the time of the exodus. And that ancestor had a common ancestor in the Middle East about 7,800 years ago from whom most people in the Middle East are descended.

Could Ashkenazi Levite males be descendants of the Sorbs/Wends/Lusatians? If the genetic analysis is right and they are close genetically to the Sorbs of today, it would show how enriched the tapestry is of the mosaic of various Jewish communities of the world all acting as a catalyst, coming together, intermarrying, and forming a quilt. Let's look at the Sorbian language.

There are two versions of Sorbian, also called Sorbic, Wendish or Lusatian, corresponding to the divisions of the Lusatian region. Both versions belong to the Western Slavic group. The southern area called Upper Lusatia speaks a dialect nearer to Czech (Luther's Catechism was translated into Upper Sorbian); the northern area, or Lower Lusatia, a dialect nearer to Polish.

Which version is closest to Yiddish? Traditionally the Wends call themselves Srbi (Sorbee) in their own language, but the Germans call them Wenden, a term widely used both by others and by, many of the Slavic Lusatians themselves, including those who migrated to foreign lands in the 19th century.

When the Jews left the Rhineland in medieval times to move a little to the East, say in East Germany or Western Poland, Wend was the German name for all West Slavs. The German word, "Wend" eventually symbolized the feared Germanization of the Wends that began in the 9th century with the Carolingians and continued through the Weimar Republic and the Nazi period. So if you were a Srbi a Sorb (Wend) in the 9th century, and a Jewish village from the Rhineland sprung up near you, and you were resisting Germanization, forced Christianity on your Pagan beliefs, wouldn't you at least consider becoming Jewish? You'd automatically get the chance to write your language with newly learned Hebrew letters.

The alternative would be the German alphabet, but you've just been defeated by the Germans and told to become Christian, to replace your Slavic language with German words. What would you do? Comprise, and start speaking what would develop later into Yiddish? Does this possibility sound more plausible than 500,000 Khazars turning Jewish and rushing into Poland after the destruction of Khazaria in 965 CE? Make up your own mind. Chances are a little bit of each might have happened, with traces of this enriched mosaic of genes joining the towns of the Jews fleeing oppression from the Middle East or Spain.

Lusatia was ruled at times by non-German princes. Since the Peace of Prague in 1635, it has remained under German control. In the 19th century when Jews were seeking surnames, many of these surnames came from Prussia such as

Lewin, Lewinsky, Levine, Levene, Levin, and Levenstein. Any book on genealogy will give Prussia as the place of origin for many names now used by Ashkenazim. Some genealogy books will give surnames as originated in both Prussia and Austria for these same names.

Before German unification in 1871 Lusatia, land of the Sorbs/Wends was contained in parts of the kingdoms of Prussia and Saxony. Lower Lusatia was under Prussian administration and Upper Lusatia under that of Saxony.

After World War II, the original land of the Sorbs was in part of the German Democratic Republic (East Germany). The Sorb area was divided administratively between the districts of Dresden and Cottbus. Wendish ethnic awareness has been encouraged under the German Democratic Republic. The Slavs of Lusatia, in their own language probably would prefer to be called Sorbs. So the term Sorb has been adopted for the Slavs of Lusatia.

Sorbs may want to reflect their Slavic heritage as West Slavs of Central European ancestry. They are not the Serbs of southern Europe who are another Slavic people living in Serbia. And Sorbs have never lived in Serbia, which is near Macedonia. Sorbs live in Eastern Germany and Western Poland. In current times, nearly 60,000 people in Lusatia call themselves Sorbs. For more information, contact the Sorbian cultural center (the Domowina). Sorbs have a Sorbian-language newspaper, radio station, theater, and folklore tradition.

So what if you are an Ashkenazic Levite whose Y chromosome reveals your ancestry is close to the modern Sorbs? Do you invite a Sorb to your home to share family photos? Do you find out genetically whether the rest of your genes match by markers? Or do you take a DNA test to find out your most recent common ancestor or any medieval ancestor linking you to that Sorb you've invited for dinner exchange of family photos? How important is your DNA test result in your core identity and in your life? There are a lot of travels to ponder.

That's why the historic origin of the Ashkenazic communities is debatable. You have to let the genes tell what they can. You also have to look at linkage disequilibrium (LD). Kruglyak (1999) reported that populations don't keep their LD over long genetic distances unless there have been sharp founder effects called bottlenecks.

Posters sometimes go up at genetics conferences illustrating the bottleneck in Ashkenazic mtDNA—female lineages. And the bottlenecks usually are in the recent past. (Reich et al. (2001).

You look at the last Ice Age (LGM) or you go further back to the out-of Africa migration into the Middle East or West Asia to see bottlenecks in huge populations. The bottlenecks can be specific to male or female lineages. You see them in the mtDNA in matrilineal lineages or the Y-chromosome lineages in males.

If the bottle neck or founder effect is harsh enough, the extinctions severe enough, you see a change in the genes (Wright et al 1999). One example of a great reduction in mtDNA diversity is seen in Georgian Jewish females. When you get severe mtDNA reduction in a population, you also get long-range linkage disequilibrium. Only Georgian Jewish females showing the great reduction in mtDNA are not Ashkenazic females from Central and Eastern Europe, especially North Eastern Europe. Also, South Eastern non-Jews are genetically close to North Eastern non-Jews.

So you have to look at Ashkenazic women and men in their own community and see how close or not close their genes are to the host populations. You already know the males cluster with other Jews and with males in the Middle East in 70 percent to 80 percent of individuals studied. What about the origin of Jewish mothers from Ashkenazic communities? Are they related to anyone in the Middle East? Are they related to one another?

Or are they formed from independent local women in independent communities that eventually merged in medieval times? You be the judge after reading the latest genetic findings. If you want to dig further, read the latest articles. Many findings on Ashkenazic mtDNA are unpublished at the time this book is being written, so there's no way to read the articles of the very latest findings. One thing is certain:

The mosaic of communities forms a rich tapestry of having merged together. By the time of publication, the articles will probably be available to the public in the various journals of human genetics. Read them. I've learned a lot from reading them, and I highly recommend the articles and the books. For now, until any more information comes in, the mothers of the Ashkenazic communities present a mosaic of communities that have merged. As Dr. Mark Thomas wrote, "Ashkenazi Jews were made up of a mosaic of different, independently founded communities that has since homogenised."

Also, I highly recommend the audio tapes of the conferences on Jewish genealogy. Visit audioiotapes.com on the Web at http://www.audiotapes.com/conf.asp?ProductCon=77 to see the 111 available audio tapes for the 19th Annual Conference on Jewish Genealogy recorded in 1999.

Check out the Y-chromosome haplogroups at: http://freepages.genealogy.rootsweb.com/~dgarvey/DNA/markers.htm

Check out your mtDNA at:
http://www.stats.ox.ac.uk/~macaulay/founder2000/tableA.html

http://shelob.bioanth.cam.ac.uk/mtDNA/toc.html

Also see the geographical index at: http://shelob.bioanth.cam.ac.uk/mtDNA/geogind.html

You can view the CRS online at: http://www.bioanth.cam.ac.uk/mtDNA/anderst.html. Also see the Web site on how to read female-line DNA tables at: http://family.nf/english/projects/female-lines/how-to-read-female-line-dna-tables.html.

Below is an mtDNA list of sequences from one person descending from a family of orthodox Jewish great grandparents who have been in rabbinical, scholarly families for dozens of generations according to traditions. The individual's mtDNA mutations below from the low-resolution HVR1 and the high-resolution HVR2 mutations are compared with the Cambridge Reference Sequence (CRS) to check for variability.

HVR1 Haplogroup H

HVR1 Mutations:

16189C

16356C

16362C

16519C

HVR2 Mutations:

263G

309.1C

315.1C

523-

524-

Where is the individual's ancestral geographic origin? Since family tradition has a cultural component and mtDNA has a biological component, where do these genes appear geographically in the ancient past, the recent past, and the present? The mtDNA doesn't show up in a table of Ashkenazi mtDNA from various tests performed. Is the female descended from a convert of Northern European ancestry?

Or because on a table, one sampled Palestinian had similar mtDNA sequences, does it mean the female is "really Jewish?" It's these kinds of questions that people actually ponder. The actuality is that a "real Jew" is someone who takes Judaism seriously and whose mother or grandmother is Jewish or has converted to Judaism according to tradition. Would it make a difference if one Northern European woman became Jewish 1,000 years ago in Prague rather than 3,500 years ago in Jerusalem? Does the individual descend from a matrilineal line in the Middle East, in West Asia, in Northern Europe, or in Southern Europe?

For DNA from a Moslem, would it make a difference if the person was from Europe or the Middle East? Of course not. What about a Christian? Can a Christian of a particular church be a Christian whether an ancestor came from one country or another? So why should would it be important to pin point the country of origin when we all pretty much come from the same place if we go back far enough to that one common ancestor.

Let's take a look at how online research can give some clues, but not a definite decision on where the matrilineal line originated. First we'll look at HVS-1, the low-resolution haplogroup mutations in the mtDNA that is, the matrilineal lines that go back about 21,000 years in Europe, and perhaps are even older before the ancestor migrated to Europe. Somewhere mtDNA haplogroup H hand a previous ancestor, possibly in the Middle East who was pre-HV. That ancestor gave rise to another ancestor HV, which in time gave rise to H.

Finally, H migrated from the Middle East or Western Asia to Europe and settled in the Ice Age "refugium" in southern France or Spain, near the Mediterranean in the foothills of the Pyrenees. About 13,000 years ago, V mtDNA (split off from H and migrated to Scandinavia and to the Berbers in N. Africa. H mtDNA became a "clan mother" during the Ice Age by successfully reproducing enough daughters to pass on the haplogroup. After the Ice Age, H expanded all over Europe from Iceland to the Urals and is a "pan European" type today. H mtDNA also is found in the Middle East. About 46% of Europeans and about 25% of Middle Eastern peoples currently have H mtDNA. V mtDNA possibly arose in Europe.

Searching the Mitomap Table at: http://shelob.bioanth.cam.ac.uk/mtDNA/hvr1n.html we find the slowest mutating sequence, 356 shows up in individuals from the following geographic locations: UK, Havik, Karelina, Portuguese, Turkish and Volga-Finnic.

Then we look at the next sequence which would be 356C and 362C and find it shows up in a Bulgar and a Karelian. When I get to the exact sequences 189C, 356C, 362C, it shows up in a person from the UK, Spain, Austria, and Bulgaria.

We see that the main mutation is 356 or actually 16356C in the individual with mtDNA H haplogroup, mutations at 16189C, 16356C, 16362C, 16519C. The 189 mutation or 16189C is a fast mutating site. So is the mutation 362 or to be exact, 16362C as it's usually written. So what we focus on for ethnicity is the slowest mutating site, which is 356 or 16356C.

In the tables at http://shelob.bioanth.cam.ac.uk/mtDNA/hvr1n.html on the Web, we see that 16356C is found in the Volga Finnic people of North Eastern Europe, but also in Turks, Bulgarians, and Portuguese. So does this very frum (religiously obedient) orthodox Ashkenazi Jewish person with ancestors from Bialystock, Poland and Bessarabia Rumania have a female ancestor who in ancient times—very ancient times came from Karelia (nation within and just east of Finland)? Or would the individual's Yiddish speaking ancestors have come from Bulgaria, Turkey, or Portugal? People of Southeastern Europe are closely related genetically to people of Northeastern Europe.

The time frame here could be tens of thousands of years or as recent as a common ancestor perhaps 250 years ago. Let's look a bit deeper into the ancestry and the sequences. Keep in mind that H haplogroup is pan-European and found all over the Middle East. The sequences place the individual in various possible geographic locations as far as ancestry.

These particular sequences also show up in one to four individuals recorded in other databases in Siena, Italy, in Crete, in Norway, Germany, Poland, Scotland, Bulgaria, Spain, England, Iceland, Croatia, Albania, Portugal, Austria, Bashkortostan in the Urals, the Ukraine, and among the Komi of Finland.

How can you tell where (geographically) the person's female ancestral line originated? That's part of the history and geography of human genes.

You can see where the mtDNA haplogroup started out, going from the Middle East to Europe, probably to the north of Spain or south of France 20,000–21,000 years ago. You see H in the Middle East about 28,000 years ago in the Fertile Crescent and in Anatolia and what was Armenia. You see it in the refugium in the Pyrenees 21,000 years ago, and in England 12,000 years ago where a young male skeleton was found in Gough's Cave in Somerset having H mtDNA haplogroup.

At the end of the Ice Age 12,500 years ago, H mtDNA traveled from the Cromagnon caves of southern France and Spain to what was to become England. All people in with European ancestors with H mtDNA descend from one single female with H mtDNA haplogroup who lived about 20,000 years ago in the Pyrenees area where there was a "refugium" from the Ice Age where the fishing was abundant and the campsites offered good shelter.

Yet, we still have to look further to get a handle on what happened to these particular sequences of H mtDNA. We know by looking at databases of Eastern Europe that those particular sequences 189C, 356C, 362C, 519C are found in North Central and North Eastern Europe primarily. They show up in Europe at a very low level, but where they show up most frequently is in Germany, Poland, Scotland, Norway, and Sweden.

Today, matches for these sequences are found frequently in England, Belgium, the Netherlands, the US, and Germany. The sequences are found all around the Adriatic Sea. So it's pan-European. On a low level, the sequences also show up in Turkey, Bulgaria, England, Spain, Portugal, Crete, and Italy. On a slightly higher level the sequences show up in Germany, Scotland, Poland, the Ukraine, and among the Komi in Finland.

We know Finland has one of the least diverse mtDNA pool. So all we can surmise from looking at the mtDNA databases is that the mtDNA haplogroup with those particular sequences show up at a low level in Europe and show up at a slightly higher level in North Central and North Eastern Europe. The difference in levels would be four individuals from Scotland and Germany have this sequence verses three individuals from Poland, Norway, Sweden for example. And the source would be a database with about 10,000 sequences in it.

We also know that without examining any particular sequence, H mtDNA in general, appears 25% of the time in the Middle East and more than 46% of the time all over Europe—from Iceland to the Urals. Those particular sequences of the individual do appear in Iceland, Norway, Sweden, Scotland, England, Germany, the Ukraine, (Komi group) of Finland, and Austria....but also in Bulgaria, Turkey, and as far east as Bashkortostan in the Urals. So we have to look at where it appears most—North Central Europe and North Eastern Europe.

The problem in looking at ancestry is that the point of origin is not necessarily where the mtDNA sequences appear in the largest numbers today, but where it is found most diverse. The more diverse the sequences the longer it has been in that place. This gives a clue to the origin or coalescence point.

H mtDNA in Turkey (ancient Anatolia) has a coalescence point of about 28,000 years or more compared to 20,000 years in Europe. However, the sequences of H in the Middle East would be different from the sequences of H in Europe in many cases, but not all.

You have this little movement call back-migration, where from ancient times people traveled from Europe back to the Middle East and stayed there. And you have waves of migration moving from southwest to northeast. About 15% of the Middle East is comprised of Europeans moving back there in prehistoric times, and about 20% to 26% of Middle Easterners, mostly Neolithic farmers after the end of the Ice Age moved into Europe. It took them much longer to reach the northern countries, but some did arrive and stay, introducing by trade the idea of farming to the Paleolithic hunters.

Where else can you check the history and geography of your mtDNA or Y chromosome? There are several excellent databases on the Web where you can check your sequences to see how many individuals from which countries have the same sequences as your own. Keep in mind that this information does not necessarily tell you where your particular ancestors came from, but the databases give you an idea where sequences like yours are found.

The question is, when you find someone with your sequences, does it mean that at one time you and that person shared the same common ancestor perhaps 300 generations ago or more? If you share the same single female mtDNA H haplogroup ancestor who lived 20–21,000 year ago in Europe, yes, you share at least the same first H mtDNA clan mother.

And perhaps if your sequences match today, you share a slightly more recent ancestor. However, those mutations could pop up anywhere in anyone's line, related or not with or without the same mtDNA H. It all depends on what the other mutations are along with your sequences. So you'd have to check out that person's lineage to see how it might have crossed the path of your ancestors to get a handle on your search.

Let's look further at HVS-1 sequences. First I searched the Internet at Macaulay's Founder Tables to see where my exact mtDNA sequences are showing up at: http://www.stats.ox.ac.uk/~macaulay/founder2000/tableA.html

Be aware that this table from the United Kingdom may not necessarily contain the same sequences from the same countries as some of the databases in Eastern Europe. So check out as many databases online or in scientific journals as you are able to access. For example, I found the exact sequences in Macaulay's Table listing the following sequences found in individuals claiming ancestry from the following geographic areas 189 356 and 362 for England, Spain, Austria, and Bulgaria. The tables at the Web site list abbreviated names for the countries.

How you search in what country currently your mtDNA HVS-1 haplogroup appears is by realizing that the letters stand for names of countries. For example: Nu means Nubia. Eg stands for Egypt. Be stands for Bedouin. Ye is Yemen. Iq is Iraq. In is India. Sy stands for Syria. Pl stands for Palestine (Arab Palestinian). Dz is Druze, a tribe of people living in Lebanon. Tk is Turkey. Ku is Kurd. Ar is Armenia. Az is Azerbaijan (in Central Asia), Cauc stands for people living in the areas of the Caucasus mountains such as Georgia, Armenia, Ossetia, Chechnya, Kabarda, Adyge, the Circassians, for example, the peoples of the north and south Caucasus mountains. MdE stands for Eastern Mediterranean.

SE is Southeastern Europe. MdC is central Mediterranean—Italy. Alp means the area of the Alps, such as Austria. NC stands for North Central Europe—Germany. MdW stands for Western Mediterranean, such as Spain and Portugal. Bs stands for Basque. NW stands for Northwestern Europe, namely, England/Britain. Sca means Scandinavia—Sweden, Iceland, Norway, Finland, and Denmark. NE is North Eastern Europe.

Look at the sequences of H mtDNA 189, 356, 362. The mutation (519C) wasn't included as some mtDNA research testing only test 400 or so base pairs. You'll see where the exact sequences appear in the table in only four countries: Spain, England, Austria, and Bulgaria. If you look at the sequences that contain the 356C mutation without the 362 mutation, you'll see it appears in more places and that more people have that sequence. The conclusion is that H mtDNA 189C, 356C, 362C, 519C appears at low levels in Europe.

Perhaps it went through a bottleneck. Perhaps it went through extinctions, even though it's the most frequent mtDNA haplogroup in Europe—which is H. However, it does appear in Europe in those four areas in that particular database. In an Estonian unpublished database, it appears in many more countries, including the one's in Macaulay's database.

The Estonian database has those exact sequences appearing among the Komi of Finland, in the Ukraine, in Croatia, Albania, Bulgaria, Turkey, Crete, but more frequently in Germany, Poland and Scotland, and also in England, Iceland, Sweden, Norway, and in Bashkortostan, a country in the Urals. According to the Macaulay database, those exact sequences aren't found east of Bulgaria. In the unpublished Estonian database Turkey and Bashkortostan are added, but also Crete. Since Albania and Crete show these sequences in the Estonian unpublished database, history notes there was a migration in medieval times from Albania to Greece and to Crete, and the population was absorbed.

So what are the origins of this person—Volga Finnic? Germanic? Polish? Bulgarian? Can we ever know for sure? The exact sequences are found in England, Netherlands, and Belgium. Where did the most recent ancestor of this individual originate? Will we know more in the future about tracing our ancestors from a great grandparent back in time several hundred or several thousand years?

We have the first ancestor—H mtDNA and the present, with the particular sequences living in the US. We know for generations the ancestors lived in Poland and then in Rumania. When did the ancestors arrive in Poland, and did they come from Germany or Lithuania? If Lithuania, when did they arrive there from what other geographic place? It's a fascinating migration as the sequences reveal.

So if you want to match your own sequences to a table that shows what nations your sequences appear in today, click on Macaulay's statistical tables from Oxford University in England and see whether your particular sequences are found in that database. The Web site again, is: http://www.stats.ox.ac.uk/~macaulay/founder2000/tableA.html.

Note that to the left of the table all the countries of the Middle East are listed starting with Nubia (in Africa) at the extreme left with Egypt next and then Bedouins, Yemen, Iraq, India, Syria, Palestine, Druze, Turkish, Kurdish, Armenian, Azerbaijan, Caucasus, Mediterranean East. Then you have to the right half of the table all the European countries going from the central Mediterranean—Italy north to the Alps and Austria followed by Germany, then down to Spain and Portugal and then to the Basques in Western Europe, then up again to England in NW Europe, then northeast to Scandinavia and finally to North East Europe.

The table more or less follows several of the routes of migrations of ancient and prehistoric peoples out of Africa (Nubia) into Egypt an then into the Middle East, to India, and migrating west to the Middle East and then north to the Caucasus, then back to Europe and finally, the last migration route from southwest Europe to Northeastern Europe passing through central Europe, England, Scandinavia, and finally reaching Northeastern Europe. Where are you on any of the databases? Also check out the mtDNA Concordance Tables at: http://shelob.bioanth.cam.ac.uk/mtDNA/hvr1o.html.

The individual from a long line of orthodox Jewish families was concerned that the mtDNA sequences didn't show up on the left side of the Macaulay Database statistical tables. Why didn't they show up with an ancestry in Iraq, Palestine, or Syria? Did the Jews flee oppression from those areas and move into Western and then Eastern Europe?

Why is the ancestral mother matching with all those Central and Eastern Europeans and also with individuals in Spain and Portugal and England? Note that only one person from Spain, one person from Austria, one person from England, and one person from Bulgaria shows up for that exact mtDNA sequences of HVS-1. So we dig a little further and look at the high resolution mtDNA mutations for HVS-2. And what do we find? This table below is from the individual's personal DNA reading for the high-resolution HVR2 mutations regarding deep maternal ancestry.

HVR2 Mutations   263G

309.1C

315.1C

523-

524-

We find that the HVR2 Mutations (or HVS-2) are found in most people all over Europe and all over Western Asia and the Middle East, or are they? Look where they do appear. The HVR2 mutations also are very common sequences. Remember that the HVS-1 appears only at a low level in Europe. But look at the high-resolution HVR2 mutations. They appear in France and in the Orkney Islands, in Scotland, Bulgaria, and Turkey.

HVR2 can distinguish mtDNA haplogroup H from mtDNA haplogroup U4. If you see the letter "A" at position 00073 in HVR2 (or HVS2) the mtDNA haplogroup is H. If you see a "G" at position 00073 in HVR2, the mtDNA haplogroup is U4. Both H and U4 contain the mutation sequence 356 or 16356C. However, U4 and H show up in different countries but they also show up in the same geographic ancestral areas. For example, U4 doesn't show up among the Ossetians of the Caucasus Mountains, but H shows up among this ethnic group. Sequences 189, 356, 362 haplogroup H doesn't show up in the Caucasus, at least in the databases, but again, you have to think about how many people are in the sample. Some databases contain at least 10,000 individuals from a variety of countries.

Check out some of the founders at: http://www.stats.ox.ac.uk/~macaulay/founder2000/tableB.html.

Note that the tables of founders at V. Macaulay's site of Oxford University, UK is excellent for checking your sequences on the Internet. I highly recommend looking at all the tables on these sites. So, is this individual with mtDNA haplogroup H, sequences at 16189C, 16356C, 16362C, 16519C Germanic, Northeastern European, Southeastern European, Middle Eastern or what do you think? What we are looking at here is the person's ancient female ancestor with the latest mutations since H mtDNA evolved thousands of years ago and is found all over West Eurasia.

What we have to narrow down is the current mutation sequences. That's the mutations or transitions in the sequences that evolved away from the Cambridge Reference Sequence (CRS) and see where in geographic location the sequences as they appear today turn up. Most helpful are tables online you can check out and the various statistical databases that match your mtDNA sequences to the actual parts of the world in which they appear. However, it won't tell you for sure whether you're related to anyone in that location today. Check out Vincent Macaulay's Web site at:

http://www.stats.ox.ac.uk/~macaulay/ and look over his tables. Perhaps you'll find your mtDNA sequences there. Also for males, interested also in Y chromosome haplogroups, check out the various Y chromosome tables at: http://freepages.genealogy.rootsweb.com/~dgarvey/DNA/markers.htm

If you want to see how genetically close Ashkenazim are to other nationalities, look at the Human Races Calculator on the Web at:

http://racearchives.com/calc/jewsychroms.asp?popid1=1&popid2=9&dbname=jewsychroms

Compare 6 Jewish and 23 non Jewish Y-Chromosome Analysis. You'll see that Ashkenazic male Y chromosomes match 95% with Syrian male Y-chromosomes, 94% with Greek Y-chromosomes, and 95% with Roman Jews.

Also see at that site: http://racearchives.com/calc/haplo_profiles.asp?dbname=europeanmtdnabyregion&po

You can select a population and view its profile as far as how distant or close the population is from another population. You can also view Y-chromosome haplotype frequency tables from the Hammer study at http://www.rasch.org/rmt/rmt161g.htm. The article is titled, "DNA and the Origins of Jewish Ethnic Groups. In the article at this Web site, the Ashkenazi male Y chromosomes are positioned on a table between the Jewish non-Ashkenazi and the Turks. Other studies report Ashkenazi male Y chromosomes close to the Greeks and still other studies close to the Kurds. So you have to look at a large number of studies to see whether there is agreement over time where the Ashkenazi stand.

The article, "In DNA, New Clues to Jewish Roots," by Nicholas Wade, at: http://www.racesci.org/in_media/raceanddna/dna_jewish_nyt_May2002.htm reports that the Ashkenazim show "less diversity in its mitochondrial DNA, perhaps reflecting the maternal definition of Jewishness. But unlike the other Jewish populations, it does not sow signs of having had very few female founders."

What the pattern in the Ashkenazic population does suggest is that it's a mosaic of separate populations "formed the same way as the others." According to the article, it reports that Dr. Harry Ostrer, a medical geneticist at New York

University said, "the 26 specific genetic diseases found among Ashkenazim usually attributed to 'founder effects' could be explained by the idea of small populations."

So what you get from reading more and more research articles on Ashkenazic genetic origins is that the whole idea of Jewish communities founded by Jewish men and local women is against the Jewish tradition. What do the genes say? Tradition says the first Jewish communities in Eastern Europe were formed by families who fled oppression from one land and were invited by princes to populate other lands, usually to the East.

What was the primary catalyst that brought the Jewish communities together in medieval times through the 18th century? How do you trace Jewish DNA for ancestry and family history through 3,000 years by looking at a merging mosaic of communities? How much trade, traffic, intermarriage, migration, and rapport occurred between the Ashkenazic and non-Ashkenazic Jewish communities of Europe, the Middle East, Africa, Central Asia, India, and China in historic times? And when the records can't be readily accessible, how much detail can we read in the DNA?

10

Merging a Mosaic of Jewish Communities by DNA

Say you're Jewish with ancestors from Eastern Europe, an Ashkenazim whose ancestors spoke Yiddish in the old country. How do you interpret your own DNA test results to look at not only your own family history, but your ancestors as far back as you can go genetically? You know the records may stop at one point back in time, but the DNA will not stop. It will mutate over thousands of years, but it will show you an open road on where you came from, even in a general sense.

I highly recommend the book, *The Beginnings of Jewishness* by Dr. Shaye Choen, professor of Jewish literature and philosophy at Harvard. When you begin to trace your DNA think about when the Jewish communities were formed. Were they formed in Southern Italy in the third and fourth century? Or were the communities formed soon after the Islamic conquests from the seventh to the ninth centuries CE?

If you consider Jewish tradition that says families practiced matrilineal descent to determine Jewishness, and your DNA search takes you to the seventh to ninth centuries CE, you can see how small communities were formed in places such as Alsace in France or in the Rhine Valley. Look at articles written by Dr. Hammer, Dr. Goldstein, and the population geneticists who are researching Ashkenazic mtDNA, the founding mothers.

Look at DNA to see founding events. Read the article by M.F. Hammer, A.J. Redd, et al. (2000) "Jewish and Middle Eastern non-Jewish populations Share a Common Pool of Y-Chromosome Biallelic Haplotypes." Proc. National Academy of Science, USA, Vol 97, Issue 12, 6769–6774, June 6, 2000. Then compare the study with later articles such as ""High-resolution Y chromosome haplotypes of Israeli and Palestinian Arabs reveal geographic substructure and substantial overlap with haplotypes of Jews." Oppenheim, Ariella, et al. *Human Genetics* 107(6) (December 2000): 630–641.

Check out "The Y Chromosome Pool of Jews as Part of the Genetic Landscape of the Middle East." Oppenheim, Ariella, et al. *The American Journal of Human Genetics* 69:5 (November 2001): 1095–1112. I also recommend reading the following articles: "Study finds close genetic connection between Jews, Kurds." Traubman, Tamara. *Ha'aretz* (November 21, 2001).

According to the article, it's the Sephardic Jewish males who closely resemble the Kurdish Jewish males. The Ashkenazim were found to differ from the Sephardic and Kurdish males, even though in most previous studies, the Y chromosome of Ashkenazim clusters closely with Sephardic Jews. Yet in this study the Kurdish and Sephardic Jewish populations differed to some degree from Ashkenazic Jews. Studies are still suggesting Ashkenazic males mixed with European peoples during their diaspora in varying degrees, except for the Ashkenazic males with the Cohen Modal Haplotype on their Y chromosomes.

The researchers suggested that the approximately 12.7 percent of Ashkenazic Jews carrying the Eu 19 chromosomes—signature of Eastern Europeans, descend paternally from eastern Europeans. The Eu 19 chromosome shows up in 56% of Polish men and 60% of Hungarian men. Not all Ashkenazic males carry the Eu19 chromosome.

Read the article, "Are today's Jewish priests descended from the old ones?" Zoossmann-Diskin, Avshalom. *HOMO: Journal of Comparative Human Biology* 51:2–3 (2000): 156–162. See the article at: http://www.ariga.com/genes.shtml titled, "Doctor finds fault in the contentions that the "Cohen modal haplotype" designates Israelites and that most Jewish priests have a common ancestor." 27 February 2001.

According to the article at the Web site, "Zoossmann disputes point that the Cohen Modal Haplotype is the signature for the Hebrew nation. * The Cohen modal haplotype is the most common haplotype among Southern and Central Italians*1, Hungarians*2, and Iraqi Kurds*3, and is also found among many Armenians*4 and South African Lembas*5. This calls into question the notion that the haplotype was a marker for the ancient Hebrew population."

You'd have to compare Dr. Zoossmann's article with the articles that discuss the Cohen Modal Haplotype such as "*Y Chromosomes of Jewish Priests*," in Nature volume 385 by Michael F. Hammer, Karl Skorecki, and their colleagues, January 2, 1997, and the article, "*Origins of Old Testament Priests*" by Karl Skorecki, David Goldstein, et al. in Nature volume 394. Before you begin your research, look at the Cohen Modal Haplotype Web site at: http://www.geocities.com/hrhdavid/cmhindex.html.

The point is that whenever you have a research study and a resulting article, another scientist will find some flaw in it. That's the way the scientific process moves forward. My highest recommendation on how to understand all this is to look at articles and research done by scientists with enough genetics background to consider the possibilities. There are many sites on the Web discussing Jewish genetics, many written by historians and many written by scientists and physicians. Then there are articles summarizing secondary sources. You have to do your own homework and be the judge. New studies come out each year with new information. The door is open for new results and findings.

The majority of Ashkenazic Jewish men carrying the Eu 9 chromosomes and similar markers descend paternally from Judeans who lived in Israel two thousand years ago. So the point is you can't make a judgment about the ancestry of any particular Jewish male—or female—until you look at all the genetic markers and match them to the geographic location where they are or were.

There's always the Cohen Modal Haplotype found in some Ashkenazic males to research. I recommend the article, "The Priests' Chromosome? DNA analysis supports the biblical story of the Jewish priesthood." Travis, J. *Science News* 154:14 (October 3, 1998): 218. Jewish women don't have a Cohen Modal Haplotype because it's a male Y-chromosome passed from father to son for thousands of years. The new puzzle to solve is the Ashkenazic females. Since Jewish tradition passes the Jewish heritage as a religion and ethnic community from mother to children, what geographic areas did the women come from?

I suggest following studies on mtDNA and other markers to see where the mothers came from or at least who the mothers' genes are closest to in current times. So much has been studied and written about male Y-chromosomes and ancestry and so little on women. The door is just opening and currently much of the data is yet unpublished.

So patience will reveal new information on women as soon as the newer studies are published. In the meantime, keep informed by looking at the latest articles in the various human genetics journals. Contact your local Jewish genealogy society and see what speaker is available who is researching mtDNA and other female ancestry markers. Universities around the world have population genetics departments doing research. Keep in contact with them and their publications and/or conferences.

Once you found your DNA trail—mtDNA for women, Y-chromosomes for men, and even if you took a racial percentages DNA test, what do you do with the information? You create a time capsule, a scrap book, a type of DNA and oral history journal. You use photography, text, sound, music, speech, video, and you put your ancestral record archive in an oral history—transcribed and put to audio or video, to sound, text and imagery. You even may want to put your information on the Web or in an archive to be viewed by future descendants. The whole tapestry links you back to that first ancestor and to the one in the future. It's a rich experience in history and time.

How do you write, tape, and transcribe an oral history of your DNA along with your genealogy and family history records and photos? Assuming you're a beginner in genealogy with no science background and interested in family history, where do you begin your search? What's the cultural component behind a trait as biological as your genes?

If you're a family historian, an oral history researcher, or a person fascinated with ancestry, here's how to understand the results of DNA tests. Different people have different, sometimes opposite opinions on whether DNA testing is a useful tool in the hands of family historians. If you are a carrier of a genetic disorder, DNA testing is useful in researching your family history to find out who was the first carrier in your ancestry back in time.

Here the debate unfolds as scientists, authors, physicians, media people, owners of DNA testing companies, genealogists, historians and researchers comment, write, and opine on DNA testing and genealogy.

What is the distribution of mtDNA haplogroup K? We know that haplogroup K is a clade of haplogroup U. Previous studies revealed that 27% to 32% of Ashkenazim have haplogroup K and that 9.0 of Ashkenazim have the mtDNA haplogroup H that follows the CRS. The rest have mutations of haplogroup H that does not follow the sequences of the CRS without mutations. What is the distribution of mtDNA haplogroup K in the rest of the populations sampled?

Take for example one sample appearing in the chapter, *Anatolian and Trans-Caucasus Populations*, Archaeogenetics: DNA and the Population Pehistory of Europe, McDonald Institute Monographs, 2002, page 223. The highest figure is 31.7% in Georgians sampled have haplogroup K mtDNA. Next are Armenians sampled with 27.8% haplogroup K mtDNA. Following are Turks with 24.7%, and Siena, Italy samples, Tuscans, Saradinians, French, and Albanian samples with 35.8% haplogroup K mtDNA. Haplogroup K mtDNA also appears at 25% in the Nile Valley, and at 20% in Ethiopians, and 1.2% of Indians. It also appears at 11% in Estonians, Finns, and Karelians, and at 18.6% in Russians, Poles, Czechs, and Slovaks.

Where did it originate? In the Middle East, probably, but about 17,000 years ago it developed in Europe in the area where Venice, Italy is today and then migrated into the Alps.

How do you use DNA testing to interpret family history records? How eager are people to take a DNA test for family history research? Most DNA tests require only that someone swish mouthwash around in his or her mouth and send it for testing to a laboratory. So what can a DNA test really tell you about your own ancestry—distant or not so distant? And most of all, how do you interpret and use the results?

Here's a letter from Dr. Mark Humphrys:
Lecturer
School of Computer Applications,
Dublin City University,
Glasnevin, Dublin 9, Ireland.

"Dear Anne:

Here's a summary of the position as I see it:
Why everybody in the west is descended from Charlemagne:
We all know that all humans are related. So a good question is: When was our Most Recent Common Ancestor (MRCA)?

Surprisingly, the answer to that question is a lot more recent than DNA studies would suggest, since we are searching all lines of descent, rather than just the lines genes traveled on. You do not inherit all your ancestor's DNA, but only a small part of it. And yet, even if you inherit NONE of their DNA (which is not only possible, but probable, as you go back far enough), they are still your ancestor.

To find the answer to the MRCA, we need to look beyond DNA studies. Mathematical models suggest that, if humans picked mates randomly, the MRCA is in historical times, perhaps c. 1200 AD! This is an amazing result, suggesting that we do not have to go back into prehistory to find an ancestor of every single human! But obviously humans do not pick mates randomly—they tend to mate with people in their local geographic area.

Computer simulations that take this into account suggest that even with a high degree of local mating, the MRCA is still in historical times, perhaps c. 300 AD. If we consider just the West, the MRCA may be as recent as c. 1000 AD.

How realistic are these models?
Well, there has been a growing collection of REAL, proven descents from medieval figures in genealogy. For instance, my own children have proven descents—through many different lines—from Charlemagne, who lived around 800 AD. He is the ancestor of most of the royal houses of Europe and so is a natural focal point for the genealogies of the West.

My web page, Royal Descents of Famous People, is a large and growing list of famous people in the west who are all proven descendants of Charlemagne. And if all these people have proven descents, every step of the way, how many more people must have descents in reality that cannot be proved because of the scarcity of records? It must be a much greater number. My work is a strong indicator that everyone in the West descends from medieval royalty.

In short, work by a number of people—my genealogical study, other people's computer simulations and mathematical models—all confirm each other's findings that the MRCA for a large, interbreeding area such as the West, is within recent recorded history. Another finding of those models is that not long before the MRCA, if someone is the ancestor of anyone alive today, they are the ancestor of all people alive today. Since Charlemagne is probably around that early date for the West, and since he is a proven ancestor of some people, it is likely that he is the ancestor of all people in the West.

Everybody in the West is descended from Charlemagne:
In conclusion, if you have west European ancestry at all, it seems virtually impossible for you not to be descended from Charlemagne, who
How to Interpret Your DNA Test Results For Family History & Ancestry xii
lived around 800 AD. 90 percent of the world (including all the West) is descended from Confucius:

For the MRCA of the whole world, we need to consider extremely isolate daboriginal populations. If they were truly isolated, we may have to go back thousands of years to get a common ancestor with them. For people who did not live in isolated enclaves though—the West, Middle East, more or less all of Asia, most of Africa—the MRCA is highly likely to be in recent historical times (late BC, possibly even AD). Anyone with ancestry from these areas is, for example, almost certainly a descendant of Confucius, who lived around 500 BC and who is a proven ancestor of some people alive today in China, hence probably ancestor of all people in the world except the extremely isolated.

This exciting consensus is fairly new, and is supported by three independent fieldsof (a) genealogy, (b) mathematical models, and (c) computer simulations.

The findings are robust with respect to barriers such as religion, class difference, etc. All one needs is a tiny amount of crossing of such barriers in the population in the past in order to get everyone today (of different religions etc.) with a recent common ancestor.

The only thing that can push back the MRCA before historical times is total geographic isolation of populations from each other, which we know did not happen for most of the world.
People are inspired (rightly so) by DNA studies of ancient common human ancestors tens of thousands of years ago. And yet the fact is that we are almost certainly all descended from any historical figure in classical times that left descendants."

---

end quote

Web pages on MRCAs:
http://computing.dcu.ie/~humphrys/FamTree/Royal/ca.html
http://computing.dcu.ie/~humphrys/FamTree/Royal/ca.genetic.html
http://computing.dcu.ie/~humphrys/FamTree/Royal/ca.math.html
http://computing.dcu.ie/~humphrys/FamTree/Royal/famous.descents.html

The Web pages include a fantastic computer simulation by a gentleman named Rohde at MIT to work out the MRCA for a non-random mating model. He confirms much of Chang's work, and in general it is another strong indicator that the MRCA for the world (or 99 percent of it) is post-1000 BC—maybe even AD.

Regards
—Mark
Dr.Mark Humphrys

Lecturer
School of Computer Applications,
Dublin City University,
Glasnevin, Dublin 9, Ireland.
http://computing.dcu.ie/~humphrys/

Steve Olson, author of the book, Mapping Human History in a telephone interview with me on December 3, 2002 at 1:50 PM EST answered my question—What do you say about using DNA as a tool for genealogy—to extend family history research?

"The most valuable use of DNA testing is to demonstrate how closely related we are to each other, both as individuals and as members of human groups," Steve Olson says. "I'm a skeptic about the Seven Daughters of Eve (book) because I believe that everyone in the world is descended from all seven of those women. As I point out in my book, Mapping Human History."

"As I point out in the book, I believe that everyone living today is descended from most people who lived a few millennia ago," Olson explains. "So genetic tests need to be interpreted very carefully or you draw false conclusions about being descended from a relatively small number of people."

Does Steve Olson think DNA testing as a tool is useful to genealogists? "No, I don't feel DNA testing can tell you things that can't be discovered in other ways. I should probably say here, though, that I'm fairly skeptical about DNA testing for genealogical purposes, and I'm particularly critical of the Seven Daughters of Eve idea."

The Seven Daughters of Eve, is a book written by Bryan Sykes, from Oxford Ancestors. Bryan Sykes, MA PhD DSc, is Professor of Human Genetics, University of Oxford, and with Oxford Ancestors, who comments in this book. Sykes has a different opinion about DNA testing and genealogy/family history research.

Oxford Ancestors is the world's first company to harness the power and precision of modern DNA-based genetics for use in genealogy. The motto on the Oxford Ancestors Web site at:
<http://www.oxfordancestors.com/> reads: "Putting the genes in genealogy."

Oxford ancestors is based on more than a decade of research into human populations and their origins carried out by Professor Bryan Sykes, Professor of Human Genetics at the University of Oxford and his team in the world-renowned Institute of Molecular Medicine in Oxford, England.

So as you read in this book, and any other books you research, there are many different experts in genetics, medicine, and the media with different opinions.

Science is supposed to be skeptical by nature as well as open-minded for change. Facts provide an open door to further inquiry, and facts need to be checked as new information comes in. So what stance will you take? Will you take the skeptical side on DNA testing? Or do you reason that DNA testing is one more tool that adds genes to genealogy? Where will you stand in this debate—observer, skeptic, or DNA researcher working with genealogy and genetics?

Perhaps you're a genealogist or oral historian doing family history research and you have no science background in genetics. Now that the molecular revolution has introduced DNA testing for ancestry research, here's how to use your curiosity.

You may want to find information about tests of racial percentages or DNA testing and ancestry. Make up your own mind. Now you can combine DNA research and oral history research into one archive. How do you interpret DNA tests and how do you plan, record, and transcribe an oral history for your family or others?

DNA testing for ancestry is offered by companies that combine DNA testing (done by commercial laboratories and/or university laboratories) with surname genealogy. Various surname groups on the Web also offer discounts with DNA testing companies and laboratories. Ask for the facts.

Whom do you go to first, assuming you have no background in either science or genealogy? Scientists? The media? DNA testing companies? University laboratories? Oral historians? Genealogists? Biological anthropologists? DNA mailing lists on the Web? Whom can you trust?

And where does the truth lie—in technology? It's like twelve blind men asked to describe an elephant. Each touches a different part of its body and replies, "it's a tail," or "it's a trunk." Everyone has a different opinion of the value of DNA testing in researching family history or ancestry.

What do the changing scientific facts say, for now? Question authority, and do your research. Then decide what tools are the best for you in your own family history quest.

Go online to Pub Med, an NCBI research engine on the Internet for medical and scientific articles in professional journals. Read the article titled, "The common, Near-Eastern Origin of Ashkenazi and Sephardi Jews Supported by Y-Chromosome Similarity," Santachiara Benerecette, AS, Semino O, Passarino G, Torroni A, Brdicka R, Fellous M., Modiano G, Diparrtimento de Biologia Cellulare, University della Calabria, Cosenza, Italy. Annals of Human Genetics Jan; 57 (Pt 1): 55–64, 1993. Compare the study to studies done on Jewish Y-chromosomes a decade later. What new information did you find?

In the 1993 study about 80 Sephardim, 80 Ashkenazim and 100 Czechosolvaks had a DNA test of their Y-chromosomes. These males were examined for the Y-specific RFLPs. The aim of the study was to look at the origin of the Ashkenazi gene pool by looking at specific genetic markers useful to estimate the paternal gene contribution to these men's origins. To find out ancestry, scientists examine specific genetic markers in the DNA.

The genetic markers of the Ashkenazim and the Sephardim were compared with each other and with the Czechoslovakians. The Czechoslovakians turned out to be very different from the two Jewish groups. Who are the Ashkenazim closest to? The Sephardim first, and then the Lebanese. Both the Ashkenazim and the Sephardim appeared to be closely related to the Lebanese. The conclusion of the study was that Ashkenazi and Sephardi are both close genetically to the Lebanese as far as their Y-chromosome-specific RFLP markers. According to the Pub Med abstract, "A preliminary evaluation suggests that the contribution of foreign males to the Ashkenazi gene pool has been very low (1% or less per generation.)

Also check out, Santachiara Benerecetti AS, Semino O, Passarino G, Morpurgo GP, Fellous M, Modiano G (1992) "*Y-chromosome DNA polymorphisms in Ashkenazi and Sepharadi Jews.*" In: Bonné-Tamir B, Adam A (eds) Genetic diversity among Jews: diseases and markers at the DNA level. Oxford University Press, New York, pp 45–50

In the nineties decade, most of the studies of Ashkenazic DNA ancestry markers focused on looking at the paternal lineages, the Y-chromosomes, unless the studies were specific for genetic diseases research. Population genetics that looks at ancestry focused widely on the male line of descen. Articles or research tracing the maternal lineages were difficult to find in public searches of scientific journals or even in the media.

With the new decade, more studies of the maternal lineages of Ashkenazim and non-Ashkenazic Jews are more readily available. Still, there is research yet unpublished that continuously adds new information to the research.

The question remains, who were our founding mothers and from where did they come—from ancient Israel, from Western Asia, from Europe or are we what we appear to be—a mosaic of Jewish communities that merged and intermarried over the centuries? Is there yet to be found an unbroken line yet found that links us to any one ancient civilization, or is there? Or are we mixed with the memories of expansions and migrations over thousands of years?

The mtNDA reveals the haplogroups found among non-Jews with similar origins predating any organized religion. We females are part of the K mtDNA haplogroup clan and the H mtDNA haplogroup clan that gave rise to millions of Europeans, West Asians, and Middle Eastern peoples. What new information. Are Jews a race?

The answer is they are part of the human race. The debate will go on regarding how many genes tie Jews to their ancestral palm-latitudes home in the Levant and before that in the Fertile Crescent. Is there unity in diversity? Why such a debate on origins at all? It's more political than religious. Anyone who takes Judaism seriously can become a Jew, have a child and rear it as Jewish, and so on for thousands of years since Abraham smashed the idols in his dad's sculpture shop in ancient Sumeria.

If Jews weren't linked to the Middle East, why would caricature stereotyped images portray them in cartoons with typical Semite features and Assyroid skulls? And yet if European Jews didn't look Northern European as well, why would they be forced to wear armbands with six-pointed stars in Germany and North Eastern Europe during World War II, unless they looked so much like Germans you couldn't point them out in public as appearing different in coloring or features?

Seeking a core identity is the reason why Jews want to explore ancestry by DNA testing. The feeling you belong to a certain group of people who wrote certain books of wisdom in ancient times is powerful. You want to belong to a family, a family within the family of humankind. You want to celebrate holidays with others celebrating the same holidays.

Jews come in all colors and in all types of DNA. And yet, there is this paternal lineage link to the Lebanese for the Ashkenazim and the Sephardim. Now what about our founding mothers? Like my former teacher once remarked, "How could a young, Jewish merchant from Baghdad or Persia traveling to Poland or to the Jewish communities in the Rhine Valley in the ninth century resist marrying a redheaded or blonde 'shiksa' goddess on the road to Speyer?" The answer could be, more genes outflowed from the Jewish males into the general local population than came in and remained.

So the origin of Ashkenazic communities will always be up for debate and theory. The details remain in the genes that reveal ancestral lines. How would historians account for the Ashkenazic Levites some, but not all, of which have genes close to Sorb males? Did Sorb males convert to Judaism to escape oppression from the Germans who invaded their Western Slavic territories to convert them to Christianity and Germanize them at a time when they were pagans resisting Christianity and the German language?

Did they team up with the Jewish communities living in East Germany in those early medieval centuries, perhaps around the year 800 CE? All scientists know is that the many Jewish communities founded independently eventually merged as more and more people flowed east into Poland upon invitation from the Polish princes. The Ashkenazic families migrated from Germany, France, and Hungary eastward. By 1000 CE, most Jewish communities were already founded and scholarship began to flourish, such as the writings of Rashi.

Who were these Ashkenazic Jews of Germany and France? They were the Roman Jews, the Jews who lived in ancient Rome who migrated northward from Southern Italy and Rome after the fall of Rome. They went were the trade flourished—trade that didn't require owning land. They minted coins and changed money, cut diamonds, or worked with gold. They sewed clothing and peddled wares. They traveled and wrote books.

They were musicians and healers, rabbis and scholars. And they went were they were welcome. Some followed the northward movements of the Roman army. Sephardic Jews traveled the same routes, but instead of going north, went to Spain and N. Africa. Other Jews fleeing oppression branched into Iraq, Syria, Greece, and Persia. Some went out to Bukhara and Central Asia from villages in Iraq. Some went to India and some to Ethiopia.

Sometimes they found local women and married them, and other times, the women came from other Jewish communities. So you can't at least at this time in research make a sweeping statement of where all the women came from. You can only say they came mostly from other merging Jewish communities. Further scientific research again, will let the details in the genes speak their ancestral history. So keep updated and read the emerging articles in the human genetics journals.

You can access them online through most of the medical research engines on the Internet. Or you can visit a university library, especially a medical school library, and read the newest articles at the library as well as the latest books on Jewish genetic diversity or any other topic in genetics. The particular field looks at population genetics and evolutionary genetics. Read the article that will take you back before there were borders or organized religions titled, "*Tracing European Founder Lineages in the Near Eastern mtDNA Pool.*" Martin Richards, Vincent Macaulay, et al. American Journal of Human Genetics, 67: 1251–1276, 2000.

See where your mother really came from. (The term "our mothers" refers to the human race.) You'll notice in the articles you read that the British often use the term "Near Eastern" and that the Americans use the term "Middle Eastern" for the same area.

Perhaps you want to find out the percentage of various races in your ancestry. How do know where to begin your journey into the past and future? What if you're a foundling, an orphan, or have no knowledge of your own ethnicity? Can a DNA test at least tell you how many races are in your recent or ancient past? What facts do genetic markers really tell you about ancestry?

If you want to start your ancestry search with DNA testing, first you take the DNA tests along with tests of racial percentages if you desire. Even your DNA has a cultural component to its molecular biology. Then you interpret the results making the complex easy to understand for yourself or your clients. Your DNA testing service can help you find answers. So can many Web sites as well as this book and other books recommended here.

Next in your family history search, you collect letters, diaries, oral history transcriptions, home sources, artifacts, memorabilia, Census research, wills-and-probate records, medical histories, land records, slave ownership records, if it applies to your or your client. Pay particular attention to social histories to fill some gaps left by lack of women's records.

Search through church, synagogue, mosque, pagoda, or temple records, vital records from the US government such as military records, social security information, and government pensions for retired government employees, employment and tax records, if any exist and are available. Check school records from elementary through college, if any, social histories, ethnic histories, and religious school records.

Go to the family history Web sites, the ships' passenger lists. I highly recommend a book for searching women's ancestry, titled, *Discovering Your Female*

Ancestors, by Sharon DeBartolo Carmack, Betterway Books, Ohio 1998, ISBN # 1-55870-472-8. The book's subtitle emphasizes "Special strategies for uncovering hard-to-find information about your female lineage."

Marriage records often were in different languages representing the former country or languages of the ethnic group. You may need to translate a different alphabet to find a maiden name on a marriage certificate never registered, but obtained from clergy.

Then you review and analyze the records. Study the social history of the times and location of this individual.Add family history and migrations to social history, and you have the beginnings of an outline to write a biography of the ancestor as a family history.

Learn to interpret the results of your own DNA test and expand your historical research ability to trace your ancestry. "An interesting idea was expressed by a colleague from Canada, Dr. Charles Scriver," explains geneticist, Dr. Batsheva Bonné-Temir. "At a meeting which I organized
here in Israel on Genetic Diversity Among Jews in 1990, Dr. Scriver gave a paper on 'What Are Genes Like that Doing in a Place Like This? Human History and Molecular Prosopography.' He claimed that a biological trait has two histories, a biological component and a cultural
component." Dr. Charles Scriver is founder of the DeBelle Laboratory of Biochemical Genetics in Canada. He also established screening programs in Montreal for thalassaemia and Tay Sachs Disease.

According to Bonné-Tamir, at the 1990 meeting in Israel on Genetic Diversity Among Jews, Dr. Charles Scriver stated, "When the event clusters and an important cause of it is biological, the cultural history also is likely to be important because it may explain why the persons carrying the gene are in the particular place at the time."

The term, "when the event clusters" refers to an event when genes cluster together in a DNA test because the genes are similar in origin, that is, they have a common ancestral origin in a particular area, a common ancestor.

"When I look at my own papers throughout the years," says Bonné-Tamir. "I find that I have been quite a pioneer in realizing the significance of combining the history of individuals or of populations with their biological attributes. This is now a leading undertaking in many studies which use, for example, mutations to estimate time to the most recent ancestors and alike."

What lines of inquiry are used in genetics? Dr. Charles R. Scriver wrote a chapter in Batsheva Bonné-Temir's book, titled What are genes like that doing in a place like this? Human History and Molecular Prosopography. The book title is: Genetic Diversity Among Jews:

Diseases and Markers at the DNA Level. Bonné-Tamir, B. and Adam, A. Oxford University Press. 1992. With permission, an excerpt is reprinted below from page 319:

"When a disease clusters in a particular community, two lines of inquiry follow:

1. Is the clustering caused by shared environmental exposure? Or is it explained by host susceptibility accountable to biological and/or cultural inheritance? 2. If the explanation is biological, how are the determinants inherited? These lines of inquiry imply that a disease has two

different histories, one biological, the other cultural. One involves genes (heredity), pathways of development (ontogeny), and constitutional factors; the other, demography, migration and cultural practice.

Neither history is mutually exclusive. Such thinking shifts the focus of inquiry from sick populations and incidence of disease to sick individuals and the cause of their particular disease. The person with the disease becomes the object of concern which is not the same as the disease the person has." (Page. 319).

After hearing from Dr. Scriver by email, I then emailed Stanley M. Diamond. He contacted writer, Barbara Khait, and got permission for me to reprint in this book some of what she wrote about Diamond's project. It's the chapter, "Genetics Study Identifies At-risk relatives" from Celebrating the Family published by Ancestry.com Publishing.

Check out the Web site at:

http://shops.ancestry.com/product.asp?productid=2625&shopid=128.

Here's the reprinted article. Persons interested may go to the Web site for more information. I found out about Stanley M. Diamond from Dr. Scriver, since he mentioned Stanley M. Diamond's project in the book chapter Scriver wrote for Batsheva Bonné-Temir's book on Genetic Diversity Among Jews: Diseases and Markers at the DNA Level. Barbara Khait's chapter follows.

◆ ◆ ◆

"In 1977, Stanley Diamond of Montreal learned he carried the betathalassemia

genetic trait. Though common among people of Mediterranean, Middle Eastern, Southeast Asian and African descent, the trait is rare among descendants of eastern European Jews like Stan. His doctor made a full study of the family and identified Stanley's father as the source.

"Stan was spurred to action by a letter his brother received in 1991 from a previously unknown first cousin. Stan asked the cousin, "Do you carry the beta-thalassemia trait?" Though the answer was no, Stan began his journey to find out what other members of his family might
be unsuspecting carriers.

"Later that year, Stan found a relative from his paternal grandmother's family, the Widelitz family. Again he asked, "Is there any incidence of anemia in your family?"His newfound cousin answered, "Oh, you mean beta-thalassemia? It's all over the family!"

"There was no question now that the trait could now be traced to Stan's grandmother, Masha Widelitz Diamond and that Masha's older brother Aaron also had to have been a carrier. Stan's next question: who passed the trait onto Masha and Aaron? Was it their mother, Sura
Nowes, or their father, Jankiel Widelec?

"At the 1992 annual summer seminar on Jewish genealogy in New York City, Stan conferred with Or. Robert Desnick, who suggested that Stan's first step should be to determine whether the trait was related to a known mutation or a gene unique to his family.He advised Stan to seek out another Montrealer, Dr. Charles Scriver of McGill University-Montreal Children's Hospital. With the help of a grant, Dr. Scriver undertook the necessary DNA screening with the goal of determining the beta-thalassemia mutation.

"During this time, Stan began to research his family's history in earnest and identified their nineteenth century home town of Ostrow Mazowiecka in Poland. With the help of birth, marriage, and death records for the Jewish population of Ostrow Mazowiecka filmed by The Church of Jesus Christ of Latter-day Saints (LOS), Stan was able to construct his family tree.

"Late in 1993, Dr. Scriver faxed the news that the mutation had been identified and that it was, in fact, a novel mutation. Independently, Dr. Ariella Oppenheim at Jerusalem's Hebrew University-Hadassah Hospital mad e a similar discovery about a woman who had recently
emigrated from the former Soviet Union.

""The likelihood that we were witnessing a DNA region 'identical by descent' in the two families was impressive.We had apparently discovered a familial relationship between Stanley and the woman in Jerusalem, previously unknown to either family," says Dr. Scriver.

"It wasn't very long ago when children born with thalassemia major seldom made it past the age of ten. Recent advances have increased life span but, to stay alive, these children must undergo blood transfusions every two to four weeks. And every night, they must receive painful
transfusions of a special drug for up to twelve hours.
"The repeated blood transfusions lead to a buildup of iron in the body that can damage the heart, liver, and other organs. That's why, when the disease is misdiagnosed as mild chronic anemia, the prescription of additional iron is even more harmful. Right now, no cure exists
for the disease, though medical experts say experimental bone-marrow transplants and gene-therapy procedures may one day lead to one.
"Stan's primary concern is that carriers of thalassemia trait may marry, often unaware that their mild chronic anemia may be something else. To aid in his search for carriers of his family's gene mutation of the beta-thalassemia trait, he founded and coordinates an initiative known
as Jewish Records Indexing-Poland, an award-winning Internet-based index of Jewish vital records in Poland, with more than one million references. This database is helping Jewish families, particularly those at increased risk for hereditary conditions and diseases, trace their medical
histories, as well as geneticists."
Says Dr. Robert Burk, professor of epidemiology at the Albert Einstein College of Medicine at Yeshiva University, and principal investigator for the Cancer Longevity, Ancestry and Lifestyle (CLAL) study in the Jewish population (currently focusing on prostate cancer), "Through the establishment of a searchable database from Poland, careful analysis of the relationship between individuals will be possible at both the familial and the molecular level.

"This will afford us the opportunity to learn not only more about the Creator's great work, but will also allow (us) researchers new opportunities to dissect the cause of many diseases in large established pedigrees."
Several other medical institutions, including Yale University's Cancer Genetics Program, the Epidemiology-Genetics Program at the Johns Hopkins School of Medicine, and Mount Sinai Hospital's School of Medicine have recognized Diamond's work as an outstanding application
of knowing one's family history and as a guide to others who may be trying to trace their medical histories, particularly those at increased risk for hereditary conditions and diseases.

In February 1998, in a breakthrough effort, Stanley discovered another member of his family who carried the trait. He found the descendants of Jankiel's niece and nephew—first cousins who married—David Lustig and his wife, Fanny Bengelsdorf. This was no ordinary

find—he located the graves by using a map of the Ostrow Mazowiecka section of Chicago's Waldheim Cemetery and contacted the person listed as the one paying for perpetual care, David and Fanny's grandson, Alex.

"It turned out Alex, too, had been diagnosed as a beta-thalassemia carrier by his personal physician fifteen years earlier. The discovery that David and Fanny's descendants were carriers of the beta-thalassemia trait convinced Stan, Dr. Scriver, and Dr.Oppenheim that Hersz Widelec, born in 1785,must be the source of the family's novel mutation.

"'This groundbreaking work helps geneticists all over the world understand the trait and its effects on one family,' says Dr. Oppenheim. "A most important contribution of Stanley Diamond's work is increasing the awareness among his relatives and others to the possibility that

they carry a genetic trait which with proper measures, can be prevented in future generations. In addition, the work has demonstrated the power of modern genetics in identifying distant relatives, and helps to clarify how genetic diseases are being spread throughout the world."

For more information about thalassemia, contact Cooley's Anemia Foundation (129–09 26th Avenue. Flushing,New York, 11354; by phone 800-522-7222; or online at www.cooleysanemia.org). For more about Stanley Diamond's research. visit his Web site (www.diamondgen.org).

Thalassemia is not only carried by people living today in Mediterranean lands. The first Polish (not Jewish) carrier of Beta-Thal was discovered in the last few years in Bialystok, Poland. Stanley Diamond met with the Director of the Hematology Institute in Warsaw in November 2002, and the Director of the Hematology Institute in Warsaw indicated that they now have identified 52 carriers. Check out these Web sites listed below if the subject intrigues you.

"Genealogy with an extra reason"...Beta-Thalassemia Research Project.
http://www.diamondgen.org/
JTA genetic disorder and Polish Jewish history
www.jta.org/page_view_story.asp?intarticleid=11608&intcategoryid=5
IAJGS Lifetime Achievement Award
http://www.jewishgen.org/ajgs/awards.html
Jewish Records Indexing—Poland

http://www.jri-poland.org/

11

Molecular Revolution

Geneticists today are making inroads in new areas such as phenomics and ancestral genetics. Batsheva Bonné-Tamir, PhD, http://www.tau.ac.il/medicine/USR/bonnétamirb.htm or
http://www.tau.ac.il/medicine/at Tel-Aviv University, Israel, is Head of the National Laboratory for the Genetics of Israeli Populations (with Mia Horowitz) and Director of the Shalom and Varda Yoran Institute for Genome Research Tel-Aviv. She is also on the faculty of the Department of Human Genetics and Molecular Medicine, Sackler School of Medicine.

Dr. Bonné-Tamir states that "One of my most impressive conclusions from the advancement in the last few years and the accumulation of knowledge in the fields of genetics and medicine, is the molecular revolution based on immense sophistication of lab techniques. This is really responsible for the recent increased emphasis on the human-socialanthropological aspects that affect biological diversity."

Bonné-Tamir explains, "At a meeting in 1973, in my paper on Merits and Difficulties in Studies of Middle Eastern Isolates, I said that 'The Middle Eastern isolates have emphasized again the fertile and necessary interrelationship between history and genetics.'"

Do historical events influence genes? "Comparative studies in population genetics are often undertaken in order to attempt reconstruction of historical and migratory movements based on gene frequencies," says Bonné-Tamir.

"The Samaritans and Karaites offer opportunities in the opposite direction, for example, to learn the influence of historical events on gene frequencies." In another paper in 1979 on Analysis of Genetic Data on Jewish Populations, Dr. Bonné-Temir wrote that "Our purpose in studying the differences and similarities between various Jewish populations was not to determine whether a Jewish race exists. Nor was it to discover the original genes of 'ancient Hebrews,' or to retrieve genetic characteristics in the historical development of the Jews.

"Rather, it was to evaluate the extent of 'heterogeneity' in the separate populations, to construct a profile of each population as shaped by the genetic data, and to draw inferences about the possible influences of dispersion, migration, and admixture processes on the genetic composition of these populations."

In 1999, Dr. Bonné-Temir organized an international symposium on Genomic Views of Jewish History. "And unfortunately, the many papers presented were never published," says Bonné-Temir.

Molecular Genealogy Research Projects

Certain mtDNA haplogroups and mutations or markers within the haplogroups turn up in research studies of Ashkenazim when scientists look at the maternal lineages. For example, 9.0 of Ashkenazic (Jewish) women have mtDNA haplogroups that follow the Cambride Reference Sequence (CRS) (Anderson et al. 1981).

That means their matrilineal ancestry lines follow the reference sequence that all other mtDNA haplogroup markers are compared with. The CRS shows a specific sequence of mtDNA haplogroup H found in more than 46% of all Europeans and 6% of Middle Eastern peoples. You can view a table of mtDNA sequences titled "Frequently Encountered mtDNA Hapotypes" at Table 3 in the article, *"Founding Mothers of Jewish Communities: Geographically Separated Jewish Groups Were Independently Founded by Very Few Female Ancestors,"* Mark G. Thomas et al, American Journal of Human Genetics, 70:1411-1420, 2002.

The only exception is that the Ashkenazic mtDNA haplogroup maternal ancestral lines, show up at only 2.6% with one mutation away from the CRS 343 creating U3 mtDNA haplogroup instead of the H mtDNA haplogroup. The CRS is H haplogroup. Where does U3 mtDNA show up at the higher rate of 17%?

In Iraqi Jews. Ashkenazi mtDNA shows up at 9.0 percent following the CRS with H mtDNA haplogroup. Yet 27.0% of Moroccan Jews have mtDNA following the CRS. So does more than 46% of all Europeans and 25% of all Middle Eastern people have MtDNA following the CRS. That's haplogroup H of the Cambridge Reference Sequence.

The table in the article mentioned above has many sequences of mtDNA listed. Ashkenazi mtDNA was compared to MtDNA in other Jewish groups—Moroccan, Iraqi, Iranian, Georgian, Bukharan, Yemenite, Ethopian, and Indian. These were compared to non-Jewish Germans, Berbers, Syrians, Georgian non-Jews, Uzbeks, Yemenites, Ethiopian non-Jews, Hindus, and Israeli

Arabs. The percentage of frequencies of HSV-1 mtDNA sequences were listed in the samples from sites 16090–16365.

Looking only at Ashkenazi mtDNA, the mutations 184 and 265T show up in 2.6% of the Ashkenazi mtDNA. Yet in Jews from Bukhara, these same mutations show up in 15.2% of mtDNA.

And 129 and 223 mutations show up in 2.6% of the Ashkenazi mtDNA. Yet in Bukharian Jewish mtDNA, this mutation shows up at 12.1%. The rest of the Ashkenazi mtDNA stands at 9.0% for matching the CRS. That's H haplogroup, the most frequent mtDNA haplogroup found in Europe. Only 1.3% of Ashkenazic mtDNA has one mutation at 274. Yet 20% of Yemenite Jewish mtDNA shows this same mutation at 274.

Be aware that not every Jewish person has been tested for mtDNA or Y-chromosomes. You first have to research how significant samples are in speaking for the majority of any population. They do have scientific credibility, but you must always look at the sample size.

Men carry their mother's mtDNA but pass on to their sons their Y-chromosome. Women pass on their mtDNA haplogroup only to their daughters.

Genomic views of any ethnic group's history are important for further study. Whether you are taking the skeptic's position or the genomic view of your cultural history, biology does have a cultural component that needs to be analyzed scientifically. Finding flaws or benefits in research studies of any kind is the way to find inroads to truths. How else can facts change and knowledge progress?

Molecular genealogy has joined efforts with molecular genetics. How can this information help you in family history research? Ugo A. Perego, MS. Senior Project Administrator, Molecular Genealogy Research

Project, Brigham Young University, http://molecular-genealogy.byu.edu, says, "I believe that DNA is the next thing in genealogy—the tool fo the 21st century family historians. In the past 20 years, the genealogical world has been revolutionized by the introduction of the Internet.

"An increasing number of people are becoming interested in searching for their ancestors because through emails and websites a large world of family history information is now available to them. The greatest contribution of molecular methods to family history is the fact

that in some instances family relationships and blocked genealogies can be extended even in the absence of written records.

"Adoptions, illegitimacies, names that have been changes, migrations, wars, fire, flood, etc. are all situations in which a record may become unavailable. However, no one can change our genetic composition, which we have received by those that came before us.

"Currently, DNA testing is an effective approach to help with strict paternal and maternal lines thanks to the analysis and comparison of the Y chromosome (male line) and mitochondrial DNA (female line) in individuals that have reason to believe the existence of a common paternal or maternal ancestor.

"A large database of genetic and genealogical data is currently been built by the BYU Center for Molecular Genealogy and the Sorenson Molecular Genealogy Foundation. This database will contain thousands of pedigree charts and DNA from people from all over the world.

Currently it has already over 35,000 participants in it.

"The purpose of this database is to provide additional knowledge in reconstructing family lines other than the paternal and maternal, by using a large number of autosomal DNA (the DNA found in the non-sex chromosomes).

This research, known as the Molecular Genealogy Research Project is destined to take DNA for genealogists to the next level." For additional reading, please visit the BYU's Molecular Genealogy Research Project's two Web sites. Another good source of information is at www.relativegenetics.com, a company specialized in Y chromosome analysis for family studies.

12

What Are Your Genes Doing In That Holding Tank?

Are your genes thinking outside their box? Have you ever wondered what your genes are doing in your "temporary container" before they move on and change and where they have traveled during the past 40,000 years or more? When you have your DNA tested, work with the lab and DNA testing company, and ask them to explain to you how the 37 or 43 Y-chromosome markers you had tested as a male or 400+ base pairs you had tested in your mtDNA you had tested for female lineage sequences can help you determine your ancestry or find any matches similar to your DNA in a database. Read the frequently asked questions files of DNA testing companies online. Ask questions by email.

Sons inherit their mtDNA from their own mothers. Then mothers pass mtDNA on to their daughters. Sons also inherit the Y-chromosome from their fathers, but do not pass it to their daughters. Women don't have Y chromosomes.

The mtDNA is passed down from mother to son and mother to daughter through the cytoplasm (the cell contents surrounding the nucleus) in the egg. Only the daughters pass on their mtDNA to their daughters. And sons pass their Y-chromosomes to their sons, but those sons carry the mtDNA of their own mothers.

Even though both sons and daughters are formed from the union of a sperm and an egg, only the daughters will pass their mtDNA (which is the same as their great grandmother's on their maternal side and still further back to the first founder of their mtDNA group. Only daughters
will pass the mtDNA on to the next generation.

Each lab has different methods of reporting their results, but you can use DNA test results as a tool for learning family history. Join DNA mailing lists and research or ask questions of the DNA testing firms specializing in genealogy by genetics about how many mutations occur in how many generations.

Here's how you can do your own research independently of any laboratory that tested your own DNA if you're curious about Y-chromosome DNA tests. Males take Y-chromosome DNA tests to find out paternal ancestry lineages. Males also can have their mtDNA checked, but women don't have a Y chromosome. So women only can check their maternal lineages with mitochondrial (mtDNA) tests

Understanding HLA Genes (White Blood Cells)

HLA genes are white blood cells. Anthropologists look at white blood cells called by the scientific name of HLA genes to study genetic drift. If you have a research need to learn about tissue typing, you might want to read about understanding the HLA genes. Tissue typing is usually done on white blood cells, or leukocytes. The markers are referred to as human leukocyte antigens (HLA). A good starting point is to read the definitions and excerpts about tissue typing testing on the 'About' Health and Fitness Web site at: http://thyroid.about.com/library/immune/blimm25.htm?terms=Human+Leukocyte+Antigen.

Using Your Own DNA Test Results as a Genealogy Tool

It's good to have a mentor to answer questions about your test results until you are able to do your own research on the Web. If you're a lay person, where can you learn enough molecular genetics to get a handle on DNA test results and untangle ancestral roots? If you've ever wondered why your genes are not where you thought they were supposed to be (in geographic location on a map), that topic of research is called molecular prosopography. See the Web site:
www.linacre.ox.ac.uk/research/prosop/prosopo.stm.

Prosopography is an independent science of social history embracing genealogy, onomastics and demography. Prosopography is all about human history and genes that travel because your genes have both a cultural and a biological component. The cultural component includes onomastics which is the study of the origin of a name and its geographical and historical utilization.

Onomastics includes the study of how and when place-names were originated and used. Then there's toponymics. Toponymics is the study of names related to a place or region. See http://libraryweb.utep.edu/onomastics.html or http://www.kami.demon.co.uk/gesithas/biblio/bib08.html. And you probably know demography, is the interdisciplinary study of human populations. Demography deals with social characteristics of the population and their development. So you'd find more information on demography by researching population studies.

What Are Your Genes Doing In That Holding Tank?   121

Phenomics is the science of customizing, tailoring, and individualizing medicines and other health treatments to the total human genome of one person.

The age of one medicine or hormone fits all is gone. As a tool, phenomics also can be applied to herbal remedies, food supplements, vitamins and minerals, hormones, and other formulas adjusted to an individual's total genome. If you have a genetic risk for a certain disease, perhaps you can find out what way there is to prevent it by using phenomics as a tool for customizing your treatment or working on prevention strategies of lifestyle, diet, or medicine.

Family history DNA testing is a new way to approach biological research. Genealogy and genetics are forms of hunting and gathering that persist. First you start with transcribed oral history. We are foragers in molecular family history.

Molecular genealogy uses DNA testing (human genetics) as a tool for untangling ancestral and recent family roots. Here's an introduction to family DNA testing to be used with oral history gathering and genealogy.

Start your family history time capsule, gift basket, scrapbook, genetic genealogy, or begin a small business publicizing DNA testing for genealogy. The place for genetic genealogy is in an archives, library, museum, or good storage place.

Future generations need a DNA history of as many ancestors as they can find willing to participate and to create oral histories. Genetics is the most mathematical/statistical of the biological sciences.

The public now has access to fields such as bioinformatics that combine computers and biological information. Family historians need a bridge to fill the gap between such a mathematical science as genetics and genealogy, often based on records and oral histories.

The oral history would be transcribed on acid-free paper in hard, bound copy. Photos and other memorabilia could be added. Then the basic archive would be copied onto disks such as a CD, DVD, or other, stored in a computer and on video and audio tape.

Another copy would be saved as a multimedia presentation with text, sound, voice, photos, illustrations, and video/audio and saved on a disk to be played on screen with a home entertainment player or in a computer.

You could put a smaller file online on a Web site. This molecular biography would represent not only the life of a person, but a history of the person's DNA test results, racial percentages, ethnicity, if known, and anything else about the DNA sequence as far as geographic location or even medical history, if desired, in a more private file for relatives.

This is where genetics joins with genealogy.

We not only have a family history to archive, but now a genome, or at least a record of the matrilineal and patrilineal ancestry by DNA. We have the markers and the sequences. The idea is to learn enough about DNA testing and genealogy to understand what those sequences and
markers mean.

What can we learn about ancestry through the mitochondrial DNA (for women and men) the Y chromosome only for men, and other markers on the genome? What should we look at to view the percentages of races such as Native American, African, East Asian, or Indo-European (Europe, Middle East, and India)?

What do these sequences tell us about our ancestry? If there's no such thing as race, what geographic locations of our ancestors are we viewing back in time when we look at the genetic markers?

What dates are we looking at—a few generations ago or 21,000 years? What do our transitions and mutations mean over a long span of time? What foods, medicines, therapies, and climates are best for our customized, individual molecular profiles?

How do we read and interpret those genetic markers? Where does genealogy and oral history fit in? Family history—genealogy—now has joined up with molecular genetics and evolutionary anthropology. And included with genealogy is the tradition of transcribing and recording oral history, diary journaling and restoration, time capsules, biography, scrap booking, videography, and photography.

The genome has reached the genealogist. Family history today is multimedia and molecular, historical and futuristic. "Progress in our knowledge of the genome and of its function has been extremely rapid since the development, in the mid-eighties, of the Polymerase Chain Reaction," says Professor of Genetics, Guido Barbujani, (Department of Biology, University of Ferrara, Italy.) Dipartimento di Biologia, Universita' di Ferrara via L. Borsari 46, I-44100 Ferrara, Italia. See his Web site at:
http://www.unife.it/genetica/Guido/Guido.html.

Dr. Barbujani's fields of interest include human population and molecular genetics and evolution, and I've read many of his articles in the various journals of genetics and research books, such as Archaeogenetics: DNA and the population prehistory of Europe published by the McDonald Institute Monographs.

"By that method, minimal quantities of DNA can be studied, which has opened the field for a number of previously hard-to-imagine applications, ranging from gene therapy to the prediction of interactions among genes, from the sequencing of entire genomes to the retrieval of DNA sequences from extinct organisms," Barbujani explains.

"DNA technologies proved so powerful that people tend to forget about their limitations. Still, limitations exist, especially in the field of genealogical reconstructions, and future technical advancements are unlikely to be of great help.

"Consider this: Each of us has two parents, four grandparents, eight grand-grandparents, and so on. In principle, only ten generations ago (around 1750 AD) we had 1024 different ancestors. In fact, chances are our ancestors were less than 1024, because consanguineous marriages likely occurred at various stages. But even if we had only 200 independent ancestors ten generations ago, each of them contributed to our 30,000 or so genes.

"On the other hand, only one of them transmitted to us her mitochondrial DNA and, if we are males, from only one of them did we inherit our Y chromosome," Barbujani reveals. "The other 198 or 199 ancestors' contributions to our genotype are of course equally important, but there is no easy way to figure them out."

"Indeed, at every generation recombination created new associations of genes along our chromosomes, except for the mitochondrial DNA and for part of the Y chromosome, which do not recombine. In this way, traits of DNA coming from different ancestors have been assembled in a mosaic that cannot be disentangled a posteriori, in which each piece has a different, and possibly very different, origin. In short, it is an illusion to think that our mitochondrial DNA (or our Y chromosome) may allow us to understand our family history.

"These are small parts of our genome, and hence contain information on but a small bit of our biological history," says Barbujani. "Other ancestors have transmitted to us many more genes than the ancestors from whom we inherited our mitochondrial DNA, and they may have come from different parts of the world."

"That may sound frustrating to some, but population genetics has something important to tell us in this regard. Population histories are much easier to reconstruct than individual histories, because chance phenomena have a much greater impact on the latter.

"When a large number of individuals are jointly analyzed, rather robust evolutionary inferences may be drawn, even if some members of the sample have had an unusual family history. By combining measures of genetic diversity, among populations and among individuals, with the evidence coming from mitochondrial and Y-chromosome genealogies, population geneticists have shown very clearly that each population contains a large proportion of all humankind's alleles, around 85 percent, on average.

"This finding has several implications. One is: should most humans disappear because of some global catastrophe, and should only one community survive, the loss of genetic diversity would be very limited, around 15 percent. That might or might not be reassuring, but is true.

"Secondly, although many tend to think that humans come in clear racial clusters, that is not true; if, on average, populations contain 85 percent of the global human diversity, two individuals from very distant localities can be just 15 percent more different genetically than members of the same population (unless the latter are relatives, of course). Thirdly, genetic diversity is so high among members of the same population, that the only possible explanation is those populations incorporated, through time, contributions from other populations at a rather high rate.

"In other words, our ancestors spent most of their evolutionary time in communities connected by extensive migratory exchanges, and not in isolated groups. Through migration, alleles of African, Asian and European origin ended up all over the world, and no biologically recognizable race evolved in our species. Therefore, it is impossible to define our origin by studying our DNA, but if it were possible, we would probably find that our roots are spread over much of the world.

"As Jonathan Marks remarked, today convincing people that there is no such thing as a human race is probably as difficult as, in the 17th century, to convince people that the earth rotates around the sun and not vice versa. However, this is a scientific fact, and perhaps the single most significant result of human evolutionary studies. Everybody can tell a Nigerian from a Japanese person, but if we move from Nigeria to Japan we shall never find a sharp boundary separating two well-distinct groups.

"Rather, we shall notice that the genetic features of people change continuously, in a gradient, and that each community harbors substantial biological differences among its members. The best way to summarize these concepts, I think, is by a slogan invented by the French anthropologist André Langaney: Tous parents, tous différents. We are all relatives, and we are all different."

13

The Cohen Modal Haplotype and the Armenian Modal Haplotype

If you want to look for signatures of Middle Eastern origin in Ashkenazic males you first look for repeat patterns that support the hypothesis that haplotypes with high DYS388 repeat. If they repeat, then you can hypothesize that there is an origin in the Middle East. The DYS388 repeat becomes one of the signatures of ancestry of Middle Eastern or Southeast Asian origin (Bradman et al. 2000).

For example, in Armenians, the DYS388 marker of the Y-chromosome repeats 15 times. In Georgians the repeat is 12 times. Does it repeat in the majority of Ashkenazic males? The Armenian modal hg2 haplotype is shared with other Middle Eastern countries, but the Armenian modal hg1 haplotype is a one-step relative of the English modal haplotype 3 and the Frisan modal haplotype 50 of the hg1 haplotypes. The Armenian hg1 haplotype also is the Turkish modal hg1 haplotype.

Scientists know that the Cohen Modal Haplotype shows up in non-Jews in Hungary, Italy, and Armenia, but there's also the modal hg2 haplotype in Turkey and Azerbaijan. Armenians share haplotypes that occur frequently in Jews and in other populations. The Cohen Modal Haplotype is strikingly similar in Sephardic and Ashkenazic Y-chromosomes—the paternal lines. There are regional DNA differences in Armenia. And Armenia had a vibrant Jewish community in medieval times that disappeared several hundred years ago.

The community existed contemporaneously with Jewish communities at the tail end of the era of the Khazars (a few were still around in 1200 after Khazaria was destroyed in 965 CE). Jewish communities flourished in the 13th century in neighboring Georgia and also in the Caucasus, in Iran, Azerbaijan, Daghestan (original homeland of the Khazars), the Crimea, (the refugium for Byzantine Jews and people fleeing Germany and Hungary).

The Armenian Jewish community was a neighbor to the Jewish communities of the Ukraine, where Jews from Germany and Central Europe joined existing communities of Jews from Anatolia and Greece fleeing to the Ukraine from both West and South. Byzantine Jews lived in the Ukraine and the Crimea, as well as Khazars who may have joined the nearby Jewish communities. What is known is that Jewish men traveled far and wide within existing Jewish communities. Medieval Armenian Jews had Hebrew names. The city of Eghegis contains 62 medieval Armenian Jewish gravestones dated around the year 1266 CE with Aramaic and Hebrew inscriptions.

The medieval Armenian Jewish community was small—perhaps consisting of only about 150 people, according to Frank Brown, writing in the Jerusalem Report ("Stones from the River"). The stone inscriptions contain dates ranging from the middle of the 13th century to 1337.

See the Web site on Jewish Armenian communities in medieval times at: http://www.sefarad.org/publication/lm/045/4.html.

14

DNA of the Levites

The Levites are different. Levites, unlike Cohanims, have some Y-chromosomes in three different groups showing a heterogeneous, a diverse, variable origin. Some contemporary Levites may not be direct patrilineal descendants of a paternally related group. There is a term, "the Ashkenazic Levite Modal Haplotype." See the Scientific Correspondence section of Nature, Vol. 394, 9 July 1998.

Studies look at the marker DYS 388 in the Y-chromosome to see its repeat patterns. Scientists also use a model as a method to estimate the coalescence time of Cohanim chromosomes and in certain studies have dropped DYS388 in analyzing Cohanim chromosomes to estimate coaslescent time. Ashkenazic and Sephardic Cohanim chromosomes have been dated to an estimate of 2,684 to 3,221 years before present.

The earlier date goes back to the Exodus and the latter date goes back to the destruction of the first Temple in 586 BCE. Studies conclude that the origin of "priestly Cohanim Y-chromosomes" originated sometime during or right before the Temple period in the history of Judaism. There's always uncertainty because the mutation rate varies.

In some of the older anthropology textbooks, Jews and Armenians have been classed together as "Armenoid or Assyrian" in characteristics such as skull shape and features.

What actually happens is when a broad-skulled person from any country marries a long and narrow-skulled person, the child sometimes is born with an "Armenoid" skull, that is a flattened occiput, narrow skull, long or oval face, and a convex nose with complexions varying from fair to swarthy and hair color from blonde or red to brown or black. These characteristics for decades had been assigned to the "Armenoid" peoples where Ashkenazim and Armenians had been grouped together before DNA testing was used by physical anthropologists, population geneticists, or archaeogeneticists.

For more information on DNA studies of the Levites see the article, "The Origins Of Ashkenazic Levites: Many Ashkenazic Levites Probably Have A Paternal Descent From East Europeans Or West Asians," Bradman, N1, Rosengarten, D and Skorecki, K21, The Centre for Genetic Anthropology, Departments of Biology and Anthropology, University College London, London, UK. And 2 Bruce Rappaport Faculty of Medicine and Research Institute, Technion, Haifa 31096, Israel and Rambam Medical Center, Haifa 31096, Israel. (See the Bradman Index at http://dna6.com/abstracts/bradman.htm which is online as part of an index to a list of abstracts and posters at http://dna6.com/abstracts/index.htm

Here are some definitions you might want to peruse before we go into the next chapter on personalizing family history records with theresults of DNA tests. If you are a historian or genealogist, it would be useful to be able to discuss possible DNA testing with your clients.

Molecular tools to family history research open doors to new subjects. Be sure to read the updates to these articles, as research brings out new information.

15

Life Story Genealogy: Writing and Marketing People's Life Story Highlights

Here's how to systematically collect, record, and preserve living peoples' testimonies about their own experiences. After you record in audio and/or video the highlights of anyone's experiences, try to verify your findings. See whether you can check any facts in order to find out whether the person being recorded is making up the story or whether it really did happen.

This is going to be difficult unless you have witnesses or other historical records. Once you have verified your findings to the best of your ability, note whether the findings have been verified. Then analyze what you found. Put the oral history recordings in an accurate historical context.

Mark the recordings with the dates and places. Watch where you store your findings so scholars in the future will be able to access the transcript or recording and convert the recording to another, newer technology. For instance, if you have a transcript on paper, have it saved digitally on a disk and somewhere else on tape and perhaps a written transcript on acid-free good paper in case technology moves ahead before the transcript or recording is converted to the new technology.

For example, if you only put your recording on a phonograph record, within a generation or two, there may not be any phonographs around to play the record. The same goes for CDs, DVDs and audio or video tapes.

So make sure you have a readable paper copy to be transcribed or scanned into the new technology as well as the recordings on disk and tape. For example, if you record someone's experiences in a live interview with your video camera, use a cable to save the video in the hard disk of a computer and then burn the file to a CD or DVD.

Keep a copy of audio tape and a copy of regular video tape—all in a safe place such as a time capsule, and make a copy for various archives in libraries and university oral history preservation centers. Be sure scholars in the future can find a way to enjoy the experiences in your time capsule, scrapbook, or other storage device for oral histories.

Events move from the person being interviewed to you, the interviewer, and then into various historical records. In this way you can combine results of DNA testing with actual memories of events. If it's possible, also take notes or have someone take notes in case the tape doesn't pick up sounds clearly.

Writing Skits from Oral and Personal History Transcripts

Emphasize the commitment to family and faith. To create readers' and media attention to an oral history, it should have some redemptive value to a universal audience. That's the most important point. Make your oral history simple and earthy. Write about real people who have values, morals, and a faith in something greater than themselves that is equally valuable to readers or viewers.

Publishers who buy an oral history written as a book on its buzz value are buying simplicity. It is simplicity that sells and nothing else but simplicity. This is true for oral histories, instructional materials, and fiction. It's good storytelling to say it simply.

Simplicity means the oral history or memoirs book or story gives you all the answers you were looking for in your life in exotic places, but found it close by. What's the great proverb that your oral history is telling the world?

Is it to stand on your own two feet and put bread on your own table for your family? That's the moral point, to pull your own weight, and pulling your own weight is a buzz word that sells oral histories and fiction that won't preach, but instead teach and reach through simplicity.

That's the backbone of the oral historian's new media. Buzz means the story is simple to understand. You make the complex easier to grasp. And buzz means you can sell your story or book, script or narrative by focusing on the values of simplicity, morals, faith, and universal values that hold true for everyone.

Doing the best to take care of your family sells and is buzz appeal, hot stuff in the publishing market of today and in the oral history archives. This is true, regardless of genre. Publishers go through fads every two years—angel books, managing techniques books, computer home-based business books, novels about ancient historical characters or tribes, science fiction, children's programming, biography, and oral history transcribed into a book or play.

Life Story Genealogy: Writing and Marketing People's Life Story Highlights

The genres shift emphasis, but values are consistent in the bestselling books. Perhaps your oral history will be simple enough to become a bestselling book or script. In the new media, simplicity is buzz along with values.

Oral history, like best-selling novels and true stories is built on simplicity, values, morals, and commitment. Include how one person dealt with about trends. Focus your own oral history about life in the lane of your choice. Develop one central issue and divide that issue into a few important questions that highlight or focus on that one central issue.

When you write or speak a personal history either alone or in an interview, you focus on determining the order of your life story. Don't use flashbacks. Focus on the highlights and turning points. Organize what you'll say or write. An autobiography deals in people's relationships. Your autobiography deals as much with what doesn't change—the essentials—as what life changes you and those around you go through.

Your personal history should be more concrete than abstract. You want the majority of people to understand what you mean. Say what you mean, and mean what you say. More people understand concrete details than understand abstract ideas.

16

Personalizing Ethnic Family History Records with DNA Testing

You can choose a DNA testing company that provides a database for you to find DNA matches to your mtDNA or Y-chromosome or let you take racial percentages tests. Then you can find your match and interview the individual or chat and create DNA Match time capsules of your own, a journal, audio tape, video, or other archive where your family and the other family shares ancestral history events in an oral or transcribed archive or record.

Or you can work with famiy diaries of events uniting ancestors. Diaries and DNA testing personalize family history records. DNA family databases and scrap booking are more valuable when linked together. It's time to compile a written and illustrated family tree time capsule in any or all of various media—print, pictures, video, audio, for the Web, in a scrapbook form of stories, anecdotes, experiences, photos, journal writings, and memorabilia that also includes DNA testing.

DNA test results and autobiographies also may highlight the important events that you want remembered. In the future, families may be able to archive the sequences of their entire genome—all their genes—into a database to be kept along with photos, video, audio, crafts, and memorabilia marking the life experiences, events, rites of passage, and highlights focused around a central issue.

You can piece together records of women's clubs, diaries, and DNA tests and look at your maternal lineages. String together military pension or service records, village societies, or Census records and city directories, and link your paternal lineage from voter lists and court records to Y-chromosome test results.

The file or database could be passed onto other family members and the genome given to health care professionals to customize therapy or treatment, tailor foods and vitamins or supplements, or create a living video biography. For now, whole genome DNA testing is expensive, and what are affordable include the matrilineal and patrilineal lineages and the percentages of races.

For family historians, there are also the surname databases and message boards on the Web. And for tracing female ancestors, there are marriage certificates, birth records, court records, church and synagogue records, records of teachers, factory workers, census records, social and immigrant records, women's publications, clubs, insurance records, deeds and wills, and other records that reveal more than the words, "and wife."

The 1850 US Census was the first census to name all members of a household, their birthplaces, and whether married within the year. By 1870, the US Census asked whether one's parents were foreign born. And a decade later, the 1880 US Census named relationships to the head-of-household.

By 1900, the US Census included the number of years married, number of children born and who of the children were living. They also added immigration and naturalization data. Native Americans had special censuses. So you can also look at school censuses and state and local censuses as well as city directories published until 1976.

Years ago when people had no phones, the city directory was one way to locate families. In creating a "family history memorabilia time capsule" or database that includes DNA testing, you can include small crafts such as braided hair embroidery as art, craft, needlework, preserved clothing or wedding gowns restored and wrapped.

You'd index where the craft work or clothing is located, and the index or list of memorabilia would go into your scrapbook, database, or time capsule. What new item that you might add, would be the family's DNA, the male and female mtDNA and the male Y chromosome, plus a racial percentages DNA test.

Records may be copies and stored in many ways—as Web sites, printed books, diaries, on CDs and DVDs, as video and audio tapes, as oral history transcripts printed out in text, or as a photo scrapbook with captions. Or you can create a multimedia presentation combining text, voice, video, photographs, music, and commentary.

You would ask as many relatives as you can find to lightly rub a felt tip or pad, cytobrush, or a swish of mouthwash in their mouths and send the samples packaged and labeled separately to a DNA for genealogy testing company. With all those entries in your time capsule, your descendants (or your clients' if you do family history research) will have a better idea of who any particular family was as people (rather than some anonymous photos).

You can even search antique stores and flea markets and the people listed on the Web. Some genealogists rescue old photos and are listed on the Web. Check to see whether any photos found in certain locations might be your family members or those of your clients if you are a genealogist or family history researcher.

So you wipe a felt swab or small brush across the inside of your cheek and mail it to a DNA testing company. Or you swish a type of mouth wash and expectorate it into a container and mail it back to a DNA testing company emphasizing testing and/or researching genealogy by DNA analysis. Some of these companies may also have a division that tests DNA for forensic purposes, and other firms may give the DNA to a laboratory for actual testing and then send you the results with information on how to further research your ancient lineages or genealogy for more recent DNA matches.

What comes back to you in the mail a few weeks later are a print out, perhaps a CD, or a mailing on paper and/or email table of some of your DNA sequences. Now it's your job to find out what the sequences mean. Most companies have frequently answered questions message boards and some firms will email you answers to your questions. Other companies may offer to store your DNA or a certain length of time. So check with the company on what it offers regarding DNA testing and genealogy questions answered.

"The state of identity testing is such that people should have a specific hypothesis that they want to test," says Harry Ostrer, M.D, Professor of Pediatrics, Pathology, and Medicine Director, Human Genetics Program New York University School of Medicine.

"Do Susan Smith and I share a common matrilineal ancestor?"

"Do Jeffrey Jones and I (if male) share a common patrilineal ancestor?" Dr. Ostrer asks. "Hoping to discover something unanticipated is unrealistic. It is very unlikely that amateur genealogists will discover that they had Amerindian ancestry unless they had a strong reason to expect so.

"The problem of course is that many people are searching for roots and hoping that genetic testing will fill the gap for absence of familial oral histories," Dr. Ostrer explains. "Unfortunately, there are no shortcuts to the work of the genealogist. With the Internet, email and a heightened awareness of genealogy, the tools—word-of-mouth and access to vital records—are more accessible."

According to Dr. Harry Ostrer's article, "A Genetic Profile of Contemporary Jewish Populations," in Nature Reviews/Genetics, Vol. 2, November 2001 (Science and Society), p. 895, Macmillan Magazines Ltd, "The Ashkenazi Jewish population in Eastern Europe expanded rapidly, growing from an estimated

10,000–15,000 people in 1500 to 2 million in 1800 and 8 million in 1939 (REF.34)."

Compare that profile to the group of people you're researching. What's the individual's genetic profile? How does it compare to the oral history profile or the written record profile, either social or medical, ethnic, or industrial?

Consider the group of people you may belong to on one or both sides of your family. Then find out about the genetic history of your people in the same way as you research the genealogy or family history—through reading articles on the molecular genetics history of your ethnic group. You can also talk to relatives and even trace each ancestor's medical histories as far back as oral history or written records take you.

How can you use DNA testing information together with oral histories, diaries, military and court records? You can do online genealogy searches. You can explore by reading and interviewing scientists or listening to tapes or videos. Research your own genetic origins or any ethnic group you want to study. If you're not Jewish, the techniques are universal. Learn about how DNA techniques and molecular genealogy meet. Apply the methods to your own family history research.

Dr. Ostrer of New York University School of Medicine, Human Genetics Program conducted genetic analysis of Jewish origins. See the Web site at: http://www.med.nyu.edu/genetics/jewishorigins.html

According to the Web site, "The next step in Jewish genetic demography will be to understand the patterns of Jewish migration that formed the historical communities. Clearly most of these communities no longer exist, but their genetic structure can be discerned by studying the DNA of their descendants."

Consider looking at any other family memorabilia such as photographs or paintings, even crafts made in the past. Oral history, DNA testing, and genetic history work together with written, medical, and oral family history. Consider the times and background of the dates.

Search the industrial revolution era or before up to the present. What conditions did the person you're searching live under—agricultural or industrial? Was the family confined to a tiny apartment in an urban setting or on a farm?

Once you receive the results of DNA testing, you'll have a collection of sequences. Now is your chance to learn how to interpret those equences by asking questions on the DNA mailing lists and reading up on the subject of what the sequences mean in plain words.

To find out where to get your questions answered about interpreting the sequences, first check with the company that tested your DNA as various labs use different markings. Then contact the message board at Roots Web.com and subscribe to the genealogy digest known as GENEALOGY-DNA-D.

Subscribe to the mailing list and receive frequent email, or just the digest, or read the messages at the Web site. There, you may ask your questions about how to interpret your own sequences or others. To subscribe to GENEALOGY-DNA-D, send a message to GENEALOGY-DNA-D-request@rootsweb.com that contains in the body of the message the command subscribe and no other text.

No subject line is necessary, but if your software requires one, just use subscribe in the subject, too. To contact the GENEALOGY-DNA-D list administrator, send mail to:

GENEALOGY-DNA-admin@rootsweb.com. Your first step is to ask the company who tested your DNA to tell you how to interpret your sequences. Most companies have a frequently asked questions section on the Web site, and others ask to be emailed questions.

Are you interested in researching, collecting information, scrap booking, genealogy, or writing about family histories or your genetic history? How can you create a time capsule for future generations of printouts of part of your DNA or mtDNA or Y chromosome sequences?

What will future generations do with this information? Can it help unite people who are distant or close relatives or those with the same common ancestor in the very distant past? Family historians and genealogists now have a new branch of genealogy to learn—molecular family history.

If you're interested in DNA and Jewish genealogy, write to: JewishGen, Inc. 2951 Marina Bay Dr., Suite 130–472 League City, Texas 77573. On the Internet, the Web site is at: http://www.jewishgen.org/. There is a special interest group on Jewish DNA research and genealogy. It's called Genealogy by Genetics, and the Web site is at: http://www.jewishgen.org/dna/. You can subscribe to the mailing list.

The Genealogy by Genetics special interest group of the Jewish Genealogy Web mailing lists on the Web have a partner, Family Tree DNA (FTDNA) that tests your DNA and if you select, racial percentages. The DNA testing partner maintains databases. They will be integrating the FTDNA database library with existing JewishGen databases to provide users with the ability to connect with lost branches of their families.

There are several excellent books written on how to interpret DNA tests for people without a science background. See the bibliography at the back of this book. I particularly found Alan Savin's book very informative in bringing together DNA testing knowledge to genealogists.

Alan Savin of Maidenhead, England, is author of the 32-page book, DNA for Family Historians (ISBN 0-9539171-0-X). See the Web site: http://www.savin.org/dna/dna-book.html.

This excellent book that I highly recommend explains and explores in layman's language how family historians-genealogists can use DNA research and test results for family history research. The book also has case studies and makes genetic theory easier to understand by those without a background in genetics. It discusses the practicality of DNA testing for family historians as genetics joins genealogy. And it includes discussion of some of the problems of using DNA testing as a tool for family history research.

What I like about this book is that it's written at a reading level that is clear to understand without a science background. And the reader will find a good introduction, historical background, explanation of DNA fingerprinting, mitochondrial DNA testing, Y chromosome DNA testing (for males), collecting and analyzing DNA, future developments, and an excellent bibliography that includes Web sites, magazine articles, and books. So when I contacted Alan Savin by email, he related to me his story of how he introduced genetics into genealogy.

"I believe I was the first family historian in the world to use DNA for genealogical research back in 1997," says Alan Savin. "I originated the phrase 'genetic genealogy'. Realizing its potential, I wished to share this with everybody, hence the writing of the book. It is still selling well, especially in the USA, with orders being received worldwide. I have been approached recently for the book to be translated into German. It has been well received and recommended by a spectrum of reviewers from many genealogical publications, DNA testing companies themselves, e.g. Family Tree DNA and the media, e.g. the BBC."

"As stated in its introduction 'one of my primary aims is to explain this area of genetics in a language easily understood by a genealogist or any lay person'. Further books are planned in the series to develop the themes."

Savin says, "I could be said to be the father of genetic genealogy and I have seen my idea grow with the help of others. I keep a close watch on its development, behind the scenes, and look forward to seeing the science reach its maturity."

Aside from reading books on DNA, what else can a family historian do when there are no records to be found? Hobbyists and professional genealogists who wish to extend their family trees by confirming a link where no conventional source records exist would be interesting in having their DNA tested. Sometimes

DNA tests may be used to determine whether a person is part of a larger group of people: for example, Jews will be able to confirm they are of Cohanim lineage. DNA tests are excellent for individuals who want to perform surname-based family tree reconstruction projects.

An excellent article containing another version of the quote below (used with permission) titled, "Tangled Roots? Genetics Meets Genealogy" by Kathryn Brown appeared in the publication, Science, 1 Mar 2002.

Commenting on the role of DNA testing companies, Peter Underhill, a molecular anthropologist at Stanford University admits, "My concern is that people comprehend the relatively low level of resolution offered by these tests. Because the tests analyze relatively few markers along Y DNA or mtDNA, millions of people may share a given molecular profile. I think these companies have a role to play, as long as the science is done well."

Terry Melton, PhD is President/CEO/Laboratory Director of Mitotyping Technologies, LLC, 1981 Pine Hall Drive, State College, PA 16801. "The most important contribution of this science to genealogy is the ability of mtDNA to trace the maternal line long distances throughout a family tree," says Dr.Melton."My favorite pedigree is one from a paper by Sigurdardottir (American Journal of Human Genetics 66:1599) showing fifteen generations of an Icelandic family where living individuals typed from extreme tips of the family (whose ancestral female dates back to 1560) have the same mtDNA profile.

"In addition, mtDNA can sometimes be used to illuminate ethnic ancestry (in a very general way). Mitochondrial DNA types are correlated with the region of the world where the ancestral lineages originate. There have been dozens of scientific papers written on this subject. "Unlike Y chromosome typing, which should follow the patriline and family name), mitochondrial DNA is more difficult to correlate with recorded genealogy, since female names are lost in marriages,"

Melton explains. "However, the possibility remains that if a family can locate two (even very distant) maternal relatives in their tree, the mtDNA typing can confirm the matrilineal connection."

In addition to checking DNA test results with databases and tables on the World Wide Web or in other records, the family historian can compare results and read further about DNA to learn more.

Family members who have their DNA tested also can also track lineages and more recent genealogy by looking at the tell-tale clues that old, antique photos offer as well as use old and new city directories that list people who may not even have had a telephone.

Marjorie Rice rescues old family photos from antique stores and flea markets using the skills and sharp eye of a genealogy researcher to get them back into the hands of family members. An article about her work is on the Web at: http://www.ancestry.com/library/view/news/articles/6590.asp.

She looks on the back of the photos to see whether there are family names and/or photographer imprints on the front. She posts the names and locations on surname message boards on the Internet. To date, she has restored 409 photos to family members. See article about her work

at: http://www.ancestry.com/library/view/news/articles/6590.asp .

Besides putting dozens of family photos from the early 20th century in my own computer database by scanning and saving, I wrote to various genetic scientists, physicians, and researchers in the field of evolutionary biology and genetics for their opinions regarding the application and use of DNA testing for family historians and genealogists, even for people who want to track and record their own lineages, family trees not only by surname, but by DNA to find out what they can.

Some people are puzzled when "and wife" is listed instead of a female and her maiden name on documents. And with women for hundreds of years taking their father's or husband's surname, doors can open to researching female lines when mtDNA is tested.

Ancient ancestry in female lineages may be traced somewhat by mtDNA. It is inherited by women and passed on to their daughters. Y chromosomes are inherited by men and passed on to their sons. Both show us clues to ancient ancestry or ethnicity even in some small ways that show expansions and migrations of people across geographic distances for thousands of years. Mutation rates and genetic drift due to isolation of small communities show the researcher where the people had sought refuge and how they expanded in clines or gradients of genes.

Where the genes are most diversified shows researchers a clue to where the genes originated rather than where they might be today. Where the genes look alike or very close, shows the people have migrated to an area only recently in the eons of time. What are various geneticists' and genome scientists' opinions of DNA testing for genealogy research?

Richard Villems, MD, Dr. Sci, head of the Department and Professor of Evolutionary Biology at the Institute of Molecular and Cell Biology, Tartu University, Tartu, Estonia, replied to my question about DNA-driven genealogy testing by email, noting that, "The answer is straightforward and short: yes, DNA 'testing' is a very powerful method for genealogy research—specifically so as far as maternally inherited mitochondrial BSA and paternally inherited Y chromosome, are concerned.

"Although the current practical use is, technically speaking, far from a possible state-of-art level in case of mtDNA, the latter is, if a full sequence of mtDNA is analyzed, a very precise tool to resolve genealogy in a phylogenetically correct way already. As far as Y chromosome is involved, it would be even more so, because Y chromosome is huge compared to mtDNA—some 60 millions of nucleotides compared to about 16,500 in mtDNA. However, realistically speaking, it would take a huge technological effort to reach a stage where a phylogenetic resolution would be "final"; we are just at the beginning of a long way.

"In theory, even a son will differ from his father, in average, in a few Y-chromosomal mutations—therefore the ideal resolution would indeed allow reconstructing the biological history of this chromosome in minute details. At present, this time is still far away because of an enormous cost of such a work. Nevertheless, the fact that we do know what is possible, one may predict that any man can calculate how exactly he is related to, say, to his contemporary PM of the country—or, say, to the Secretary General of the Chinese Communist Party (if that exists at that future time anyway).

"As far as autosomal genes are involved, I am pessimistic—Mendelian segregation and recombination are probably too powerful in creating noise that such a clear-cut resolution cannot be expected—never.

"Hobbyists and professional genealogists who wish to extend their family trees by confirming a link where no conventional source records exist would be interesting in having their DNA tested. Sometimes DNA tests may be used to determine whether a person is part of a larger group of people: for example, Jews will be able to confirm they are of Cohanim lineage. DNA tests are excellent for individuals who want to perform surname-based family tree reconstruction projects."

Dr. Richard Villems also wrote me this reply, when I inquired about what ethnicities my own mtDNA might reveal, "Your motif in HVS-1 is beyond any reasonable doubt within haplogroup H. Every even slightly experienced in mtDNA researcher knows that although transition in 16356 is a good guess that a particular mtDNA belongs to U4, there are enough 16356 mutations also within H. And what does it mean that 'research showed recently' that 16356C is U4—this is a very well known fact already at least for 4–5 years! But there are exceptions one ought to know as well.

Moreover, this combination you have is well present all over Europe—plenty in Scandinavia, in Estonia as well—but also in Germany and, to make it really a pan-European—also in the Adriatic area as well as in Eastern Europe down to the slopes of the southern Urals, among Turkic-speaking Bashkirs."

I also wrote to another scientist who works with human genetics, Dr. Vincent A. Macaulay, Dept of Statistics, University of Oxford, UK, who replied similarly, "Your sequence (16189-16356-16362) is almost certainly in haplogroup H. I have several exact matches to your sequence my database which are confirmed as H using other markers in the mtDNA molecule.

"Position 00073 is in HVSII, which is not in the part of the molecule that Oxford Ancestors sequenced. I think they have confused 00073 and 16073 (which is in HVSI) in their reply to you. If you had HVSII sequenced, I would be confident that 00073 would display an "A". The 16356 mutation has happened more than once, so it does not always imply haplogroup U4.

"For your information this sequence has not been observed east of Bulgaria. In my database, there are sequence matches in UK, Spain, Portugal, Germany, Austria and Bulgaria. I hope this helps: I would suggest that you seek further clarification from Oxford Ancestors."

Another scientist in genetics, Dr. Antonio Torroni, Institute of Biochemistry, University of Urbino, Italy, also wrote to me that he found one person from Crete in his mtDNA database with my mtDNA sequences. So where did my own founding female lineage come from and which country represented my direct ancestor—or did all of those countries?

Since only a sample from each country was tested and put in the various database, I wondered whether an ancestor might have been not yet tested, not in the database, and in some geographic area not yet mentioned. The journeys for the founder types have only just begun. What geographic part on Earth, what ethnicity could I ultimately call my own down to the bones? Would I ever find out?

Dr Peter Reed has a PhD in Human Genetics from the University of Oxford and was a pioneer in the use of STR genetic markers in medical research. "To non-enthusiasts genealogy is considered an obsession with the past," says Reed. "Yet the combination of genetics and genealogy enforces how family history is integral to what we are today."

All our ancestors have contributed to our personal genetic makeup, and by examining our own genes we are viewing the DNA of our ancestors.

"Current uses of genetics in genealogy only examine a fraction of our entire genetic makeup and have largely developed from anthropological research," Reed explains. "However, the driving force of the current 'genetic revolution' has been research into human physiology and psychology, and it is from this work that new applications for genealogy will be developed."

"In five to ten years knowledge of our entire personal genetic code will be feasible, and with this knowledge will come an ability to much better understand how our ancestors contributed to our genetic makeup.

"In a few generations from now not only will knowledge of an ancestor's full genetic code be as indispensable for family history as birth and death dates are today, but family history (both genetic and social) will be a vital instrument in personal health care."

17

The Phenomics Revolution: DNA-Driven Genealogy

Is genealogy research evolving toward the use of smart cards and molecular family history reports to fill gift time capsules? "DNA testing is an exquisitely precise tool for answering certain types of genealogical questions, but it is clear that this technique is, and will continue to be, a disappointment to many who see it as a way of leaping over the 'brick walls' in their conventional research," says genealogy researcher, John F. Chandler. "DNA testing is at its best in demonstrating that two people or two lineages are not related within a genealogical time frame."

"When used for the purpose of proving that two people are related, it is notoriously often misconstrued. By itself, DNA testing can only show a general relationship, not a specific one," Chandler admits. "For the future, if the field continues to grow, there is some hope that DNA will offer a realistic chance to hunt for relations by looking for exact matches, but the growth will have to be at least three orders of magnitude before this comes to pass."

I wanted to find out more about Ancestry Informative Markers (AIMs) and my own ancestry than only what my mitochondrial DNA (mtDNA) could tell. I wanted to find out the racial percentages in my genealogy search and how this information could help me write my ancient or recent past journal. Was I Asian, African, Indo-European or Native American? What other mixtures? In what percentages? How much Roman and how much Greek? How much Portuguese am I? How much Jewish and how much Scandinavian? How much Slavic and how much Middle Eastern? What were my percentages of ancestry that accumulated over thousands of years of expansions and migrations from Ice Age refugiums? From where geographically and at which times in history did each of my ancestors contribute to my genetic markers? Could I find this out—or only a clue?

The DNA of the mitochondria is the energy generators transmitted through the egg cells, according to the New York University School of Medicine's Human

Genetics Program that offers genetic analysis in various studies. See the Web site at: http://www.med.nyu.edu/genetics/jewishorigins.html. The DNA of the Y chromosome told about male ancestry for males.

Women don't carry the Y chromosome and so are tested for DNA by either their mtDNA for ancestry, or their nuclear DNA. Most DNA testing companies offer mtDNA testing for women and Y chromosome testing for men, and men also have mtDNA, and may have that tested also to learn about their female lineages as well as their male-Y-chromosome lineages.

Some DNA testing companies also offer the racial percentages DNA testing. The racial percentages such as East Asian, Indo European, African, and Native American are DNA tests of Ancestry Informative Markers (AIMs). I wanted to find out what I could about my ancient and recent ancestry that extended beyond records in city directories and other cross-reference files.

I took the racial percentages test to find out I was 97% Indo-European and 3% East Asian. (I was told to take anything 5% or under with a grain of salt with the East Asian.) Was the test only revealing back to my great great grandmother and no further back? Or did it reveal the "real me" as I was 21,000 years ago? Or was I looking at a printout of the maternal lineages that contributed to my genes 500 years ago or one generation back from my birthdate? The search for a core identity and ancestral DNA records of the deep past was on.

Of all the three DNA tests that I took to find out what I could about my unknown ancestry, the DNA test that I found most helpful was the one that looked at the percentages of the various races in my ancestral history.

I took The DNAPrint ANCESTRYbyDNA test in order to look at my personal panel of Ancestry Informative Markers (AIMs). "Our test can only indicate to what percentage a person is Native American, African, East Asian and Indo European," says Carrie Castillo, Corporate Communications, DNAPrint genomics. For further information, contact, DNAPrint genomics, Inc. 900 Cocoanut Ave, Sarasota, FL 34236.

The test uses markers that have been characterized in a large number of well-defined population samples. These markers are selected on the bases of showing substantial differences in frequency between population groups and, as such, can tell about the origins of a particular person whose ancestry is unknown.

After the analysis of these Ancestry Informative Markers (AIMs), in a sample of a person's DNA, the probability that a person is derived from any of the parental populations and any of the possible mixes of parental populations is calculated.

The population (or combination of populations) where the likelihood is the highest is then taken to be the best estimate of the ancestral proportions of the person. Confidence intervals on these point estimates of ancestral proportions are also being calculated.

For example, the Duffy Null allele (FY*0) is very common (approaching fixation or an allele frequency of 100%) in all sub-Saharan African populations and is not found outside of Africa. So a person with this allele is very likely to have some level of African ancestry.

Knowing the percentage of your races may be one consideration when planning for personalized medicine. How many know the entire history of one's own ancestry? If your parents and grandparents had genetic-related degenerative diseases that are high in certain populations, would you want to know whether you carried genes from a particular ethnic group? I wanted answers to questions such as these because I'm a freelance writer and write novels about DNA.

Ten generations is roughly 250 years and within the time frame of genealogical interest, especially when we are considering the settlement of North America, because they only look at two (2) chromosomes. Ychromosomal analysis and mtDNA analysis each could only provide information on a very small proportion of a person's ancestors.

I went for my third and last DNA test to the AncestryByDNA test because it relies on sequences throughout one's genome. So the results I received from AncestryByDNA said more about a greater number of ancestors.

FamilyTree DNA also offers AncestryBy DNA's racial percentages test along with their mtDNA and Y-chromosome tests. My goal was to find out what I could for what I could afford, about my ancient ancestry through DNA testing. Perhaps it could tell me something more when oral and written records weren't within reach. Could these tests tell me anything other than that I resemble millions of people with the same mtDNA sequences, or if I were male, Y-chromosome markers? Could it provide a DNA match with someone who possibly shared a common ancestor with me hundreds of years ago? Who was my most recent common ancestor, and would that person show up in a database? The answer is only if that person took the test and asked for his or her email to be made public for contact with another DNA match.

After all, my entire genome wasn't being tested. That's not affordable on my budget. And my entire genome would reveal more personal information that the mtDNA, even the high and low resolution HVS-1 and HVS-2 sites. I still matched with millions of people. Only in my case, my mtDNA sequences are found only at a low frequency in Europe. What caused their extinctions? Or did they have more sons than daughters?

The places where my recent relatives lived were mostly unknown to me, and all I could go by was looks as perceived by others based on stereotypes based on cartoons and caricatures. Online database tables told me someone with my matrilineal DNA (mtDNA) lived in Crete. It was as good a starting point as any. So I went out and bought feta cheese for lunch melted on pizza dough.

Then one to four people per thousand with my exact sequences of mtDNA also lived in Scotland and Norway and Siena, Italy (Tuscany) and Turkey and Bulgaria, and Iceland and Austria. What part of the world did my ancestors belong to for any length of time? What would it mean to me other than an ethnic costume for Halloween or a trip to an ethnic restaurant or listening to music of that geographic place?

The first table I researched contained my HVS-1, low resolution sequences of mtDNA. Yet when I had my mtDNA tested for HVS-2, high resolution, different geographical places turned up—the Orkney Islands off the coast of Scotland, France, England, Bulgaria, and Turkey. Well which is the real me—Bulgaria and Turkey or Scotland and Orkney Islands?

In 2002 I received a certificate from Oxford Ancestors saying I was an Ulrike (haplogroup U4). I wrote Vincent Macaulay asking how can one tell which is which with the same mutations? From his tables and email, he said to find out whether I had a G at position 00073 at HVS-2. He emailed me a note saying that chances are almost certain that I had an A at that position 00073 on HVS-2, if I'd look. Certainly the three mutations I had were in his online database tables.An A at position 00073 of HVS-2 would make me H haplogroup. A G at position 00073 would make me a U4, but the only way to be sure is to do a high resolution test of the mtDNA for HVS-2.

So I wrote to Dr. Villems from Estonia, where Kristiina Tambets database sequences came from and to Bryan Sykes, from Oxford Ancestors. Bryan Sykes, MA PhD DSc, is Professor of Human Genetics, University of Oxford, and with Oxford Ancestors. He has written several books on the history and geography of human genes, including The Seven Daughters of Eve and a book on the sons of Adam, genetically speaking. Anyway, Villems also agreed I'm probably an H, not a U4 (what Oxford Ancestors named Ulrike).

The question came up because one of my sequences, 16356C also is found in mtDNA haplogroup U4. Dr. Sykes and I corresponded by email several times, and Dr. Sykes is most helpful and emailed me on January 15, 2002. He wrote, "David Ashworth from Oxford Ancestors has shown me you message and the replies you received from Drs. Macaulay and Villems about whether your DNA sequence places you in the clade of U4 Ulrike or H Helena.

"David tells me that on your original certificate, issued in August 2000, you were placed in the clan of Helena but that when you were sent a replacement you had become a daughter of Ulrike instead. Of course your actual DNA sequence hadn't changed, but the assignment of your clan had.

"It may help if I explain how that is done. Clans are defined by a mixture of two sorts of genetic markers, the variants in the control region sequence and the variants at a number of other sites around the mtDNA molecule now generally called SNPs (short for Single Nucleotide Polymorphisms). These are usually designated as +4643Rsa1 or +11329Alu1 etc as you have pointed out in your messages.

"Vincent's classification on the website and in the papers you refer to contain a complete list of these variants. What they mean is that a restriction enzyme recognises the variation and either cuts or does not cut the DNA at that point. Since your hobby is reading about DNA, I am sure I don't need to explain what a restriction enzyme is. So, take +4643Rsa1. That means the enzyme Rsa1 cuts at base number 4643. The variant-4643Rsa1 means that the enzyme does not cut the DNA.

"Vincent and I, with Martin Richards, spent a great deal of time correlating the control region variants with the SNPs by analysing both on several hundred (it may even have been thousands) of mtDNAs and this was an important part of distinguishing the different clans. On the whole these types of variant are more stable than some of the control region sequence variants but not always and ideally every DNA should be tested for both. However, that would put the price to customers up hugely because each one of the SNPs had to be done separately—although I know that Oxford Ancestors are looking into offering this service.

"But even that would not guarantee completely accurate assignment in every single case. Only sequencing the entire mtDNA circle of sixteen and a half thousand bases at astronomical cost would do that—though even that would not be any good unless you had at your fingertips a database of thousands of other complete sequences with which to compare it and only a handful have been completely sequenced to date.

Also, as more work is reported, the evolutionary networks will change. "What I am getting at is that no system is foolproof. The Oxford Ancestors service, to keep it affordable, only sequences the control region. Then the sequence is compared to a database which holds other sequences which have been examined for

SNP variants. If the customers control sequence matches up with one of these then it is assigned to the same clan.

In other cases, where there is not an exact match, the database is searched for close matches or sites which are characteristic of particular clans. In the case of your sequence which has variants from the reference sequence at 189, 356, 362 (we delete the 16 prefix for HVS1) two of the three variants are quite unstable—that means they can mutate back and forth. Position 189 is one of the least stable of all and position 362 is not very far behind. Position 356 is far more stable and is also characteristic of clade U4, whose clan mother is Ulrike. However, it is not completely stable and does crop up in other clans—one of which is Helena.

"So the sequence 189, 356, 362 could be in the clan of Ulrike mutating at the unstable positions 189 and 362 away from the U4 root sequence of 356. Or it could be in the clan of Helena with a rare variant at 356 taking it away from 189, 362.

One way of telling the two apart is to look at the variant at 073. This is actually in HVSII and not HVSI and that was a source of confusion in some of the email exchanges I have read.

"Oxford Ancestors doesn't do the 073 test, as you know, so the sequence was assigned on the balance of probabilities to Ulrike. I have now had a chance to compare the sequence to some new research data of my own from Britain in which we did do the 073 test and found five exact matches which carry A at 073, indicative of clade H. So I think you are probably correct and are indeed a daughter of Helena rather than Ulrike. This means that the mutation at 356 would have occurred on a Helena background rather than the 189 and 362 variants occurring on an Ulrike background.

"That might explain why you were originally issued with a Helena certificate in August 2000. At that time, the service was being sent out from my laboratory before Oxford Ancestors acquired its own premises. That means that whoever did that first assignment, and it may well

have been me, did recognize the ambiguous nature of the 356 mutation in that particular sequence but that piece of information was not properly transferred to the new set-up—and that is my fault.

"I must thank you for clarifying the assignment of this particular sequence. It is a changing field and your observation has helped it move on one more stage further. I am sure Dr Ashworth will want to issue a new Helena certificate. And of course, I hope you are pleased to have moved back to your original clan."

◆   ◆   ◆

E-Letter from Bryan Sykes:

From: Bryan Sykes
To: Anne Hart
Sent: Wednesday, December 01, 2004 4:28 PM

Subject: Re: Thank you for starting us to search for English ancestors

Dear Anne
Well I suppose that's what academics are for. I'm so thrilled that my research has led to something useful. It certainly didn't seem so at the time.

On a serious vein, what has happened in 'genetic genealogy' is extremely unusual. Blue sky scientific research has opened up a field which is now being championed by yourself and others. The research that counts is now being done by enthusiastic practitioners—mainly unpaid. It is the return of the long forgotten 19th century paragon—the amateur scientist. I feel a ponderous and pompous article coming on!
Best wishes—and a very happy Christmas.

Bryan

Belonging to Helena's clan sounds more personal that what it means—a member of haplogroup H, presumably one of the Seven Daughters of Eve, the founding "clans" or haplogroups found in Europe in prehistoric times. But even H haplogroup had to have a common ancestor before heading for Europe in the middle of the Ice Age 21,000 years ago. And that ancestor had to come from presumably somewhere in the Middle East.

Haplogroup H is the most frequent cluster in the Middle East and the Caucasus. It's present at a frequency 25 percent. In Europe, it's found much more frequently at around 46 percent. There are more haplogroup H people in Europe than there are in any other part of the world.

The mtDNA haplogroup H represents a female ancestor who lived in the Middle East up to 28,400 years ago. Some surviving daughters then went to Europe, and some stayed in the Middle East. However, the European daughters' mtDNA with Haplogroup H have an "age estimate" of only up to 21,400 years. So the arrival of or mutation to H in Europe began more recently in Europe than it did in the Middle East. Yet today there are more Europeans with haplogroup H than there are in the Middle East with the same matrilineal lines of mtDNA haplogroup H.

Other mtDNA haplogroups of female lineages are much older, if we look at mtDNA coalescence times and founder effects. For example, mtDNA haplogroups T and J both date to around 50,000 years before the present in the Middle East, but more recent dates in Europe. Haplogroup J is found today at its highest frequency in Arabia, making up 25 percent of the Bedouin and Yemeni population.

It's also found in Europe, also a more recent arrival. Perhaps mtDNA haplogroup J entered Europe around 10,000 years ago or less, probably with the agricultural revolution of the Neolithic age, after the last Ice Age ended around 12,500 years ago.

The oldest mtDNA in Europe is the female lineage of U mtDNA haplogroup. It's around 50,000 years old in the Middle East, perhaps around 45,000 years ago in Europe, and from U comes many sub divisions such as European-specific U5, North African U6, and Indian U2i, all showing an origin of around 50,000 years ago. The first female lineage out of East Africa into the Middle East was L3, but mtDNA haplogroup U also followed out of Northern Africa and went to Europe as well as most of the Middle East, where it's found today.

An interesting theory is that 50,000 years ago, the route from Northern Africa was closed until 44,000 years ago, so people coming from Asia or Africa into Europe through the Middle East had to come from India across the southern route until the route from the Middle East opened up to get to Europe, and that was around 44,000 years ago.

At that time the Fertile Crescent around what is today Iraq opened up as well as the Levant. By then, people could use a northern route across the Bosphorus from Turkey to Greece and enter Europe. Those in what is today Greece then would have gotten trapped in the Balkans by 25,000 years ago, unless they made it to the refugiums in southwestern France and northwestern Spain near the Mediterranean and at the foot of the Pyrenees. Some made it.

That's why we have the wonderful cave paintings of large animals in southwestern France, particularly the Dordogne valley. Art bloomed when the Ice Age was raging at its maximum and the open tundra or fields of grass was a steppe for animals and hunters. As soon as the Ice Age ended and forests took over most of Europe, the wonderful art subsided into a dark age that began around 12,000 years ago. Then the early farmers came up from the Middle East. They now make up about 20 percent of Europe's population, and the idea of farming caught on during the next few thousand years. There was an agricultural frontier that separated hunters from farmers, and it lasted thousands of years.

What puzzled me is why today H haplogroup is nearly missing from the Arabian Peninsula. What made it leave, the changing climate or low population frequency? For more information I turned to an excellent article titled "Tracing European Founder mtDNAs" by Richards, et al published in the American Journal of Human Genetics, 67:1251–1276, 2000. I read about mtDNA haplogroup V, which appears to have expanded in Europe around 13,000 years ago. Then I re-read Bryan Sykes's book, The Seven Daughters of Eve. It was time to take the next step.

So I went to Family Tree DNA for more information. I had my HVS-2 (high resolution) mtDNA tested to find out more about what my ancestry might be and whether I was a U4 or an H haplogroup. The two single female ancestors who founded H and U4 in prehistoric times came from different parts of Eurasia.

Family Tree DNA sent two small felt-tipped serrated pads with a push stick that pushes the felt pad from the holder into a small vial of preservative solution. I brushed the inside of my cheek several times, put the two pads into the two tiny vials of solution, and sent it back. I had a little difficulty poking the stick to drop the pads, and in the end had to pull the pads firmly from the sticks and drop them into the vials with my fingers. (I washed my hands first.)

Family Tree DNA tested more base pairs. I found that indeed there was an A at position 00073 in HVS-2, just like Victor Macaulay told me I'd probably find if I looked. That made me a member of H1b mtDNA haplogroup (origin on the Eastern coast of the Baltic Sea). Family Tree DNA also found a new transition to the letter C at position 16519. Family Tree DNA tested 540 base pairs as compared to the 400 tested at Oxford Ancestors, which is close to the minimum that needs to be tested to find out one's mtDNA haplogroup results.

Bennett Greenspan of Family Tree DNA emailed me an answer to my inquiry of what question he would like to see answered in a book on genealogy through DNA testing. "It would be to explain the direct line of descent...male to male to male, with no mixing of the genders. That's what people seem to have a hard time with."

What I learned from email correspondence from Family Tree DNA is that my mtDNA won't tell me when the last mutation on a string happened, but H haplogroup in its form as H haplogroup appears on the CRS (Cambridge Reference Sequence) without all the mutations that I have occurring over thousands of years of evolution, is a little over 20,000 years old. (I visualized H as the sequence of the Cro-Magnons of the Mesolithic caves of SW France and Northern Spain.)

Could my ancestors have painted that fine art work on caves at Lascaux or Altamira during the height of the Ice Age? Since then my mtDNA has mutated away from the Cambridge Reference Sequence (CRS), and perhaps the last mutation that occurred in my HVR-sequence happened 2–10,000 years ago.

There are about 3 billion DNA letters (technical name: "base pairs") in human DNA. You can picture these letters as beads on a keychain, each one labeled with an A, C, G, or T. The letters stand for adenine, cytidine, guanine, and thymidine, always referred to as A,C,G, and T. These nucleotide bases are joined together, one after the other like a molecular string of pearls called DNA (deoxyribonucleic acid).

Oxford Ancestors tested only 400 of my HVS-1 sequences. Family Tree DNA tested 540 and found a new mutation or transition16519C in HVS-1. Then when I had HVS-2 tested at Family Tree DNA, I found the transitions also were very common on the CRS and were 309.1C, 315.1C, and deletions at 523-and 524-. Any mutations I had that showed up in my HVS-2 results were more common in the population, and the rare sequence was on the CRS.

I looked up HVS-2 sequences on Victor Macaulay's tables on the Web and found additional countries such as Orkney Islands off the coast of Scotland, Norway, Turkey, Bulgaria, Scotland, and England matching my HVS-2 results. So far, I had no clue as to whether my maternal line was European or Middle Eastern or both. You have to look at HVS-1 and HVS-2 together and not look at them separately when you are trying to find out your nearest common ancestor.

That's when I turned to a BioGeographical Ancestry test from AncestryByDNA. It's a company that recently presented a complex genetics classifier for personalized medicine. AncestryByDNA's CEO is Dr. Tony Frudakis, of DNAPrint genomics, Inc. 900 Cocoanut Ave, Sarasota, FL . The Web site is at http://www.dnaprint.com/.

The Web site for testing ancestry such as percentages of various races is located at: www.ancestrybydna.com. They even have a chat room. DNA testing is about personalized medicine as well as finding out about ancestry and other genetic-related questions. It's also about an informatics platform for genotype pattern recognition.

Here's your gateway to understanding the genetic basis for complex trait determination. DNA testing is about looking at pioneers in the emerging field of post-human genome phenomics. By putting the genomics puzzle together, you become part of the phenomics revolution with ancestry testing or other genotyping services. It's about research on individual genetic responses to certain medications as much as about finding your ancient or racial percentage ancestry.

From the DNA kit I was sent with printed information, I mailed in a DNA sample obtained from rubbing a soft piece of felt inside my cheek on a felt-tipped, serrated swab, which I air-dried and placed in an addressed return envelope and mailed back to DNA Print genomics and asked to be tested for percentages of various racial groups such as African, East Asian, European, and Native American.

Let's say you tested your mtDNA to find your female lineage, but you want to look up female relatives and don't know their maiden names. My own great grandmother's death certificate didn't list a maiden name. The next step would be to look at her marriage certificate.

I could also look at the City Directory for a particular city in 1889 to see where she lived, looking first under her father's name. I could try the US Census records for 1890 also in that city.

My grandparents were small children at that time living in a large house and farm in upstate New York, and all I know to begin my search is my great grandmother's first name and her father's last name, and I have my mtDNA, female lineage high and low resolution sequences.

Those would be the same in my great grandmother as in my present grand daughter. The mtDNA stretches back to a single female founder 21,000 years ago in Europe and further back in time, the usual cereal belt. I know my sequences are quite popular in Crete.

City Directories often list maiden names and the names of all residents living in a home, particular before homes had telephones. Where else can you look on the Web to start besides the usual beginning genealogy Web sites? You might order marriage certificates or death certificates as well as birth certificates to find maiden names.

The National Center for Health Statistics in Hyattsville, Maryland is also on the World Wide Web at: http://www.cdc.gov/nchs/howto/w2w/newyork.htm. For example, to view an address where to write to in order to purchase a copy of a marriage certificate for New York State, the Web site will help provide information as to where to write to in order to purchase copies of marriage licenses for New York, for example, from the year 1880 forward.

For other states, check the Web site at The National Center for Health Statistics under each state. You can also search foreign countries for records. You could also look at the Ellis Islands records, if a relative came to Ellis Island, and even view a picture of the ship at the Ellis Island Online Web site at: http://www.ellisisland.org/.

One good place to start is http://www.cdc.gov/nchs/products.htm for publications and products. Click on http://www.cdc.gov/nchs/nvss.htm for Vital Statistics. Click here http://www.cdc.gov/nchs/releases/96facts/mardiv.htm for marriage and divorce statistics.

18

Molecular Genealogy & DNA Testing Firms

The Power of DNA Technology in Every Home. This is the slogan of the GeneTree DNA Testing Center that supplies DNA testing applications directly to the consumer. "We would like to demonstrate how we provide the science of DNA analysis applications directly to the consumer, allowing them to conduct their own research projects in the comfort of their own home," says Terrence C. Carmichael, MS, founder of GeneTree DNA Testing Center.

"By examining the Autosomal STRs, Y-chromosome STRs and mtDNA sequence analysis and RFLP, GeneTree is helping people (such as genealogists, anthropologists, and just those generally interested) uncover their deep ancestral migration patterns, establish biological relationships with relatives 1–50 generations apart, and uncover the mysteries of past and present relationships. These services are wonderful, and prove to be of great value to the consumer, whether it is for immigration purposes, assistance with genealogy or anthropology research, or for answering the simplest of questions, such as 'are you my father?'"

After receiving his MS degree, Carmichael went on to receive a Professional Designation in Marketing and Sales from UCLA. Terry has worked at the DNA laboratory bench for 4 years and spent 9 years providing Product Development, Technical Consulting, and Marketing for the DNA purification industry, working for companies such as Bio-Rad and QIAGEN. In 2000, Carmichael co-authored a book titled, "How to DNA Test your Family Relationships".

Having started 2 successful businesses, Terry is a visionary. He has applications submitted for 2 separate patents; one for applying DNA profiles to identification cards and the other for a new high-throughput DNA purification product held by Bio-Rad Laboratories. Below are the Web sites for some of the products offered by GeneTree DNA Testing Center.

GeneTree Products:

http://www.genetree.com/servlet/moonshine/goto?page_url=/products/ productgroups.jsp
Y-Chromosome Information:
http://www.genetree.com/servlet/moonshine/goto?page_url=/products/ product.jsp&id=7
mtDNA Information:
http://www.genetree.com/servlet/moonshine/goto?page_url=/products/ product.jsp&id=8
Native American Assessment:
http://www.genetree.com/servlet/moonshine/goto?page_url=/products/ product.jsp&id=20
Biography: Terrence C. Carmichael,MS
Terrence Carmichael, MS
(888) 404-GENE (ext. 207)

****

GeneTree DNA Testing Center

3150 Almaden Expressway, #203
San Jose, CA 95118-1253
Phone: (888) 404-GENE/(408) 723-2670
Fax: (408) 723-2671 http://www.genetree.com/

****

19

What is DNA? Should Genealogists Take an Interest?

"The human genome is about 3×10^9 base pairs long, which would weigh about 40 pg picograms: 1 pg=10^{-12} grams) per genome," reports Michael Onken, and this description appears on the science Web site of Ricky J. Sethi, MadSci.ORG Administrator at MadSci.ORG (http://www.madsci.org/) at the Washington University School of Medicine, http://www.madsci.org/. "Human cells are diploid, i.e. each contains two copies of the genome, so the nuclear DNA from a human cell would weigh about 80 pg. If we want total cellular DNA, then we need to include mitochondrial DNA (mtDNA).

"The human mitochondrial genome is about 16,000 base pairs long. There are about 10 copies of the genome per mitochondrion, and there are on the order of 1,000 mitochondria per cell. This gives us about 0.2 pg of mtDNA per human cell.

"There are on the order of 10^{14} cells per adult human, many of which are without nuclei, like skin cells and red blood cells. This would give us just under a kilogram of chromosomal DNA and on the order of a few grams of mitochondrial DNA in the average human body." (This excerpt is reprinted with permission of Ricky J. Sethi, MadSci.ORG Administrator, at the Washington University School of Medicine. See the Web site at http://www.madsci.org/.)

Knowing how many genes a human has in the future will help not only genealogists and other family and oral historians trace ancestors and keep records of lineages, but physicians will be able to tailor medicines to help people based on how their individual genes react to different elixirs, drugs, natural supplements, herbs, foods, and medicines.

Combined with the knowledge of rainforest tropical plants and their cures, the human genome is headed towards individualization and customization, with an appropriate mixture of food, medicine, or therapy based on one's individual genetic makeup.

To the person without a science background, knowing one's genes also is a way to connect people to their common ancestors in the past and to those descendants when written records cannot be found or when a person lived in a land that didn't require a last name be recorded at a particular time in history. Family history can be researched not only for medical reasons, but for historical reasons, and to show how people are related to one another down through the ages.

Useful DNA Definitions for Historians and Genealogists Interested in Molecular Anthropology/Archaeology

* Genome. A person's genome is one set of his (or her) | genes. The human genes, which control a cell's structure, | operation, and division, are located in the cell's nucleus. The | full human genome (estimated at 50,000 to 100,000 genes) is present in every cell-nucleus, even though many genes are| inactive in cells which have some specialized functions (the| "differentiated" cells).

* Genes and Chromosomes. Genes are composed of segments of DNA. In normal cell-nuclei, the DNA is distributed among 46 chromosomes (23 inherited at conception from a person's father, and 23 from the mother). Each chromosome consists of one very long strand of DNA and numerous proteins, which are required for successful management of the long DNA molecule. The longest chromosomes each "carry" thousands of genes. Every time a cell divides, the cell must duplicate the 46 chromosomes and must distribute one copy of each to the two resulting cells.

* The Code. The DNA of each chromosome is composed of units—nucleotides" of four different types (A, T, G, C). These nucleotides are linked to each other in linear fashion. The sequence of the four types of nucleotides is critical, because the sequence produces the "code" which
(a) determines the function of each particular gene, (b) identifies the gene's start-point and stop-point along the DNA strand, and (c) permits certain regulatory functions. The code of the human genome consists of more than a billion nucleotides.

* The Mitochondrial DNA (mtDNA). Outside the nucleus, human cells also have some "foreign" DNA located in structures called the mitochondria. This

small and separate set of DNA does not participate in the 46 human chromosomes, and is not part of "the genomic DNA." The mitochondria are inherited from the mother.

These genetic term definitions are from the book titled: Confirmation that Ionizing Radiation Can Induce Genomic Instability: What is Genomic Instability, and Why Is It So Important? John W. Gofman, M.D., Ph.D., and Egan O'Connor, Executive Director, CNR. Spring, 1998. The excerpt of definitions from Dr. Gofman's essays, such as what is quoted above is reprinted with permission. See excerpts from the book at the Web site at: http://www.ratical.org/radiation/CNR/GenomicInst.html.

All the definitions from Dr. Gofman's essays are available for reproduction in other publications. Please do cite the title and above URL so people who wish to study the complete work can do so. For more information see the Web site at: CNR page (http://www.ratical.org/radiation/CNR/). For further information, contact the publisher, David Ratcliffe, "rat haus reality press" at: http://www.ratical.org/rhrPress.html.

20

How to Interview for Intergenerational Writing

STEP 1: Send adults or students in any grade from age 9 to 17 accompanied by supervising adults to senior community centers, nursing homes, or senior apartment complexes activity rooms.

STEP 2: Have each student bring a tape recorder with tape and a note pad.

STEP 3: Assign each student one or two older persons to interview with the following questions.

1. List and discuss the most significant experiences, events, or turning points or events in your life.

2. How did you survive the Wars?

3. What were the highlights, turning points, or significant events that you experienced during the economic downturn of 1929–1939? How did you cope or solve your problems?

4. What did you do to solve your problems during the significant stages of your life at age 10, 20, 30, 40, 50, 60 and 70-plus? Or pick a year that you want to talk about.

5. What changes in your life do you want to remember and pass on to future generations?

6. What was the highlight of your life?

7. How is it best to live your life after 70?

8. What years do you remember most?

9. What was your favorite stage of life?

10. What would you like people to remember about you and the times you lived through?

STEP 3:

Have the student record the older person's answers. Select the most significant events, experiences, or turning points the person chooses to emphasize. Then write the story of that significant event in ten pages or less.

STEP 4: Ask the older person to supply the younger student photos, art work, audio tapes, or video clips. Usually photos, pressed flowers, or art work will be supplied. Have the student or teacher scan the photos onto a disk and return the original photos or
art work or music to the owner.

STEP 5: The student and/or teacher scans the photos and puts them onto a Web site on the Internet at one of the free communities that give away Web site to the public at no cost....some include http://www.tripod.com/, http://www.fortunecity.com/, http://www.angelfire.com/, http://www.geocities.com/, and others. Most search engines will give a list of communities at offering free Web sites to the public. Microsoft also offers free family Web sites for family photos and newsletters or information. Ask your Internet service provider whether it offers free Web site space to subscribers.

1. Create a Web site with text from the older person's significant life events
2. Add photos.
3. Add sound or .wav files with the voice of the older person speaking in small clips or sound bites.
4. Intersperse text and photos or art work with sound, if available.
Add video clips, if available and won't take too much bandwidth.

5. Put Web site on line as TIME CAPSULE of (insert name of person) interviewed and edited by, insert name of student who interviewed older person.

STEP 6: Label each Web site Time Capsule and collect them in a history archives on the lives of older adults at the turn of the millennium. Make sure the older person and all relatives and friends are emailed the Web site link. You have now created a time capsule for future generations.

This can be used as a classroom exercise in elementary and high schools to teach the following:

1. Making friends with older adults.
2. Learning to write on intergenerational topics.
3. Bringing community together of all generations.
4. Learning about foster grandparents.
5. History lessons from those who lived through history.
6. Learning about diversity and how people of diverse origins lived through the 20th century.
7. Preserving the significant events in the lives of people as time capsules for future generations to know what it was like to live between 1900 and 2000 at any age.
8. Learning to write skits and plays from the life stories of older adults taken down by young students.
9. Teaching older adults skills in creative writing at senior centers.
10. Learning what grandma did during World War 2 or the stock market crash of 1929 followed by the economic downturn of 1930–1938.

What to Ask People about Their Lives

Step 1
When you interview, ask for facts and concrete details. Look for statistics, and research whether statistics are deceptive in your case.

Step 2

To write a plan, write one sentence for each topic that moves the story or piece forward. Then summarize for each topic in a paragraph. Use dialogue at least in every third paragraph.

Step 3

Look for the following facts or headings to organize your plan for a biography or life story.

1. SLOGAN. Ask the people you interview what would be their slogan if they had to create/invent a slogan that fit themselves or their aspirations: One slogan might be something like the seventies ad for cigarettes, "We've come a long way, baby," to signify ambition. Only look for an original slogan.

2. QUEST. (This quest could be a mission, goal, result, achievement, or purpose.) How did the individual solve specific problems or come to terms with an obstacle? Ask the people you interview what purpose do they have for living or what is their mission? What was the result, objective, or goal of a specific event in their life? Is or was it equality in the workplace or something personal and different such as dealing with change—downsizing, working after retirement, or anything else? How did that person navigate the each stage or a selected stage of life? For some life has a purpose. Others are on a quest, crusade, or mission. Did they have a specific cause, purpose or goal?

3. IMPACT. Ask what makes an impact on people's lives and what impact the people you're interviewing want to make on others?

4. STATISTICS: How deceptive are they? How can you use them to focus on reality?

5. How have the people that you're interviewing influenced changes in the way people or corporations function?

6. To what is the person aspiring?

7. What kind of communication skills does the person have and how are these skills received? Are the communication skills male or female, thinking or feeling,

yin or yang, soft or steeled, and are people around these people negative or positive about those communication skills?

8. What new styles is the person using? What kind of motivational methods, structure, or leadership? Is the person a follower or leader? How does the person match his or her personality to the character of a corporation or interest?

9. How does the person handle change?

10. How is the person reinforced?

Once you have titles and summarized paragraphs for each segment of your story, you can more easily flesh out the story by adding dialogue and description to your factual information. Look for differences in style between the people you interview? How does the person want to be remembered?

Is the person a risk taker or cautious for survival? Does the person identify with her job or the people involved in the process of doing the work most creatively or originally? Does creative expression take precedence over processes of getting work out to the right place at the right time? Does the person want his ashes to spell the word "love" where the sea meets the shore?

Search the Records in the Family History Library of Salt Lake City, Utah

Make use of the database online at the Family History Library of Salt Lake City, Utah. Or visit the branches in many locations. The Family History Library (FHL) is known worldwide as the focal point of family history records preservation.

The FHL collection contains more than 2.2 million rolls of microfilmed genealogical records, 742,000 microfiche, 300,000 books, and 4,500 periodicals that represent data collected from over 105 countries. You don't have to be a member of any particular church or faith to use the library or to go online and search the records.

Family history records owe a lot to the invention of writing. And then there is oral history, but someone needs to transcribe oral history to record and archive them for the future.

Interestingly, isn't it a coincidence that writing is 6,000 years old and DNA that existed 6,000 years ago first reached such crowded conditions in the very cities that had first used writing extensively to measure accounting and trade had very little recourse but to move on to new areas where there were far less people and less use of writing?

A lot of major turning points occurred 6,000 years ago—the switch to a grain-based diet from a meat and root diet, the use of bread and fermented grain beverages, making of oil from plants, and the rise of religions based on building "god houses" in the centers of town in areas known as the "cereal belt" around the world.

Six thousand years ago in India we have the start of the Sanksrit writings, the cultivation of grain. In China, we have the recording of acupuncture points for medicine built on energy meridians that also show up in the blue tattoos of the Ice Man fossil "Otsi" in the Alps—along the same meridians as the Chinese acupuncture points.

At 6,000 years ago the Indo European languages spread out across Europe. Mass migrations expanded by the Danube leaving pottery along the trade routes that correspond to the clines and gradients of gene frequency coming out of the cereal belts.

Then something happened. There was an agricultural frontier cutting off the agriculturists from the hunters. Isn't it a coincidence that the agricultural frontiers or barriers also are genetic barriers at least to some degree?

21

Oral History/Personal History

Here's how to systematically collect, record, and preserve living peoples' testimonies about their own experiences. After you record in audio and/or video the highlights of anyone's experiences, try to verify your findings. See whether you can check any facts in order to find out whether the person being recorded is making up the story or whether it really did happen.

This is going to be difficult unless you have witnesses or other historical records. Once you have verified your findings to the best of your ability, note whether the findings have been verified. Then analyze what you found. Put the oral history recordings in an accurate historical context.

Mark the recordings with the dates and places. Watch where you store your findings so scholars in the future will be able to access the transcript or recording and convert the recording to another, newer technology. For instance, if you have a transcript on paper, have it saved digitally on a disk and somewhere else on tape and perhaps a written transcript on acid-free good paper in case technology moves ahead before the transcript or recording is converted to the new technology.

For example, if you only put your recording on a phonograph record, within a generation or two, there may not be any phonographs around to play the record. The same goes for CDs, DVDs and audio or video tapes.

So make sure you have a readable paper copy to be transcribed or scanned into the new technology as well as the recordings on disk and tape. For example, if you record someone's experiences in a live interview with your video camera, use a cable to save the video in the hard disk of a computer and then burn the file to a CD or DVD. Keep a copy of audio tape and a copy of regular video tape—all in a safe place such as a time capsule, and make a copy for various archives in libraries and university oral history preservation centers. Be sure scholars in the future can find a way to enjoy the experiences in your time capsule, scrapbook, or other storage device for oral histories.

Use your DNA testing results to add more information to a historical record. As an interviewer with a video camera and/or audio tape recorder, your task is to record as a historical record what the person who you are interviewing recollects.

The events move from the person being interviewed to you, the interviewer, and then into various historical records. In this way you can combine results of DNA testing with actual memories of events. If it's possible, also take notes or have someone take notes in case the tape doesn't pick up sounds clearly.

I had the experience of having a video camera battery go out in spite of all precautions when I was interviewing someone, and only the audio worked. So keep a backup battery on hand whether you use a tape recorder or a video camera. If at all possible, have a partner bring a spare camera and newly recharged battery. A fully charged battery left overnight has a good chance of going out when you need it.

What Should Go Into an Oral History?

Emphasize the commitment to family and faith. To create readers' and media attention to an oral history, it should have some redemptive value to a universal audience. That's the most important point. Make your oral history simple and earthy. Write about real people who have values, morals, and a faith in something greater than themselves that is equally valuable to readers or viewers.

Publishers who buy an oral history written as a book on its buzz value are buying simplicity. It is simplicity that sells and nothing else but simplicity. This is true for oral histories, instructional materials, and fiction. It's good storytelling to say it simply.

Simplicity means the oral history or memoirs book or story gives you all the answers you were looking for in your life in exotic places, but found it close by. What's the great proverb that your oral history is telling the world?

Is it to stand on your own two feet and put bread on your own table for your family? That's the moral point, to pull your own weight, and pulling your own weight is a buzz word that sells oral histories and fiction that won't preach, but instead teach and reach through simplicity.

That's the backbone of the oral historian's new media. Buzz means the story is simple to understand. You make the complex easier to grasp. And buzz means you can sell your story or book, script or narrative by focusing on the values of simplicity, morals, faith, and universal values that hold true for everyone. Doing the best to take care of your family sells and is buzz appeal, hot stuff in the publishing market of today and in the oral history archives. This is true, regardless of genre. Publishers go through fads every two years—angel books, managing techniques books, computer home-based business books, novels about ancient historical characters or tribes, science fiction, children's programming, biography, and oral history transcribed into a book or play.

The genres shift emphasis, but values are consistent in the bestselling books. Perhaps your oral history will be simple enough to become a bestselling book or script. In the new media, simplicity is buzz along with values. Oral history, like best-selling novels and true stories is built on simplicity, values, morals, and commitment. Include how one person dealt with about trends. Focus your own oral history about life in the lane of your choice.

Steps to Take in Gathering Oral Histories
Use the following sequence when gathering oral/aural histories:

1. Develop one central issue and divide that issue into a few important questions that highlight or focus on that one central issue.

2. Write out a plan just like a business plan for your oral history project. You may have to use that plan later to ask for a grant for funding, if required. Make a list of all your products that will result from the oral history when it's done.

3. Write out a plan for publicity or public relations and media relations. How are you going to get the message to the public or special audiences?

4. Develop a budget. This is important if you want a grant or to see how much you'll have to spend on creating an oral history project.

5. List the cost of video taping and editing, packaging, publicity, and help with audio or special effects and stock shot photos of required.

6. What kind of equipment will you need? List that and the time slots you give to each part of the project. How much time is available? What are your deadlines?

7. What's your plan for a research? How are you going to approach the people to get the interviews? What questions will you ask?

8. Do the interviews. Arrive prepared with a list of questions. It's okay to ask the people the kind of questions they would like to be asked. Know what dates the interviews will cover in terms of time. Are you covering the eco-

nomic depression of the thirties? World Wars? Fifties? Sixties? Pick the time parameters.

9. Edit the interviews so you get the highlights of experiences and events, the important parts. Make sure what's important to you also is important to the person you interviewed.

10. Find out what the interviewee wants to emphasize perhaps to highlight events in a life story. Create a video-biography of the highlights of one person's life or an oral history of an event or series of events.

11. Process audio as well as video, and make sure you have written transcripts of anything on audio and/or video in case the technology changes or the tapes go bad.

12. Save the tapes to compact disks, DVDs, a computer hard disk and several other ways to preserve your oral history time capsule. Donate any tapes or CDs to appropriate archives, museums, relatives of the interviewee, and one or more oral history libraries. They are usually found at universities that have an oral history department and library such as UC Berkeley and others.

13. Check the Web for oral history libraries at universities in various states and abroad.

14. Evaluate what you have edited. Make sure the central issue and central questions have been covered in the interview. Find out whether newspapers or magazines want summarized transcripts of the audio and/or video with photos.

15. Contact libraries, archives, university oral history departments and relevant associations and various ethnic genealogy societies that focus on the subject matter of your central topic.

16. Keep organizing what you have until you have long and short versions of your oral history for various archives and publications. Contact magazines and newspapers to see whether editors would assign reporters to do a story on the oral history project.

17. Create a scrapbook with photos and summarized oral histories. Write a synopsis of each oral history on a central topic or issue. Have speakers give pub-

lic presentations of what you have for each person interviewed and/or for the entire project using highlights of several interviews with the media for publicity. Be sure your project is archived properly and stored in a place devoted to oral history archives and available to researchers and authors.

Personal History Techniques

1. Begin with easy to answer questions that don't require you explore and probe deeply in your first question. Focus on one central issue when asking questions.

2. First research written or visual resources before you begin to seek an oral history of a central issue, experience, or event.

3. Who is your intended audience?

4. What kind of population niche or sample will you target?

5. What means will you select to choose who you will interview? What group of people will be central to your interview?

6. Write down how you'll explain your project. Have a script ready so you don't digress or forget what to say on your feet.

7. Consult oral history professionals if you need more information. Make sure what you write in your script will be clear to understand by your intended audience.

8. Have all the equipment you need ready and keep a list of what you'll use and the cost. Work up your budget.

9. Choose what kind of recording device is best—video, audio, multimedia, photos, and text transcript. Make sure your video is broadcast quality. I use a Sony Digital eight (high eight) camera.

10. Make sure from cable TV stations or news stations that what type of video and audio you choose ahead of time is broadcast quality.

11. Make sure you have an external microphone and also a second microphone as a second person also tapes the interview in case the quality of your camera

breaks down. You can also keep a tape recorder going to capture the audio in case your battery dies.

12. Make sure your battery is fully charged right before the interview. Many batteries die down after a day or two of nonuse.

13. Test all equipment before the interview and before you leave your office or home. I've had batteries go down unexpectedly and happy there was another person ready with another video camera waiting and also an audio tape version going.

14. Make sure the equipment works if it's raining, hot, cold, or other weather variations. Test it before the interview. Practice interviewing someone on your equipment several times to get the hang of it before you show up at the interview.

15. Make up your mind how long the interview will go before a break and use tape of that length, so you have one tape for each segment of the interview. Make several copies of your interview questions.

16. Be sure the interviewee has a copy of the questions long before the interview so the person can practice answering the questions and think of what to say or even take notes. Keep checking your list of what you need to do.

17. Let the interviewee make up his own questions if he wants. Perhaps your questions miss the point. Present your questions first. Then let him embellish the questions or change them as he wants to fit the central issue with his own experiences.

18. Call the person two days and then one day before the interview to make sure the individual will be there on time and understands how to travel to the location. Or if you are going to the person's home, make sure you understand how to get there.

19. Allow yourself one extra hour in case of traffic jams.

20. Choose a quiet place. Turn off cell phones and any ringing noises. Make sure you are away from barking dogs, street noise, and other distractions.

21. Before you interview make sure the person knows he or she is going to be video and audio-taped.

22. If you don't want anyone swearing, make that clear it's for public archives and perhaps broadcast to families.

23. Your interview questions should follow the journalist's information-seeking format of asking, who, what, where, where, how, and why. Oral history is a branch of journalistic research.

24. Let the person talk and don't interrupt. You be the listener and think of oral history as aural history from your perspective.

25. Make sure only one person speaks without being interrupted before someone else takes his turn to speak.

26. Understand silent pauses are for thinking of what to say.

27. Ask one question and let the person gather his thoughts.

28. Finish all your research on one question before jumping to the next question. Keep it organized by not jumping back to the first question after the second is done. Stay in a linear format.

29. Follow up what you can about any one question, finish with it, and move on to the next question without circling back. Focus on listening instead of asking rapid fire questions as they would confuse the speaker.

30. Ask questions that allow the speaker to begin to give a story, anecdote, life experience, or opinion along with facts. Don't ask questions that can be answered only be yes or no. This is not a courtroom. Let the speaker elaborate with facts and feelings or thoughts.

31. Late in the interview, start to ask questions that explore and probe for deeper answers.

32. Wrap up with how the person solved the problem, achieved results, reached a conclusion, or developed an attitude, or found the answer. Keep the wrap-up on a light, uplifting note.

33. Don't leave the individual hanging in emotion after any intensity of. Respect the feelings and opinions of the person. He or she may see the situation from a different point of view than someone else. So respect the person's right to feel as he does. Respect his need to recollect his own experiences.

34. Interview for only one hour at a time. If you have only one chance, interview for an hour. Take a few minutes break. Then interview for the second hour. Don't interview more than two hours at any one meeting.

35. Use prompts such as paintings, photos, music, video, diaries, vintage clothing, crafts, antiques, or memorabilia when appropriate. Carry the photos in labeled files or envelopes to show at appropriate times in order to prime the memory of the interviewee. For example, you may show a childhood photo and ask "What was it like in that orphanage where these pictures were taken?" Or travel photos might suggest a trip to America as a child, or whatever the photo suggests. For example, "Do you remember when this ice cream parlor inside the ABC movie house stood at the corner of X and Y Street? Did you go there as a teenager? What was your funniest memory of this movie theater or the ice cream store inside back in the fifties?"

36. As soon as the interview is over, label all the tapes and put the numbers in order.

37. A signed release form is required before you can broadcast anything. So have the interviewee sign a release form before the interview.

38. Make sure the interviewee gets a copy of the tape and a transcript of what he or she said on tape. If the person insists on making corrections, send the paper transcript of the tape for correction to the interviewee. Edit the tape as best you can or have it edited professionally.

39. Make sure you comply with all the corrections the interviewee wants changed. He or she may have given inaccurate facts that need to be corrected on the paper transcript.

40. Have the tape edited with the corrections, even if you have to make a tape at the end of the interviewee putting in the corrections that couldn't be edited out or changed.

41. As a last resort, have the interviewee redo the part of the tape that needs correction and have it edited in the tape at the correct place marked on the tape. Keep the paper transcript accurate and up to date, signed with a release form by the interviewee.

42. Oral historians write a journal of field notes about each interview. Make sure these get saved and archived so they can be read with the transcript.

43. Have the field notes go into a computer where someone can read them along with the transcript of the oral history tape or CD.

44. Thank the interviewee in writing for taking the time to do an interview for broadcast and transcript.

45. Put a label on everything you do from the interview to the field notes. Make a file and sub file folders and have everything stored in a computer, in archived storage, and in paper transcript.

46. Make copies and digital copies of all photos and put into the records in a computer. Return originals to owners.

47. Make sure you keep your fingerprints off the photos by wearing white cotton gloves. Use cardboard when sending the photos back and pack securely. Also photocopy the photos and scan the photos into your computer. Treat photos as antique art history in preservation.

48. Make copies for yourself of all photos, tapes, and transcripts. Use your duplicates, and store the original as the master tape in a place that won't be used often, such as a time capsule or safe, or return to a library or museum where the original belongs.

49. Return all original photos to the owners. An oral history archive library or museum also is suitable for original tapes. Use copies only to work from, copy, or distribute.

50. Index your tapes and transcripts. To use oral history library and museum terminology, recordings and transcripts are given "accession numbers."

51. Phone a librarian in an oral history library of a university for directions on how to assign accession numbers to your tapes and transcripts if the materials are going to be stored at that particular library. Store copies in separate places in case of loss or damage.

52. If you don't know where the materials will be stored, use generic accession numbers to label your tapes and transcripts. Always keep copies available for

yourself in case you have to duplicate the tapes to send to an institution, museum, or library, or to a broadcast company.

53. Make synopses available to public broadcasting radio and TV stations.

54. Check your facts.

55. Are you missing anything you want to include?

56. Is there some place you want to send these tapes and transcripts such as an ethnic museum, radio show, or TV satellite station specializing in the topics on the tapes, such as public TV stations? Would it be suitable for a world music station? A documentary station?

57. If you need more interviews, arrange them if possible.

58. Give the interviewee a copy of the finished product with the corrections. Make sure the interviewee signs a release form that he or she is satisfied with the corrections and is releasing the tape to you and your project.

59. Store the tapes and transcripts in a library or museum or at a university or other public place where it will be maintained and preserved for many generations and restored when necessary.

60. You can also send copies to a film repository or film library that takes video tapes, an archive for radio or audio tapes for radio broadcast or cable TV.

61. Copies may be sent to various archives for storage that lasts for many generations. Always ask whether there are facilities for restoring the tape. A museum would most likely have these provisions as would a large library that has an oral history library project or section.

62. Make sure the master copy is well protected and set up for long-term storage in a place where it will be protected and preserved.

63. If the oral history is about events in history, various network news TV stations might be interested. Film stock companies may be interested in copies of old photos.

64. Find out from the subject matter what type of archives, repository, or storage museums and libraries would be interested in receiving copies of the oral history tapes and transcripts.

65. Print media libraries would be interested in the hard paper copy transcripts and photos as would various ethnic associations and historical preservation societies. Find out whether the materials will go to microfiche, film, or be digitized and put on CDs and DVDs, or on the World Wide Web. If you want to create a time capsule for the Web, you can ask the interviewee whether he or she wants the materials or selected materials to be put online or on CD as multimedia or other. Then you would get a signed release from the interviewee authorizing you to put the materials or excerpts online. Also find out in whose name the materials are copyrighted and whether you have print and electronic rights to the material or do the owners-authors-interviewees—or you, the videographer-producer? Get it all in writing, signed by those who have given you any interviews, even if you have to call your local intellectual property rights attorney.

How Accurate Are Oral/Aural Histories?

Cameras give fragments, points of view, and bits and pieces. Viewers will see what the videographer or photographer intends to be seen. The interviewee will also be trying to put his point of view across and tell the story from his perspective. Will the photographer or videographer be in agreement with the interviewee? Or if you are recording for print transcript, will your point of view agree with the interviewee's perspective and experience if your basic 'premise,' where you two are coming from, are not in agreement? Think this over as you write your list of questions. Do both of you agree on your central issue on which you'll focus for the interview?

How are you going to turn spoken words into text for your paper hard copy transcript? Will you transcribe verbatim, correct the grammar, or quote as you hear the spoken words? Oral historians really need to transcribe the exact spoken word. You can leave out the 'ahs' and 'oms' or loud pauses, as the interviewee thinks what to say next. You don't want to sound like a court reporter, but you do want to have an accurate record transcribed of what was spoken.

You're also not editing for a movie, unless you have permission to turn the oral history into a TV broadcast, where a lot gets cut out of the interview for time constraints. For that, you'd need written permission so words won't be taken out of context and strung together in the editing room to say something different from what the interviewee intended to say.

Someone talking could put in wrong names, forget what they wanted to say, or repeat themselves. They could mumble, ramble, or do almost anything. So you would have to sit down and weed out redundancy when you can or decide on presenting exactly what you've heard as transcript. When someone reads the transcript in text, they won't have what you had in front of you, and they didn't see and hear the live presentation or the videotape. It's possible to misinterpret gestures or how something is spoken, the mood or tone, when reading a text transcript. Examine all your sources. Use an ice-breaker to get someone talking.

If a woman is talking about female-interest issues, she may feel more comfortable talking to another woman. Find out whether the interviewee is more comfortable speaking to someone of his or her own age. Some older persons feel they can relate better to someone close to their own age than someone in high school, but it varies. Sometimes older people can speak more freely to a teenager.

The interviewee must be able to feel comfortable with the interviewer and know he or she will not be judged. Sometimes it helps if the interviewer is the same ethnic group or there is someone present of the same group or if new to the language, a translator is present.

Read some books on oral history field techniques. Read the National Genealogical Society Quarterly (NGSQ). Also look at The American Genealogist (TAG), The Genealogist, and The New England Historical and Genealogical Register (The Register). If you don't know the maiden name of say, your grandmother's mother, and no relative knows either because it wasn't on her death certificate, try to reconstruct the lives of the males who had ever met the woman whose maiden name is unknown.

Maybe she did business with someone before marriage or went to school or court. Someone may have recorded the person's maiden name before her marriage. Try medical records if any were kept. There was no way to find my mother's grandmother's maiden name until I started searching to see whether she had any brothers in this country. She had to have come as a passenger on a ship around 1880 as she bought a farm. Did her husband come with her?

Was the farm in his name? How many brothers did she have in this country with her maiden surname? If the brothers were not in this country, what countries did they come from and what cities did they live in before they bought the farm in Albany? If I could find out what my great grandmother's maiden name was through any brothers living at the time, I could contact their descendants perhaps and see whether any male or female lines are still in this country or where else on the globe.

Perhaps a list of midwives in the village at the time is recorded in a church or training school for midwives. Fix the person in time and place. Find out whom she might have done business with and whether any records of that business exist. What businesses did she patronize? Look for divorce or court records, change of name records, and other legal documents.

Look at local sources. Did anyone save records from bills of sale for weddings, purchases of homes, furniture, debutante parties, infant supplies, or even medical records? Look at nurses' licenses, midwives' registers, employment contracts, and teachers' contracts, alumni associations for various schools, passports, passenger lists, alien registration cards, naturalization records, immigrant aid societies, city directories, and cross-references. Try religious and women's clubs, lineage and village societies, girl scouts and similar groups, orphanages, sanatoriums, hospitals, police records. Years ago there was even a Eugenics Record Office. What about the women's prisons? The first one opened in 1839—Mount Pleasant Female Prison, NY.

Try voters' lists. If your relative is from another country, try records in those villages or cities abroad. Who kept the person's diaries? Have you checked the Orphan Train records? Try ethnic and religious societies and genealogy associations for that country. Most ethnic genealogy societies have a special interest group for even the smallest villages in various countries.

You can start one and put up a Web site for people who also come from there in past centuries. Check alimony, divorce, and court records, widow's pensions of veterans, adoptions, orphanages, foster homes, medical records, birth, marriage, and death certificates, social security, immigration, pet license owners' files, prisons, alumni groups from schools, passenger lists, military, and other legal records.

When all historical records are being tied together, you can add the DNA testing to link all those cousins. Check military pensions on microfilms in the National Archives. See the bibliography section of this book for further resources on highly recommended books and articles on oral history field techniques and similar historical subjects.

22

Does Writing Your Life Story Affect Your Memory?

Oral history depends on memory and the ability to speak. I also think of oral history as aural history, based on the ability to hear someone's experiences and remember them to pass on to the next generation or the world.

To find out the effects of oral history on memory and on creative writing on memory, we'd have to ask the people who write their life story and/or genealogy in their older years what it did for them, their memory, and their ability to think and feel. Make use of introverted feeling in writing a commercial or salable life story for the new media. Think in three dimensions for older adults is a different highway. How did DNA testing influence a genealogy search for family history facts?

Did the individual create a time capsule? How was the time capsule saved—on the Web? On a CD, DVD, video, or audio tape? In a scrapbook of photos, with various memorabilia? Did anyone rescue old photos from antique stores and flea markets by searching for photographer's prints on the front or back of the photo or names on the back of the photo and dates or locations?

1. When turning your salable life story, corporate history, or biography into an adventure action romance novel, don't set up your main characters in the first chapter to be in transit traveling on board a plane, train, or ship going somewhere. The action actually starts or hits them after they have already arrived at their destination.

Start your first chapter when your characters already get to their destination place or point in time. A first chapter that opens when your main character is on a plane or train is the kiss of death from many editors point of view and the main reason why a good novel often is rejected. So cut out the traveling scene from your first chapter and begin where the action starts for real, at the destination point. Does anyone visit antique stores, malls, or flea markets to search for family history memorabilia? What about attic, basement, or garage sales?

2. Use a lot of dialogue when turning a biography or your life story into a salable novel, especially in a romance, adventure action, or suspense novel or in one where you combine romance with adventure and suspense.

Use no more than three pages of narrative without dialogue. Let characters speak through the dialogue and tell the reader what is happening. Get characters to speak as normally as possible. If the times and place dictate they speak in proverbs, so be it. Proverbs make the best novels as you turn your proverb into a story and play it out as a novel. Otherwise, have normal speech so you can be the catalyst and bring people together who understand clearly what one another means.

3. Put your characters on the stage and have them talking to one another. If you have introspection in your book, don't use introspection for your action line. Action adventure books keep characters on stage talking to the audience.

4. Use magazines and clothing catalogues to make a collage of what your character might look like. This inspiration may go up on a board in front of you or on the wall to see as you work. Get a picture in your mind of what your characters look like. If they don't exist in art history, draw them yourself or make a mixed media collage of what they look like, speak like, and stand for. Some ideas include the models in "cigar" magazines, catalogues, and fashion publications as well as multi-ethnic and historical illustrations and photos.

5. Research history and keep a loose-leaf notebook with tabs on the history of places you want to research. The history itself is great for ideas on what plot to write. Look at or visit old forts and similar places. Plug in characters to your research. Look at forts of foreign settlements in the country of your choice, U.S. or any other place. Record the dates in your files. Create a spreadsheet in Excel or any other type of spread sheet with your dates from historical research as these will relate to your characters and help you develop a real plot.

6. Keep a notebook for each novel or biography you write. Put everything related to each book in a notebook. Have one notebook for historical research and one for the novel you're writing or true storybook.

7. When sending out your book manuscript make a media kit for yourself with your resume, photo, list of works in development if you are not yet published, and any other material about your own experience in any other field. Your own biography and photo presented to the press also can be used to let an editor know when you send out your manuscript of what's in development and what you've done.

8. Write down the point of view before your book is begun. Whose point of view is it anyway? Who tells the story? If you're writing a romance novel from your life story or a military romantic suspense novel, true story, radio script, or other genre, agree on the point of view before you start.

9. Who's telling the story and how does she or he know how the other characters know what to say?

10. It's not necessary to continue ethnic stereotypes in your book. If one of your characters is a music agent, for example, and a lot of music agents are of one ethnicity or speak with a certain accent, it's not necessary to continue the stereotyping roles. Pick something new for a change. Otherwise it becomes cliché. Research diverse ways of telling the same story.

- The readers needs to learn facts or experiences, anecdotes, oral histories transcribed, and stories that have not been generalized. Use a series of incidents, action and relationship tension to balance your plot with your dialogue.

- If you're turning a biography into a romance novel, you need to balance the relationship tension with the mystery, action, or other plot. You must have some event occur on both sides, on the sexual tension side and on the mystery or action side to balance out the book.

For every action in a life story, there's an equal and opposite reaction that's primarily character-driven and secondarily plot-driven. And in an autobiography or anyone's life story, relationship tension occurs. Then the plot moves on. If it's a romantic suspense or mystery within a life story, such as true confession, true crime, or biography, usually twenty-four short chapters makes a book-length story.

A diary is written in first person as a journal or log, but a biography can be of you or your client. Even in a memoirs book or diary, you have to balance action with interaction between the heroine and the hero.

You can be the only person in your diary, but the action and interaction needs to be balanced with something out there in the external world—either forces of nature or another person—or the competition.

If you keep the competition out of your diary, put in the memories, actions, and warmth of the friends, including pets. If there are no other people, put in some force of spirit, some other push and pull, or tension, for balance with something outside yourself. This can be a job, school, a hobby, or what you choose as the force that pulls in an opposite direction existing with the force or person that pulls in your direction.

Try putting the relationship tension between the hero and heroine in the even-numbered chapters, and the mystery, historical events, or action plot events in the odd-numbered chapters.

In a 24-chapter-historical romance, this alternating action chapter, romantic tension chapter balances the plot smoothly. Most historical romance novels have 22-24 chapters. If you analyze the best-selling ones, you'll see that chapter one has an opening scene on the action side so you see what's happening.

The first action-oriented introductory chapter that shows us what's happening is followed by the second chapter on the romantic tension side showing us when and how the heroine meets the hero or has a re-union with the hero. In the second chapter, the writer takes the heroine somewhere in place or time.

The heroine in the second chapter is defined. Either she's a 90's woman, or she's in her place in history or rebelling against it. You tell the story.

If you're male, you'd use a hero. Romantic life stories featuring genealogy combined with biography usually are 10-12 chapters long. Historical romances are twice that size at 22-24 chapters. The writer decides whether it's best to turn a biography into a historical romance or a life story into a mystery, suspense, action adventure, young adult novel, romance, or other genre.

If you are not fictionalizing genealogy or biography into a story, keep your time capsule book, database, or other media true to facts and historical records only. You might want to add your DNA testing records of relatives along with a family tree or other database or time capsule.

For those who want to turn factual biography into a novel, in turning a biography into a romance, the romantic tension side is about girl meeting hero in the first chapter. In the second chapter, the hero takes her somewhere in place, space, time, or state of mind. An oral history may be written as true life story in the form of a novel or play, skit, or anecdote of experience.

The oral history highlights a life experience within a time frame set in one or more locations with all the nuances of that place. It's basically a life story, but it can be transcribed with that certain something, including—charisma, liveliness, action, forward movement, drama, tension, and unique experiences, problems solved, and goals.

23

Diaries and DNA Equal Family History Evidence

What do diaries and DNA tests have in common? Both are handled as evidence.

Diaries, like deleted files hidden in the cache pits of computers, and DNA tests can be used as evidence. Diaries also hold the seeds of a story. You could write a novel or a screenplay from a diary. A diary also is a history. So preserve a diary as you would restore and preserve a valuable work of art from the past. Diaries are meant to be passed to future generations for a glimpse into a world that can be experienced by generations far into the future. Keep a file of dates listed in the diary and any objects that surrounded the diary from the same era.

A story with a central issue needed little explanation when my mom wrote in her diary in the style of a telegram: "October 25, 1926: First day of honeymoon. On train to Miami. Today I died." What central issues and themes tell a story in the diaries that cross your path?

Keep the dates and topics organized if you are working with restoring and preserving diaries. There should be a central issue or theme. How old was the person writing the diary? How many years did the individual keep the diary? What kind of objects were near the diary, packed together?

What kind of dust or other stains were on the diary—sawdust? Farm materials and plants? The first corsage from the senior prom? How about recipes, household hints, or how-to tips for hobbies? Was the diary or journal personal and inner-reflected, or geared toward outer events in the world? Were anecdotes about people and/or pets included, or was it about the feelings of the author of the diary?

Find out what other clues the mystery of the diary unfolds, from the lipstick or nail polish stain to the sawdust and coffee stains, or that faint smell of tobacco, industrial lint, or is it lavender, jasmine or farm dust and straw? Look inside the box in which the diary was packed. It's all evidence and clues waiting to be examined just like a mystery novel. A diary is a story, and everyone life deserves a novel, story, or biography and eventually, a place in a time capsule.

How to Restore a Diary

Make a book jacket for your diary to preserve and restore it. Use acid-free paper. Call a library or museum and ask for a brand or type of long-lasting acid-free paper and where you can buy some. Put a title and label on the dust jacket with the name of the diary's author and any dates, city, state, or country.

You can also speak to the art history department of most universities and find out what kind of paper is best to use for a book jacket to restore and preserve a diary. Treat it like a work of art. The same can be done for photo scrap books.

If torn, mend the diary. Your goal is to improve its condition. Apply a protective plastic wrapper to your valuable dust jacket. Give the diary a dust jacket in good condition. It should start to look more like a valuable book in good condition. If the diary is dingy and dirty, bleach it white on the edges. Put a plastic cover on the diary. The white pages of a diary without ink can be bleached with regular household bleach, but don't let the vapors of the bleach soak through to reach the ink because it will bleach out the writing.

Repair old diaries and turn them into heirlooms for families and valuable collectibles. The current price for repair of handwritten diaries and books is about $35 and up per book or bound diary, if you like to specialize in mending old dairies and family or personal books for a fee.

Some old diaries contain recipes and also served as personal, handwritten cookbooks containing recipes created by a particular family or family cook. These were valuable books preserved as if they were family scrapbooks, unlike the recipe databases in computers we have today. They are works of art, like an old tapestry embroidered with the story of a family's major turning points and events.

For more repair tips on bound diaries and books, I recommend *How to Wrap a Book*, Fannie Merit Farmer, Boston Cooking School.

How do you repair an old diary to make it more valuable to the heirs? You'll often find a bound diary that's torn in the seams. According to Barbara Gelink, of the Collector's Old Cookbooks Club, San Diego, to repair a book, you take a bottle of Book Saver Glue (or any other book-repairing or wood glue), and spread the glue along the binder.

Run the glue along the seam and edges. Use wax paper to keep the glue from getting where it shouldn't. Put a heavy glass bottle on the inside page to hold it down while the glue dries.

To remove tape, tags, or stains from a glossy cover, use lighter fluid or cleaning fluid (away from sparks, flames, or heat lamps). Dampen a cloth with nail polish remover if lighter fluid is too smelly and flammable for you.

Another way to remove something pasted on a plastic book cover is to use the finest grade sandpaper. Many books you'll find at goodwill will have adhesive price tags on the book. It's not usual to find diaries, even bound diaries in old book stores, but they show up in garage sales and in some antique stores and flea markets along with old photos.

To bleach the "discarded book stamp" that libraries often use, or any other rubber stamp mark, price, date, or seals on the pages of a book or on the edges, use regular bleach, like Clorox. It turns the rubber stamp mark white. The household bleach also turns the edges and pages of the book white as new.

To preserve a valuable dust jacket, a tattered jacket with tears along the edges needs extra firmness. A protective plastic wrapper can improve the condition of a book if it has a jacket cover.

To look for old diaries, or old family photos, look in garage sales, flea markets, and antique shops.Attend auctions and book fairs. Two recommended auction houses for rare cookbooks include Pacific Book Auction Galleries, 139 Townsend, #305, San Francisco, CA 94107, or Sotheby's, New York, 1334 York Ave., New York, NY 10021. Pacific Book Auction Galleries recently put a large cookbook collection up for an auction.

Hunt for diaries, old photos, and other old clues to family history in thrift shops and antique stores. Some diaries also combine cookbooks with personal histories and transcribed oral histories, but these are very rare. Genealogy also can have a person's collection of favorite recipes or anything else the person collected organized and archived along with family history and genetics records.

If you're into scrap booking with family history, photos, and recipes, for nostalgia, look for cookbooks printed by high school parent-teacher associations. Some old ones may be valuable, but even the one put out by the depression era San Diego High School Parent Teacher Association for the class of 1933-34 is only worth $10.

To find out-of-print and mail-order cookbooks, contact Charlotte F. Safir, 1349 Lexington Ave #9-B, New York, NY 10128-1513, (212) 534-7933. She specializes in hard-to-find cookbooks and children's books. Astor House Books, PO Box 1701 Williamsburg, VA 23187 (804) 220-0116, specializes in cookery and gastronomy. Amber Unicorn Books, specializes in rare cookbooks. They're at 2202 W. Charleston Blvd, #2, Las Vegas, NV 89102 (702) 384-5838.

Little Treasures (Joyce Klein) Cookery Books has British and American cookbooks and general stock. They're at 7517 W. Madison, Forest Park, IL 60130 (708) 488-1212. Send your wants because they have no catalog.

Cornucopia, run by Carol A. Greenberg, has cooking and food literature and domestic history, household management, herbs and kitchen gardens, hotels and restaurants, etiquette and manners, pastimes and amusements, and needlework old and rare books. They search for out-of-print books, and are interested in material from the 19th century through 1940. Write to: Little Treasures at PO Box 742, Woodbury, NY 11797, (516) 692-7024. Greenberg is always grateful for quotations on old, rare, and unusual materials in fine condition.

The Collector's Old Cookbooks Club has half their members in other states and half in San Diego County. They send a newsletter to each member after the monthly meeting.

You could specialize in being a diary restoration specialist and book finder for genealogy groups. Perhaps you want to deal in collectors' valuable diaries, largely first editions. Mostly diaries are only editions. Some people had them bound like a blank notebook, and wrote in them. So they look like first editions of books.

Are diaries worth as much as rare cookbooks? How much are the thousands of rare cookbooks worth today? A helpful guide is the Price Guide to Cookbooks & Recipe Leaflets, 1990, by Linda J. Dickinson, published by Collector Books, at PO Box 3009, Paducah, KY 42002-3009.

See Bibliography of American Cookery Books, 1742–1860. It's based on Waldo Lincoln's American Cookery Books 1742–1860, by Eleanor Lowenstein. Over 800 books and pamphlets are listed. Order from Oak Knoll Books & Press, 414 Delaware St., Newcastle, Delaware 19720. Louis & Clark Booksellers specialize in rare and out-of-print cookery, gastronomy, wine and beverages, baking, restaurants, domestic history, etiquette, and travel books. They're at 2402 Van Hise Avenue, Madison, WI 53705. Always check for updates on addresses, Web sites, and other numbers, as they may have changed since information in this book was compiled.

Cookbooks and diaries are not that much distant from each other, although diaries of a famous person would have monetary value as would old cookbooks that are rare. Think of the events in the life story and history value of what real people's lives were like many decades or centuries ago. Any restored diaries would be valuable to descendants of anyone, and you can't put a price tag on these people's lives as expressed in diaries.

Get acid-free storage envelopes or boxes for diaries. Handle old diaries and books with gloves, and get rid of mildew safely without destroying the pages or fading the ink. It's here that a library can be helpful. Ask questions about storage from historical societies and libraries. Make copies of the diaries. Work with the photocopies when you decipher the writing.

Store old diaries in a dry, cool place where there are no bugs. Lining the storage place with plastic that's sealed will keep out vermin and bugs. Without moisture, you can keep out the mildew and mold. Store duplicates away from originals.

Call archivists and historians in your area and ask for their advice. Was something placed on a certain page, such as a dried rose, letter, or a special book mark? What meaning did it have? Date the diary. List the date it was begun and when it was ended, or look for clues for a time frame. List the geographic location of the events in the diary or the writer.

Of what kind of materials is the diary made? Is it improvised, created at low cost by the author? Or is it fancy and belonging to someone of wealth? What is the layout like? Does it show the education of the writer or anything personal? Was it a masculine almanac or calendar or a feminine expression of memorabilia and sentiment? Or was it written by a man writing poetry or letters and being romantic?

Can you tell the personality traits of the writer of that diary? What was the writing tool, a quill or a pencil? What's the handwriting like? Would a handwriting analyst know what to say about it? Does the handwriting and words express anger, joy, sadness, or what? Is it full of detail, or is the reader given the big picture? Why was the diary written? What is its central message? Do you see patterns, concepts or facts?

Transcribe the diary with your computer. What historical events influenced the writing of the diary? What language is it in or dialect? Study the historical meaning of the diary so you can get to know the writer across the chasms of decades or centuries.

Are there vital records such as deeds to real estate mentioned in the diary? What photographs are in the diary? Any artifacts mentioned or pressed between the pages? See whether you can relate to the diary author and find some type of context of the story from entry to entry. Are there any genealogical records or mention of family names, such as a great, great, great grandmother's maiden name? What about recorded events of inherited diseases or medical histories?

If the grandfather's dad went blind with glaucoma, it's has a genetic element that heirs should know about whether anyone inherited it or not. See what the diary unfolds that can be read as family history, world history, or used in the phenomics mode, to customize treatment or therapy based on genetics.

Treat the diary as a precious work of art, including the photos in there, if any. Don't touch the old right side up photos with bare fingers because the emulsion would quickly come off. Some genealogists specialize in working with old diaries, and novelists or screenwriters would probably be interested in a unique story. Restore a diary, and if a building such as a restaurant wants to hang old photos in the dining hall, let the photos be copies rather than the originals.

If you want to record the memories of relatives or friends, list 100–200 inspiring questions. Give the questions to relatives and friends. Create the questions with the goal of triggering recall of memories and experiences, events, and highlights of their life stories. Give them a diary and make a dust cover that's fancy. Put a plastic cover over the dust jacket.

Use a hardbound book with a question on each page. Or give several pages per question if the person might like to write for personal expression. You could ask the person if he or she wanted more or less pages. About 150 questions or pages are fine to last a lifetime of a minimum of one-page summarized life events or answers to the questions you ask.

The questions should be important to both you and the person who's going to write in the diary or journal. This is one way to create a genealogy diary gift that develops into a biography from a personal journal or diary.

Make sure there's enough pages and room to express what's required. Print the questions large and clear so you can elicit recorded responses to the questions. Leave room to attach photographs on acid-free, archival-quality paper.

If the person really won't write, create a tape recorded or video diary where the person can record his voice on tape, in a computer, or with a video camera on a tripod poised next to a desk to record the person talking without requiring anyone else in the room when recording.

Give the person a remote control device for the video camera to click on and off without walking toward the camera or tape recorder, or computer microphone. If the person will write at all, stick with the personal ambiance of a diary gift that someone can hold in any location or take traveling.

What questions to write? List thought-starters. Write questions about their childhood, values, dreams, and goals. Create a section for recording time as a mother or father, grandparent, how a child's name was chosen, how the marriages were arranged, or what things each child did to make a parent proud.

Put in blank pages and a place for each relative to put in the results of their DNA testing, fingerprints, print of hand or palm, or any other personal information, even medical notes or other memories in the memorabilia. Leave room for children's photos, small drawings, and meaningful relics. Use the kind of binding where someone can add pages.

File and archive the DNA test results, racial percentages tests, along with any other information from memory. Add an oral history, perhaps a pocket for a tape, or room for a transcript of an oral history to be added, such as a loose-leaf binding or similar binding so pages may be added to folders or plastic envelopes holding mementos. Have a space for the first job and for a father's memories.

The genealogy thought-starter questions can come bound in a fancy, hardbound loose-leaf that will last as pages are added. Or better yet to give each his or her own individual expression without the judgment of another relative, give a separate book to each family member so he or she can keep memories or traditions private until passed to heirs. You might want to create a separate book for each grandparent, parent, and other relative.

24

Hidden Records & Directories

Arab-American, Armenian, Greek, Turkish, Assyrian, Iranian, and Jewish Mizrahi-Sephardi-Ashkenazi Genealogy Records in the USA, Canada, and Latin America's Census Records and City Directories in the USA or in Your Ancestor's Former Lands.

If you're searching your ancestor's former nation, learn how to read the alphabet, and better yet, learn some of the language so you can read records. Glean genealogy facts from tombstone rubbings, marriage records, census records, military archives, pension applications, and city directories. The US Census population database and the Office of National Statistics of the UK database used different methodologies to come up with their results. Rare surnames will not get a search result in the US census site, whereas they will in the UK site, even if there are only a few persons with the same surname. Names shared by fewer than five people have been excluded from the UK list.

Now that you have an idea of the size of your potential prospect pool, lets assume that only 1/3 are interested in genealogy, so you now divide by 3. The end result is a very rough approximation of the number of potential participants available. If you are only using the Internet to find your participants, cut this number in half for the US. Other countries have a smaller percentage of persons on the Internet than the US.

As your first step, you have probably posted your project to as many sites and mailing lists that are applicable and allow such postings. You have probably also put up a web site, even if it is only one page. Most likely you have contacted all those persons whom you had contact with in the past regarding genealogy.

Here are some suggestions to consider in order to make more people aware of your project:

1. Consult the Directory of Family Associations. If there is a Family Association for your surname, contact them and offer to write an article for their publication about your project.

2. Register your web site with familysearch.org. Everyone searching on your surname at Familysearch.org will find your web site. You must first register yourself with familysearch.org to be able to submit your website for consideration.

3. Visit your local Family History Center, and offer to show the Genealogy by Genetics video to the staff and patrons. This might not find you any participants, but if every Group Administrator takes an hour to do this, then all the Surname Projects might find participants.

4. Review your web site. It needs to be easy to understand for those not familiar with DNA testing, and clearly present the benefits to the participant. What will they gain from participating? How will it help them in their research? What might the results tell them?

5. Find out if there are any genealogy clubs or organizations in your area, and volunteer to show the video, and answer questions.

DNA testing for genealogy is a new field, and we are all pioneers. Most likely you have learned a lot about the field as a result of your testing. Those of us who have learned about DNA testing and how to interpret the results are aware of the benefits and how the testing can assist us with our genealogy research. Convergence explains why a haplotype will match others with a different surname. DNA testing for genealogy is not a substitute for genealogy research, but is instead a companion.

The majority of those interested in Family History research may not yet be fully aware of Genetic Genealogy. If you volunteer an hour to help your fellow genealogists understand this new tool, and help more people become knowledgeable, all of us will benefit as we seek participants for our testing. Look for social histories of the ethnic group you're researching.

When you're working with DNA, you can look for historical medical records. Only a few are open to the public. You might try the microfilmed collections at The Family History Library in Salt Lake City, UT, or rent one of the microfilms from any of the worldwide family history centers, usually found in a genealogical library in various cities around the world.

Look at records from the Eugenics Record Office (ERO) that operated from 1910 to 1944. The purpose of that office was to study human genetics in order to reduce inheritable genetic disorders. You can look over the 520 rolls of microfilm. Visit the Family History Library Catalog and look under United States—Medical Records—Eugenics.

Look up the state you want, and look under Medical Records. You might want to read up on the controversial Eugenics movement. Think about how DNA testing today differs in that the test results are used today either to find relatives, ancestors, or for personalized medicine—tailoring individual therapies, diets, lifestyles, or treatments for individual genetic makeups. Personalized medicine and predictive medicine includes phenomics.

DNA Phenomics works towards the discovery and production of genomic-based personalized medical solutions for an area's region's diverse populations. Genealogy is the study of records of family history and ancestory. How times have changed. Or have they? What do you see in your own DNA and family history research?

The Family History Library in Salt Lake City also has some historical hospital records. One example is the Northwestern Memorial Hospital record, Chicago in the Family History Library, dated 1896–1933. Perhaps one of your relatives is in those files. That's one other way of finding a maiden name from the days when many people were never given a birth certificate because they were born at home and never registered. That's what happened with my mom, born in 1904 at home in NY state.

25

Understanding your Results: Ethnic Origin

Whether you are just starting a Surname Project, or want to learn about DNA testing for genealogy, everyone experiences the situation of receiving the first test result, and what now? You have one test result, and what do you do with a string of 12 or 37 numbers? Can they tell you anything? Where can you find the information you need?

In the situation of the one or first test result, most likely you will not find others to whom you are related. The odds of a random match to some one to whom you are related when you are the first of your surname to test is slim to none. Instead, you might find some clues to your ethnic origin.

To find clues about your ethnic origin, Log into FamilyTreeDna.com, and at your Personal Page click on Recent Ethnic Origins to search this data base. The results show others whom you match, or who are a near match, and their ancestor's ethnic origin.

The information on their ethnic origin is provided by each person tested (testee). The information provided for ethnic origin is only as accurate as the knowledge held by the testee regarding their ancestors. Testees are instructed to answer unknown for ethnic origin when their ancestor's origin is not known, or not certain. Sometimes the origin the testees provided is incorrect.

Incorrect origins provided by testees may lead to search results that do not seem logical. For example: Assume your ancestors are from England, but your search results show the ethnic origin of your matches as England, France, AND one match shows an origin of Native American. Does that mean that your ancestor's relatives may have lived in England and France? Yes. Does it mean that your ancestor was also a Native American? No. It means that a settler in America had a child with a Native American woman, the child was brought up as a Native

American, and that, over time, the family has "forgotten" the European ancestor, and believes their ancestry to be Native American.

During the span of generations people tend to move, as do borders, so nationality or ethnicity becomes subjective. For example, testees may enter Germany for ethnic origin, because the land of their ancestors is in Germany today, but the land had been held by Denmark for many centuries.

Your search should return at least one match, namely yourself. If your results show 3 matches from Ireland and 1 from Scotland, and you have reported to us that your ancestors came from Scotland, then you are the Scotland result. The other 3 matches are either from the Family Tree DNA database or from the databases Family Tree DNA have been supplied by the University of Arizona.

To see how your ethnic origin is recorded in our database, click on the link titled Update Contact Information. You can also update your paternal and maternal ethnic origin on this Update Contact Information page.

Exact matches show people who are the closest to you genetically. The Ethnic origin shows where they have been reported to have lived. Since many persons migrated since the beginning of time, you will typically see matches in more than one country.

For information purposes, the Recent Ethnic Origin search also displays results for those who are not exact matches, but are 'near matches'. A near match is either one step or two steps from your result. An exact match is 12/12 or 25/25. A one step match is 11/12 or 24/25. A two step match is 10/12 or 23/25. The value of the near matches is to see where those who may be related migrated over time.

Other databases available that you can search are:
European: http://ystr.charite.de/index_gr.html
US: http://www.ystr.org/usa/

In some cases you will not find any results. This is because only a very small percentage of the world population has been tested and is in the databases. The Ystr databases, plus the FamilyTreeDNA Recent Ethnic Origin database together hold about 21,000 test results. Every day more results are added, and it is only a matter of time before you will have some matches. Your test with Family Tree DNA includes access to our databases for matching.

If you do not find any results in the two YSTR databases shown above, try entering your result, and then eliminating a marker, and do this until you have a smaller set of markers that results in some matches. This might provide some clues regarding where your markers have occurred geographically.

The value of DNA testing comes from comparing your results to others. If you have started a Surname Project, you will most likely have results from others soon. If you only tested yourself, you may want to consider either using DNA testing to solve one of your Family History questions, or starting a Surname Project.

Haplotypes: Convergence

A Haplotype is the 12 Marker result from testing the Y chromosome. Some Haplotypes are common, with a high frequency of occurrence and some Haplotypes are rare, with a low frequency of occurrence.

Many people have common Haplotypes, which means that they would expect to find matches to those who do not have their surname. This occurs because we were all at one point related. As the different branches of the Adam +Eve tree evolved throughout time, mutations occurred, forming different Haplotypes. Thousands of years later, you have many different Haplotypes. Due to these mutations, you could have two branches that mutate to an identical Haplotype. This is called convergence.

If your Haplotype matches an individual with a different surname, and your genealogy research shows no evidence of an extra-marital event or adoption, your match may be the result of Convergence.

The example below shows convergence between the ABC surname and the XYZ surname, using just 3 markers to keep the example simple. Notice how the mutations over time bring two different Family Lines to the point that they match.

Time	ABC	XYZ
1000 A.D.	12 24 15	14 25 13
1200	13 24 15	14 25 13
1400	13 24 15	14 25 14
1600	13 24 15	14 24 14
1800	13 24 15	13 24 14
2000	13 24 14	13 24 14

Convergence explains why a haplotype will match others with a different surname.

DNA testing for genealogy is not a substitute for genealogy research, but is instead a companion. Results that match must be considered in light of the genealogy research. If you match someone with a different surname, most likely there wasn't an adoption or extra marital event, and your match may be the result of convergence.

Case Studies in Genetic Genealogy

In each issue of the Newsletter, Family Tree DNA looks at what Genetic Genealogy will do for your Family History research. This article is a continuation of the topic, with situations, called *"Case Studies"*, followed by a recommendation. The objective of the case studies is to present different situations you may encounter in your family history research, and how DNA testing can be applied.

Case Study

From November 21, 2002 Volume 1, Issue 5, *Family Tree DNA Newsletter*, "I have participated in a Surname Project, and had quite surprising results. All the other Lines of my surname are related, except my Line. We have all traced our ancestors to England. Not only is my line not related, but also my ethnic origin is Eastern European. What do I do now?"

Recommendation

From November 21, 2002 Volume 1, Issue 5, *Family Tree DNA Newsletter*, " I am sure you were quite surprised, and perhaps disappointed. The first step is to validate the result for your Line or family tree. Since only one person was tested for your Line, we recommend testing additional males from each branch on your tree, to see if they all match each other. If they end up matching, your result is probably due to an extra marital event, an adoption, or a name or spelling change.

"In reviewing the surnames of Eastern Europe, your surname is pronounced as the surname in England, only the spelling is different. A review of your Family History shows that the research and documentation for the time period 1800–1850 is quite sparse. Many more records are available in England for this time period, including parish registers and wills. I would suggest that more family history research might shed some light on the situation."

26

Managing a Genetic Genealogy Project: Participants with Poor Documentation

Occasionally you might run across a willing participant for your Arab American, Armenian, Greek, Turkish, Jewish, Iranian, or Eastern European Surname Project who has a poorly documented family tree, perhaps even built entirely out of the International Genealogical Index (IGI) by matching surnames. Your dilemma is that the prospective participant appears to be from a Line you haven't tested yet, but without better research you can't be sure. What comes first, the testing or the research?

This is a complex issue. If you turn away the participant and suggest that they do more research, they may become discouraged, and never return. If the participant tests, and gets unexpected results, they may become an unhappy participant.

One solution is to fill in the gaps of their research. You may not have the time to take this step. A better solution may be to communicate the situation to the participant, and let the individual make the decision to test now with the possibility of unexpected results, and also encourage the client to do further research.

Perhaps from your research experience, you may be able to suggest to the participant specific sources for them to investigate. Most likely, the individual will want to do more research, and just need information, guidance and direction. It will be favorable for your Surname Project and the participant if you are able to achieve additional research on your client's part, and that person's participation.

Haplogroups and Markers
What's a Recessive Gene?

Sometimes a recessive gene is referred to as a form of a gene called a recessive allele. The recessive allele will not express itself if combined with a dominant allele. The recessive allele is expressed by a lower-case letter. Some traits may be caused by having two recessive alleles.

Markers

How many genetic markers can tell us something for various pairings between groups of people? Markers often are great for telling multiple groups apart. For example, one marker in particular can tell Africans apart from all the other groups, but that marker can't tell Europeans from East Asians. Scientists also will look at male Y chromosomes to study various markers.

Markers are different for various ethnic groups. However, there also is some overlap as peoples become mixed. A geneticist can tell the percentages of various races by looking at the markers, even though we have come to accept there really is no such thing as a particular race because of the diversity between peoples in any one race. However, you can still look at genetic markers to see various ethnic group traits for people who have been separated for thousands of years.

African-European	54 markers
African-East Asian	50 markers
African-Native American	50 markers
European-East Asian	45 markers
European-Native American	41 markers
East Asian-Native American	24 markers

What is a Haplogroup? How is it different from a Haplotype?

Your matrilineal or female ancestors inherit the same mtDNA sequences which form a haplogroup. Look at female lineages starting with your mtDNA haplogroup today. It will be the same haplogroup letter as your common ancestor with the same haplogroup letter who lived 21,000 years ago. You are looking at a connection from a single female ancestor to all your direct female line ancestors today.

The sequences within the haplogroup may be slightly different because of the slow mutation rate of the mtDNA, but the haplogroup will be the same. And in some cases, the sequences will be similar to your ancient ancestors. While in other cases, the mutation rate may have changed your mtDNA just a little over that long span of time.

What's a Haplotype?

Let's look at the female lineages, the mitochondrial DNA clues called mtDNA for short.

Individual mitochondrial DNA called for short, mtDNA sequences, is grouped into haplotypes. A haplotype defines a series of special mutations. The mutations when lumped together are called haplogroups. Each haplogroup contains a set of haplotypes descended from the same one common ancestor. How many haplogroups of mtDNA are there? According to Bryan Syke's book, *The Seven Daughters of Eve*, at least 35 mtDNA haplogroups represented by a letter of the alphabet are listed in one of the illustrated tables. Matrilineal (female ancestral) lineages contain the mitochondria.

You can look at ancient ancestry by tracing the mtDNA lines. Some mtDNA letters belong mostly to Africa, while others belong to East Asia. Some are specific to South West Asia (India) and others are found in central and west Eurasia, which includes Europe and the Middle East. Five different mtDNA haplogroups are found in the New World—the Americas, such as ABCD and X, but the differences between the European and Middle Eastern X and the X among some Native American peoples show that they have been separated for thousands of years.

For example, in the book *Mapping Human History*, by Steve Olson, a rare and unusual haplogroup, X showed up among the Algonquian-speaking Native Americans living around the Great Lakes. It also is present in small amounts in the Lakota and Sioux. Previously mtDNA haplogroup X had been found in Finland, and in Italian, Greek, and Druze (Israel and Lebanon) peoples. Haplogroup X so far has not been found in East Asians. How did it get to the New World?

The Native American X mtDNA differed very much from the European haplogroup X to be separated by only one or two thousand years. It had to have come to the New World tens of thousands of years ago. Scientist Douglas Wallace of the Center for Molecular Medicine at Emory University in Atlanta is one of the world's leading experts on mitochondrial genetics. So when he studied two skeletons that lived in the 1300s in Illinois among the Native Americans of that time, he found the skeletons contained traces of haplogroup X.

How did he know it wasn't from mixture with a European? It was the time divergence between the European and the Native American X haplogroup that gave the answer. The haplogroup X in North America had been there for more than 10,000 years. It wasn't a "modern" European who lived in Illinois in the 14th century.

Again, you might ask, perhaps it was a Viking from Finland since X is found in Finland? The tests showed this type of X differs from the European X by mutations that reveal the X that lived in America really had been there more than 10,000 years. So it could have come more than 10,000 years ago from anywhere—central Asia, Siberia. No X haplogroups are in Siberia today as far as one can tell.

Then again, not everyone has been tested there. However, you have to draw the line somewhere, and the differences between the old world and new world X haplogroup were great as if they had been separated more than 10,000 years. It's easy to imagine someone in north central Asia could have joined up with a group of people such as hunters and traveled with them over the Bering Strait while it was still a land bridge more than 12,000 years ago.

What's a Haplogroup?

A group of related haplotypes make up a haplogroup. Haplogroups are studied especially when referring to mitochondrial DNA and Y-chromosomes. If a set of haplotypes are placed into a tree determined by the minimum number of mutations that separate them, the main branches of that tree are haplogroups. Each haplogroup in theory contains haplotypes that are all descended from a single founding individual.

Haplotypes from other regions of the genome are not studied as much because they may not always group together. Recombination makes ancestor-descendant relationships not as specific to see. You have to look for connections when you study haplotypes.

Examples: The vast majority of Native Americans belong to one of four mtDNA haplogroups: A, B, C, and D, but a few Native Americans also belong to haplogroup X. Haplogroup X is found at a low percentage in Europe, but the differences between the European haplogroup X and the Native American haplogroup X show that they separated more than 10,000 years ago.

It's more likely that someone with haplogroup X mtDNA from Southern Siberia, the Caucasus, or central Asia joined a group of hunters headed north and east more than 12,000 years ago when there was a land bridge over the Bering Strait, and settled in what is now called the North American continent.

* What's an allele?

For lots of definitions of these terms, also see the Web site: library.thinkquest.org/18258/noframes/def-allele.htm . Or See: *www.apnet.com/inscight/08271998/allele1.htm*

An allele is a form of a gene. Alleles are located at the same position (locus) on homologous chromosomes and are separated from each other during meiosis. An allele is what is actually within a region of the chromosome, and is found within a gene. *An allele is any of two or more alternative forms of a gene occupying the same chromosomal locus; such as that which determines flower petal color in peas.*

* What's a Haplogroup?

Definition: A bunch of haplotypes make up a haplogroup. The term is used usually when referring to female lineages and mitochondrial DNA or mtDNA. You might call a form of a gene an allele. An allele is an alternative form of a genetic locus. A single allele for each locus is inherited from each parent (e.g., at a locus for eye color the allele might result in blue or brown eyes).

So when a group of alleles on a single chromosome are linked together and usually inherited as a unit, these genes make up a haplogroup. Haplotypes are particularly stable in mitochondrial DNA and on the Y-chromosome, because they are not subject to recombination.

Analyses of mtDNA and Y-chromosome variation usually focus on the haplotype or haplogroup level, rather than comparing exact base pair sequences. In this case, haplotypes are defined on the basis of particular mutations shared by various individual DNA lineages.

Examples: One study of Finnish Y-chromosome variation found that 40% belonged to one of two different haplotypes, which in turn each belonged to different haplogroups and were probably introduced by different founding populations.

* **Genome.** A person's genome is one set of his (or her) genes. The human genes, which control a cell's structure, operation, and division, are located in the cell's nucleus. The full human genome (estimated at 50,000 to 100,000 genes) is present in every cell-nucleus. Many genes are inactive in cells that have some specialized functions. Many cells are differentiated to perform certain functions only.

* **Genes and Chromosomes.** Genes are composed of segments of DNA. In normal cell-nuclei, the DNA is distributed among 46 chromosomes (23 inherited at conception from a person's dad and 23 from mom). Each chromosome consists of one very long strand of DNA and numerous proteins.

The proteins are needed to manage the long DNA molecule. The longest chromosomes each support thousands of genes. Every time a cell divides, the cell must duplicate the 46 chromosomes. Every cell must distribute one copy of each chromosome to the two new cells. When cells stop dividing, that's the end of them and the organism.

* **The DNA Code.** The DNA of each chromosome is composed of units—"nucleotides" of four different types (A, T, G, C). These nucleotides are linked to each other in linear fashion. The necessary sequence of the four types of nucleotides produces the "code" which first determines the function of each particular gene. Then the sequence identifies the gene's start-point and stop-point along the DNA strand. Finally, the sequence allows specified regulatory functions. The code of the human genome consists of more than a billion nucleotides.

The Mitochondrial DNA (mtDNA). Mitochondria are needed for energy in the cell. The mitochondria are inherited from the mother. When tracing ancient and modern ancestry, geneticists look at female lineages or mtDNA. Your mtDNA is passed from mother to daughter over tens of thousands of years with few changes.

MtDNA mutates slowly during thousands of years of migrations of people across the globe. Men inherit their mtDNA from their mothers, but pass on their Y chromosomes to their sons. Women pass their mtDNA to their daughters. On very rare occasions, a few women may inherit some mtDNA from their fathers, but almost all women inherit their mtDNA from their mothers.

What mtDNA Does Not Do: It is not junk DNA. Often DNA produces more copies than it needs to function. Sometimes this is called junk DNA. MtDNA is necessary for providing energy to the cell. Outside the nucleus, human cells also have some "foreign" DNA located in structures called the mitochondria. This small and separate set of DNA does not participate in the 46 human chromosomes.

The mitochondrial DNA (mtDNA) really is not part of "the genomic DNA." According to the "out of Africa" theory that's widely held in acceptance by most scientists, all the mtDNA in the world today came from a single woman called Mitochondrial Eve who had two daughters who survived to create a line of females that expanded all over the world. Similar histories are noted for the male line using the Y chromosome. According to the book, *Mapping Human History*, by Steve Olson, (page 56) "All non-Africans descend from Africans who left the continent within the past 100,000 years."

According to a number of the latest videos on whether people took the northern or southern route out of Africa, the southern route is most favored. According to the book, *Archaeogenetics*, the flow of people varied between then and now. Today, most scientists theorize that since the north route out of Africa most likely was blocked by an Ice Age that created a dry desert in the Middle East, those leaving Africa headed toward Yemen and then along a southern route to India, Malaysia, and finally Australia.

Only when the climate changed and the Fertile Crescent of the Middle East opened up, did people expand back from India toward where the rivers met, the Middle East, such as what today are Iraq and Iran, and the Levant, reaching the coast, and from there north to what today is Europe. About 21,000 years ago, a new Ice Age began, and people who moved up from the Middle East into Europe found refuge in only a few places such as Southwest France, Northern Spain facing the Mediterranean and the Pyrenees, the Balkans and Ukraine, until the last Ice Age ended about 12,500 years ago. Then populations expanded across Europe from Spain to the Urals.

By that time, the Far East had been populated for a long time, and Central Asia was the newest land to be seen. Then by 9,000 years ago, farmers from the Levant and Anatolia moved into Europe and introduced the idea of farming so that about 80 percent of Europeans today consist of the old Paleolithic hunters and about 20 to 26 percent from the more recent arrivals from the Middle East, the cereal belt grain farmers of the Neolithic era that started about 10,000 years ago in the Levant and Fertile Crescent of the Middle East.

Genealogy, history, folklore, oral history, memoirs writing, diary journaling, demography, anthropology, and archaeology are in the midst of a molecular revolution. Has archaeology become archaeogenetics? Actually, molecular genetics biotechnology is one more *tool* in the hands of the genealogist, historian, archaeologist, folklorist, prosopographer, onomasticist, demographer, videographer, anthropologist, or family historian. And that tool, molecular genetics, is used to untangle distantly ancestral as well as recent family roots.

Now you have computer technology and Web databases to research family ties. You have molecular genetics biotechnology—DNA testing, bioinformatics, and beyond.

From ancestry by DNA to racial percentages by markers and phenomics, experts can customize medicine or therapy to an individual's genes.

You can take a paternity test. Or find out whether you're related to a distant cousin you never met. Or you can study DNA as legal evidence. Your genes are used for matching bone marrow donors to recipients.

The molecular revolution is enhancing research. From community colleges where students earn one or two-year certificates in biotechnology to perform DNA testing and bioinformatics processing on computers to the PhDs who work in research labs and universities, the molecular revolution has now joined science to history. How much do you want to know about your genome?

If you want to get at the roots of your ancestry through studies in population genetics, read the article that will take you back before there were borders or organized religions titled, "Tracing European Founder Lineages in the Near Eastern mtDNA Pool." Martin Richards, Vincent Macaulay, et al. American Journal of Human Genetics, 67: 1251–1276, 2000. See where our mothers really came from. (The term "our mothers" refers to the human race.)

Perhaps you want to find out the percentage of various races in your ancestry. How do know where to begin your journey into the past and future? What if you're a foundling, an orphan, or have no knowledge of your own ethnicity? Can a DNA test at least tell you how many races are in your recent or ancient past? What facts do genetic markers really tell you about ancestry?

If you want to start your ancestry search with DNA testing, first you take the DNA tests along with tests of racial percentages if you desire. Even your DNA has a cultural component to its molecular biology. Then you interpret the results making the complex easy to understand for yourself or your clients. Your DNA testing service can help you find answers. So can many Web sites as well as this book and other books recommended here.

Next in your family history search, you collect letters, diaries, oral history transcriptions, home sources, artifacts, memorabilia, Census research, wills-and-probate records, medical histories, land records, slave ownership records, if it applies to your or your client. Pay particular attention to social histories to fill some gaps left by lack of women's records.

Search through church, synagogue, mosque, pagoda, or temple records, vital records from the US government such as military records, social security information, and government pensions for retired government employees, employment and tax records, if any exist and are available. Check school records from elementary through college, if any, social histories, ethnic histories, and religious school records. Learn to interpret the results of your own DNA test and expand your research ability to trace ancestry.

Go to the family history Web sites, the ships' passenger lists. I highly recommend a book for searching women's ancestry, titled, Discovering Your Female Ancestors, by Sharon DeBartolo Carmack, Betterway Books, Ohio 1998, ISBN # 1-55870-472-8. The book's subtitle emphasizes "Special strategies for uncovering hard-to-find information about your female lineage."

Marriage records often were in different languages representing the former country or languages of the ethnic group. You may need to translate a different alphabet to find a maiden name on a marriage certificate never registered, but obtained from clergy.

Then you review and analyze the records. Study the social history of the times and location of your clients or ancestors. Add migrations to your history, and you have the beginnings of an outline to write a biography of the ancestor.

APPENDIX A
Directory of DNA-Testing Companies

Family Tree DNA (click on link)

1. Family Tree DNA—Genealogy by Genetics, Ltd.
World Headquarters
1919 North Loop West, Suite 110 Houston, Texas 77008, USA
Phone: (713) 868-1438 | Fax: (832) 201-7147

2. Trace Genetics LLC
PO Box 2010
Davis, CA 95617
http://www.tracegenetics.com

3. Title: Paternity DNA Testing By paternitytesters.com.
Description: Paternitytesters.com—Paternity Testing Laboratory offering AABB DNA Paternity Testing, Cheap Prices & Free DNA Banking Worldwide. For Confidential Results in 5 days, call 866-273-8323.

APPENDIX B
Ethnic Genealogy Web Sites

(Usually, there are several genealogy sites on the Web for each ethnic group.)

Acadian/Cajun: & French Canadian: http://www.acadian.org/tidbits.html

Afghanistan Genealogy: http://www.kindredtrails.com/afghanistan.html

African-American: http://www.cyndislist.com/african.htm

African Royalty Genealogy: http://www.uq.net.au/~zzhsoszy/

Albanian Research List: http://feefhs.org/al/alrl.html

Armenian Genealogical Society: http://feefhs.org/am/frg-amgs.html

Asia and the Pacific: http://www.cyndislist.com/asia.htm

Austria-Hungary Empire: http://feefhs.org/ah/indexah.html

Baltic-Russian Information Center: http://feefhs.org/blitz/frgblitz.html

Belarusian—Association of the Belarusian Nobility: http://feefhs.org/by/frg-zbs.html

Bukovina Genealogy: http://feefhs.org/bukovina/bukovina.html

Carpatho-Rusyn Knowledge Base: http://feefhs.org/rusyn/frg-crkb.html

Chinese Genealogy: http://www.chineseroots.com/.

Croatia Genealogy Cross Index: http://feefhs.org/cro/indexcro.html

Czechoslovak Genealogical Society Int'l, Inc.: http://feefhs.org/czs/cgsi/frg-cgsi.html

Eastern Europe: http://www.cyndislist.com/easteuro.htm

Eastern European Genealogical Society, Inc.: http://feefhs.org/ca/frg-eegs.html

Eastern Europe Ethnic, Religious, and National Index with Home Pages includes the FEEFHS Resource Guide that lists organizations associated with FEEFHS from 14 Countries. It also includes Finnish and Armenian genealogy resources: http://feefhs.org/ethnic.html

Ethnic, Religious, and National Index 14 countries: http://feefhs.org/ethnic.html

(Finland) Genealogical Society of Finland: http://www.genealogia.fi/indexe.htm

Finnish Genealogy Group: http://feefhs.org/misc/frgfinmn.html

Galicia Jewish SIG: http://feefhs.org/jsig/frg-gsig.html

German Genealogical Digest: http://feefhs.org/pub/frg-ggdp.html

Greek Genealogy Sources on the Internet: http://www-personal.umich.edu/~cgaunt/greece.html

Genealogy Societies Online List: http://www.daddezio.com/catalog/grkndx04.html

German Research Association: http://feefhs.org/gra/frg-gra.html

Greek Genealogy (Hellenes-Diaspora Greek Genealogy): http://www.geocities.com/SouthBeach/Cove/4537/

Greek Genealogy Home Page: http://www.daddezio.com/grekgen.html

Greek Genealogy Articles: http://www.daddezio.com/catalog/grkndx01.html

India Genealogy: http://genforum.genealogy.com/india/

India Family Histories: http://www.mycinnamontoast.com/perl/results.cgi?region=79&sort=n

India-Anglo-Indian/Europeans in India genealogy: http://members.ozemail.com.au/~clday/

Irish Travellers: http://www.pitt.edu/~alkst3/Traveller.html

Japanese Genealogy: http://www.rootsweb.com/~jpnwgw/

Jewish Genealogy: http://www.jewishgen.org/infofiles/

Latvian Jewish Genealogy Page: http://feefhs.org/jsig/frg-lsig.html

Lebanese Genealogy: http://www.rootsweb.com/~lbnwgw/

Lithuanian American Genealogy Society: http://feefhs.org/frg-lags.html

Melungeon: http://www.geocities.com/Paris/5121/melungeon.htm

Mennonite Heritage Center: http://feefhs.org/men/frg-mhc.html

Middle East Genealogy: http://www.rootsweb.com/~mdeastgw/index.html

Middle East Genealogy by country: http://www.rootsweb.com/~mdeastgw/index.html#country

Native American: http://www.cyndislist.com/native.htm

Polish Genealogical Society of America: http://feefhs.org/pol/frg-pgsa.html

Quebec and Francophone: http://www.francogene.com/quebec/amerin.html

Romanian American Heritage Center: http://feefhs.org/ro/frg-rahc.html

Slovak World: http://feefhs.org/slovak/frg-sw.html

Slavs, South: Cultural Society: http://feefhs.org/frg-csss.html

Syrian and Lebanese Genealogy: http://www.genealogytoday.com/family/syrian/

Syria Genealogy: http://www.rootsweb.com/~syrwgw/

Tibetan Genealogy: http://www.distantcousin.com/Links/Ethnic/China/Tibetan.html

Turkish Genealogy Discussion Group: http://www.turkey.com/forums/forumdisplay.php3?forumid=18

Ukrainian Genealogical and Historical Society of Canada: http://feefhs.org/ca/frgughsc.html

Unique Peoples: http://www.cyndislist.com/peoples.htm Note: The Unique People's list includes: Black Dutch, Doukhobors, Gypsy, Romani, Romany & Travellers, Melungeons, Metis, Miscellaneous, and Wends/Sorbs

Genealogy, (General):

Ancestry.com: http://www.ancestry.com/main.htm?lfl=m

Cyndi's List of Genealogy on the Internet: http://www.cyndislist.com/

Cyndi's List is a categorized & cross-referenced index to genealogical resources on the Internet with thousands of links.

DistantCousin.com (Uniting Cousins Worldwide) http://distantcousin.com/Links/surname.html

Ellis Island Online: http://www.ellisisland.org/

Family History Library: http://www.familysearch.org/Eng/default.asp

http://www.familysearch.org/Eng/Search/frameset_search.asp

(The Church of Jesus Christ of Latter Day Saints) International Genealogical Index

Female Ancestors: http://www.cyndislist.com/female.htm

Genealogist's Index to the Web: http://www.genealogytoday.com/GIWWW/?

Genealogy Web: http://www.genealogyweb.com/

Genealogy Authors and Speakers: http://feefhs.org/frg/frg-a&l.html

Genealogy Today: http://www.genealogytoday.com/

My Genealogy.com: http://www.genealogy.com/cgi-bin/my_main.cgi

Scriver, Dr. Charles: The Canadian Medical Hall of Fame http://www.virtualmuseum.ca/Exhibitions/Medicentre/en/scri_print.htm

Surname Sites: http://www.cyndislist.com/surn-gen.htm

National Genealogical Society: http://www.ngsgenealogy.org/index.htm

United States List of Local by State Genealogical Societies: http://www.daddezio.com/society/hill/index.html

United States Vital Records List: http://www.daddezio.com/records/room/index.html or

http://www.cyndislist.com/usvital.htm

APPENDIX C
Bibliographies

Bibliography 1:
Genealogy.

A Bintel Brief: Sixty Years of Letters From the Lower East Side to the Jewish Daily Forward. Metzker, Isaac, ed Doubleday and Co. 1971. Garden City, NY

Climbing Your Family Tree: Online and Offline Genealogy for Kids IRA Wolfman, Tim Robinson (Illustrator), Alex Haley (Introduction)/Paperback/ Workman Publishing Company, Inc./October 2001

Complete Beginner's Guide to Genealogy, the Internet, and Your Genealogy Computer Program Karen Clifford/Paperback/Genealogical Publishing Company, Incorporated/February 2001

Complete Idiot's Guide(R) to Online Geneology Rhonda McClure/Paperback/Pearson Education/January 2002

Creating Your Family Heritage Scrapbook : From Ancestors to Grandchildren, Your Complete Resource & Idea Book for Creating a Treasured Heirloom. Nerius, Maria Given, Bill Gardner ISBN: 0761530142 Published by Prima Publishing, Aug 2001

Cyndi's List: A Comprehensive List of 70,000 Genealogy Sites on the Internet (Vol. 1 & 2) Cyndi Howells/Paperback/Genealogical Publishing Company, Incorporated/June 2001.

Discovering Your Female Ancestors: Special strategies for uncovering your hard-to-find information about your female lineage. Carmack, Sharon DeBartolo. Conference Lecture on Audio Tape: Carmack, Sharon DeBartolo.

Folklife and Fieldwork: A Layman's Introduction to Field Techniques. Bartis, Peter. Washington, DC: Library of Congress, 1990.

Genealogy Online for Dummies Matthew L. Helm, April Leigh Helm, April Leigh Helm, Matthew L. Helm/Paperback/Wiley, John & Sons, Incorporated/ February 2001

Genealogy Online Elizabeth Powell Crowe/Paperback/McGraw-Hill Companies, November 2001

Genetic Diversity Among Jews: Diseases and Markers at the DNA Level. Bonné-Tamir, B. and Adam, A. Oxford University Press. 1992.

History From Below: How to Uncover and Tell the Story of Your Community, Association, or Union. Brecher, Jeremy. New Haven: Advocate Press/ Commonwork Pamphlets, 1988.

Iranian Genealogy Bibliography:

Iranian: Persian Watch Center: Iranian-American AntiDiscrimination Council

http://www.antidiscrimination.org/

The Iranian: http://www.iranian.com/Features/2002/December/LA2/index.html

Iran: Payvand's Iran News: http://www.payvand.com/news/00/aug/1054.html

Also see: Iranian American Jewish Federation and also the Council of Iranian American Jewish Organizations: P.O.BOX 3074, Beverly Hills, CA. 90212. See news article at Payvand's Iran News at: http://www.payvand.com/news/00/feb/1014.html

Excellent Genealogy and Related Books on Iran: Also see: http://payvand.com/books/

Another Sea, Another Shore: Stories of Iranian Migration

by Shouleh Vatanabadi, et all (2003)

Funny in Farsi: A Memoir of Growing Up Iranian in America

by Firoozeh Dumas (2003)

Wedding Song: Memoirs of an Iranian Jewish Woman

by Farideh Goldin (2003)

Exiled Memories: Stories of the Iranian Diaspora

by Zohreh Sullivan (2001)

Journey from the Land of No : A Girlhood Caught in Revolutionary Iran

by Roya Hakakian (2004)

Inside Iran: Women's Lives

by Jane Mary Howard (2002)

The National Iranian American Council: www.niacouncil.org

Genealogy and Oral History

My Family Tree Workbook: Genealogy for Beginners Rosemary A. Chorzempa/Paperback/Dover Publications, Incorporated/

National Genealogical Society Quarterly 79, no. 3 (September 19991): 183-93

"Numbering Your Genealogy: Sound and Simple Systems." Curran, Joan Ferris.

Oral History and the Law. Neuenschwander, John. Pamphlet Series #1. Albuquerque: Oral History Association, 1993.

Oral History for the Local Historical Society. Baum, Willa K. Nashville: American Association for State and Local History, 1987.

Scrapbook Storytelling: Save Family Stories & Memories with Photos, Journaling & Your Own Creativity Slan, Joanna Campbell, Published by EFG, Incorporated, ISBN: 0963022288 May 1999

"The Silent Woman: Bringing a Name to Life." NE-59. Boston, MA: New England Historic Genealogical Society Sesquicentennial Conference, 1995.

The Source: A Guidebook of American Genealogy Alice Eichholz, Loretto Dennis Szucs (Editor), Sandra Hargreaves Luebking (Editor), Sandra Hargreaves Luebking (Editor)/Hardcover/MyFamily.com, Incorporated/February 1997

To Our Children's Children: Journal of Family Members, Bob Greene, D. G. Fulford 240pp. ISBN: 038549064X Publisher: Doubleday & Company, Incorporated: October 1998.

Transcribing and Editing Oral History. Nashville: American Association for State and Local History, 1991.

Using Oral History in Community History Projects. Buckendorf, Madeline, and Laurie Mercier. Pamphlet Series #4. Albuqueque: Oral History Association, 1992.

Unpuzzling Your Past: The Best-Selling Basic Guide to Genealogy (Expanded, Updated and Revised) Emily Anne Croom, Emily Croom/Paperback/F & W Publications, Incorporated/August 2001

Writing a Woman's Life. Heilbrun, Carolyn G. New York: W.W. Norton, 1988

Your Guide to the Family History Library: How to Access the World's Largest Genealogy Resource Paula Stuart Warren, James W. Warren/Paperback/F & W Publications, Incorporated/August 2001

Your Story: A Guided Interview Through Your Personal and Family History, 2nd ed., 64pp.ISBN: 0966604105 Publisher: Stack Resources, LLC

Bibliography 2:
DNA Testing and Genetics.

A Biologist's Guide to Analysis of DNA Microarray Data Steen Knudsen/Hardcover/Wiley, John & Sons, Incorporated/April 2002

Advances and Opportunities in DNA Testing and Gene Probes Business Communications Company Incorporated (Editor)/Hardcover/Business Communications/September 1996

African Exodus, The Origins of Modern Humanity Stringer, Christopher and Robin McKie. Henry Holt And Company 1997

An A to Z of DNA Science: What Scientists Mean when They Talk about Genes and Genomes Jeffre L. Witherly, Galen P. Perry, Darryl L. Leja/Paperback/Cold Spring Harbor Laboratory Press/September 2002

An Introduction to Forensic DNA Analysis Norah Rudin, Keith Inman/Hardcover/CRC Press/December 2001

Archaeogenetics: DNA and the population prehistory of Europe, Ed. Colin Renfrew & Katie Boyle. McDonald Institute Monographs. Cambridge, UK, Distributed by Oxbow Books UK. In USA: The David Brown Book Company, Oakville, CT. 2000

Cartoon Guide to Genetics Gonick, Larry, With Mark Wheelis: Paperback/HarperInformation/July 1991

DNA Detectives, The—Working Against Time, novel, Hart, Anne. Mystery and Suspense Press, iuniverse.com paperback 248 pages at http://www.iuniverse.com/ or 1-877-823-9235.

DNA for Family Historians (ISBN 0-9539171-0-X). Savin, Alan of Maidenhead, England, is author of the 32-page book. See the Web site: http://www.savin.org/dna/dna-book.html

DNA Microarrays and Gene Expression Pierre Baldi, G. Wesley Hatfield, G. Wesley Hatfield/Hardcover/Cambridge University Press/August 2002

Microarrays for an Integrative Genomics Isaac S. Kohane, Alvin Kho, Atul J. Butte/Hardcover/MIT Press/August 2002

Does It Run in the Family?: A Consumers Guide to DNA Testing for Genetic Disorders Doris Teichler Zallen, Doris Teichler-Zallen, Doris Teichler Zallen/Hardcover/Rutgers University Press/May 1997

Double Helix, The: A Personal Account of the Discovery of the Structure of DNA James D. Watson/Paperback/Simon & Schuster Trade Paperbacks/June 2001

Genes, Peoples, and Languages Luigi Luca Cavalli-Sforza, Mark Seielstad (Translator).

Genetic Witness: Forensic Uses of DNA Tests DIANE Publishing Company (Editor)/Paperback/DIANE Publishing Company/April 1993

History and Geography of Human Genes, The [ABRIDGED] L. Luca Cavalli-Sforza, Paolo Menozzi (Contributor), Alberto Piazza (Contributor).

How to DNA Test Our Family Relationships Terry Carmichael, Alexander Ivanof Kuklin, Ed Grotjan/Paperback/Acen Press/November 2000

Introduction to Genetic Analysis Anthony J. Griffiths, Suzuki, Lewontin, Gelbart, David T. Suzuki, Richard C. Lewontin, Willi Gelbart, Miller, Jeffrey H. Miller/Hardcover/W. H. Freeman Company/February 2000

Jefferson's Children: The Story of One American Family Shannon Lanier, Jane Feldman, Lucian K. Truscott (Introduction)/Hardcover/Random House Books for Young Readers/September 2000

Medical Genetics Lynn B. B. Jorde, Michael J. Bamshad, Raymond L. White, Michael J. Bamshad, John C. Carey, John C. Carey, Raymond L. White, John C. Carey/Paperback/Mosby-Year Book, Inc./July 2000

Molecule Hunt, The: Archaeology and the Search for Ancient DNA Martin Jones/Hardcover/Arcade/April 2002

More Chemistry and Crime: From Marsh Arsenic Test to DNA Profile Richard Saferstein, Samuel M. Gerber (Editor)/Hardcover/American Chemical Society/August 1998

1996, Quest For Perfection—The Drive to Breed Better Human Beings, Maranto, Gina. Scribner, 1996

Our Molecular Future: How Nanotechnology, Robotics, Genetics, and Artificial Intelligence Will Transform Our World Mulhall, Douglas./Hardcover/Prometheus Books/March 2002

Paternity—Disputed, Typing, PCR and DNA Tests: Index of New Information Dexter Z. Franklin/Hardcover/Abbe Pub Assn of Washington Dc/January 1998

Paternity in Primates: Tests and Theories R. D. Martin (Editor), A. F. Dickson (Editor), E. J. Wickings (Editor)/Hardcover/Karger, S Publishers/December 1991

Queen Victoria's Gene: Hemophilia and the Royal Family (Pbk) D. M. Potts, W. T. Potts/Paperback/Sutton Publishing, Limited/June 1999

Redesigning Humans: Our Inevitable Genetic Future Stock, Gregory./Hardcover/Houghton Mifflin Company/April 2002

Rosalind Franklin: The Dark Lady of DNA, Brenda Maddox/Hardcover/HarperCollins Publishers/October 2002

Schaum's Outline Of Genetics Susan Elrod, William D. Stansfield/Paperback/McGraw-Hill Companies, The/December 2001

Seven Daughters of Eve, The: The Science That Reveals Our Genetic Ancestry. Sykes, Bryan. **ISBN:** 0393323145 **Publisher:** Norton, W. W. & Company, Inc. May 2002

Stedman's OB-GYN & Genetics Words Ellen Atwood (Editor), Stedmans/Paperback/Lippincott Williams & Wilkins/December 2000

APPENDIX D

Permissions

Dear Anne,
You have permission to use the primer text and the photo of the DNA molecule for your book on DNA testing for genealogists. Please prominently credit the U.S. Department of Energy Human Genome Program as the source for both and also include our website for more information on the Human Genome Project and its applications: http://www.ornl.gov/hgmis. Yes, you can use the *Dictionary of Genetic Terms* at the end of the online version of the Primer. Please provide source citations when you use each part of the document. We would appreciate having a copy of your book when it is completed.
Sincerely,

Denise Casey
Denise K. Casey
Science Writer/Editor
Human Genome News
Human Genome Management Information System
Oak Ridge National Laboratory
1060 Commerce Park, MS 6480
Oak Ridge, TN 37830
865/574-0597; Fax: 865/574-9888; Email: caseydk@ornl.gov
HGMIS World Wide Web URL: http://www.ornl.gov/hgmis
Sponsor: U.S. Department of Energy

Harry Ostrer, M.D.
Professor of Pediatrics, Pathology, and Medicine
Director, Human Genetics Program
New York University School of Medicine
550 First Avenue, MSB 136

New York, NY 10016
tel 212 263-7596
fax 212 263-3477
email harry.ostrer@med.nyu.edu

APPENDIX E

List of Published Paperback Books Written by Anne Hart. Click on underlined link to reach publisher's Web site and read each book's description.

1. <u>Predictive Medicine for Rookies: Consumer Watchdogs, Reviews, & Genetics Testing Firms Online</u>

ISBN: 0-595-35146-8

2. <u>Popular Health & Medical Writing for Magazines: How to Turn Current Research & Trends into Salable Feature Articles</u>

ISBN: 0-595-35178-6

3. <u>Writing 45-Minute One-Act Plays, Skits, Monologues, & Animation Scripts for Drama Workshops</u>: Adapting Current Events, Social Issues, Life Stories, News & Histories

ISBN: 0-595-34597-2

4. <u>Cutting Expenses and Getting More for Less</u>: 41+ Ways to Earn an Income from Opportune Living

ISBN: 0-595-34772-X

5. <u>How to Interpret Family History and Ancestry DNA Test Results for Beginners</u>: The Geography and History of Your Relatives

ISBN: 0-595-31684-0

6. <u>Cover Letters, Follow-Ups, and Book Proposals</u>: Samples with Templates

ISBN: 0-595-31663-8

7. <u>Writer's Guide to Book Proposals</u>: Templates, Query Letters, & Free Media Publicity

ISBN: 0-595-31673-5

8. <u>Search Your Middle Eastern and European Genealogy:</u> In the Former Ottoman Empire's Records and Online

ISBN: 0-595-31811-8

9. **Ancient and Medieval Teenage Diaries:** Writing, Righting, and Riding for Righteousness

ISBN: 0-595-32009-0

10. **Is Radical Liberalism or Extreme Conservatism a Character Disorder, Mental Disease, or Publicity Campaign?**—A Novel of Intrigue—

ISBN: 0-595-31751-0

11. **How to Write Plays, Monologues, and Skits from Life Stories, Social Issues, and Current Events**—for all Ages.

ISBN: 0-595-31866-5

12. **How to Make Money Organizing Information**

ISBN: 0-595-23695-2

13. **How To Stop Elderly Abuse:** A Prevention Guidebook

ISBN: 0-595-23550-6

14. **How to Make Money Teaching Online With Your Camcorder and PC:** 25 Practical and Creative How-To Start-Ups To Teach Online

ISBN: 0-595-22123-8

15. **A Private Eye Called Mama Africa:** What's an Egyptian Jewish Female Psycho-Sleuth Doing Fighting Hate Crimes in California?

ISBN: 0-595-18940-7

16. **The Freelance Writer's E-Publishing Guidebook:** 25+ E-Publishing Home-based Online Writing Businesses to Start for Freelancers

ISBN: 0-595-18952-0

17. **The Courage to Be Jewish and the Wife of an Arab Sheik:** What's a Jewish Girl from Brooklyn Doing Living as a Bedouin?

ISBN: 0-595-18790-0

18. **The Year My Whole Country Turned Jewish:** A Time-Travel Adventure Novel in Medieval Khazaria

ISBN: 0-75967-251-2

19. The Day My Whole Country Turned Jewish: The Silk Road Kids

ISBN: 0-7596-6380-7

20. Four Astronauts and a Kitten: A Mother and Daughter Astronaut Team, the Teen Twin Sons, and Patches, the Kitten: The Intergalactic Friendship Club

ISBN: 0-595-19202-5

21. The Writer's Bible: Digital and Print Media: Skills, Promotion, and Marketing for Novelists, Playwrights, and Script Writers. Writing Entertainment Content for the New and Print Media.

ISBN: 0-595-19305-6

22. New Afghanistan's TV Anchorwoman: A novel of mystery set in the New Afghanistan

ISBN: 0-595-21557-2

23. Tools for Mystery Writers: Writing Suspense Using Hidden Personality Traits

ISBN: 0-595-21747-8

24. The Khazars Will Rise Again!: Mystery Tales of the Khazars

ISBN: 0-595-21830-X

25. Murder in the Women's Studies Department: A Professor Sleuth Novel of Mystery

ISBN: 0-595-21859-8

26. Make Money With Your Camcorder and PC: 25+ Businesses: Make Money With Your Camcorder and Your Personal Computer by Linking Them.

ISBN: 0-595-21864-4

27. Writing What People Buy: 101+ Projects That Get Results

ISBN: 0-595-21936-5

28. Anne Joan Levine, Private Eye: Internal adventure through first-person mystery writer's diary novels

ISBN: 0-595-21860-1

29. Verbal Intercourse: A Darkly Humorous Novel of Interpersonal Couples and Family Communication

ISBN: 0-595-21946-2

30. The Date Who Unleashed Hell: If You Love Me, Why Do You Humiliate Me? "The Date" Mystery Fiction

ISBN: 0-595-21982-9

31. Cleopatra's Daughter: Global Intercourse

ISBN: 0-595-22021-5

32. Cyber Snoop Nation: The Adventures Of Littanie Webster, Sixteen-Year-Old Genius Private Eye On Internet Radio

ISBN: 0-595-22033-9

33. Counseling Anarchists: We All Marry Our Mirrors—Someone Who Reflects How We Feel About Ourselves. Folding Inside Ourselves: A Novel of Mystery

ISBN: 0-595-22054-1

34. Sacramento Latina: When the One Universal We Have In Common Divides Us

ISBN: 0-595-22061-4

35. Astronauts and Their Cats: At night, the space station is cat-shadow dark

ISBN: 0-595-22330-3

36. How Two Yellow Labs Saved the Space Program: When Smart Dogs Shape Shift in Space

ISBN: 0-595-23181-0

37. The DNA Detectives: Working Against Time

ISBN: 0-595-25339-3

38. How to Interpret Your DNA Test Results For Family History & Ancestry: Scientists Speak Out on Genealogy Joining Genetics

ISBN: 0-595-26334-8

39. Roman Justice: SPQR: Too Roman To Handle

ISBN: 0-595-27282-7

40. How to Make Money Selling Facts: to Non-Traditional Markets

ISBN: 0-595-27842-6

41. Tracing Your Jewish DNA For Family History & Ancestry: Merging a Mosaic of Communities

ISBN: 0-595-28127-3

42. The Beginner's Guide to Interpreting Ethnic DNA Origins for Family History: How Ashkenazi, Sephardi, Mizrahi & Europeans Are Related to Everyone Else

ISBN: 0-595-28306-3

43. Nutritional Genomics—A Consumer's Guide to How Your Genes and Ancestry Respond to Food: Tailoring What You Eat to Your DNA

ISBN: 0-595-29067-1

44. How to Safely Tailor Your Food, Medicines, & Cosmetics to Your Genes: A Consumer's Guide to Genetic Testing Kits from Ancestry to Nourishment

ISBN: 0-595-29403-0

45. One Day Some Schlemiel Will Marry Me, Pay the Bills, and Hug Me.: Parents & Children Kvetch on Arab & Jewish Intermarriage

ISBN: 0-595-29826-5

46. Find Your Personal Adam And Eve: Make DNA-Driven Genealogy Time Capsules

ISBN: 0-595-30633-0

47. Creative Genealogy Projects: Writing Salable Life Stories

ISBN: 0-595-31305-1

48. Power Dating Games: What's Important to Know About the Person You'll Marry

ISBN: 0-595-19186-X

49. Dramatizing 17th Century Family History of Deacon Stephen Hart & Other Early New England Settlers: How to Write Historical Plays, Skits, Biographies, Novels, Stories, or Monologues from Genealogy Records, Social Issues, & Current Events for All Ages

ISBN: 0-595-34345-7

50. Problem-Solving and Cat Tales for the Holidays: Historical—Time-Travel—Adventure

ISBN: 0-595-32692-7

51. 801 Action Verbs for Communicators: Position Yourself First with Action Verbs for Journalists, Speakers, Educators, Students, Resume-Writers, Editors & Travelers

ISBN: 0-595-31911-4

52. Writing 7-Minute Inspirational Life Experience Vignettes: Create and Link 1,500-Word True Stories

ISBN: 0-595-32237-9

53. Large Print Crossword Puzzles for Memory Enhancement : Neuron-Growing Stimulation for the Age-Wise Brain

ISBN: 0-595-35663-X

54. Tracing Your Baltic, Scandinavian, Eastern European, & Middle Eastern Ancestry Online: Finnish, Swedish, Norwegian, Danish, Icelandic, Estonian, Latvian, Polish, Lithuanian, Greek, Macedonian, Bulgarian, Armenian, Hungarian, Eastern European & Middle Eastern Genealogy (All Faiths)

ISBN: 0-595-35773-3

55. 32 Podcasting & Other Businesses to Open Showing People How to Cut Expenses: Get Higher Quality for Less Money

ISBN: 0-595-36083-1

56. Middle Eastern Honor Killings in the USA: (A Thriller)

ISBN: 0-595-36066-1

57. Infant Gender Selection & Personalized Medicine: Consumer's Guide

ISBN: 0-595-36539-6

58. Writing, Financing, & Producing Documentaries: Creating Salable Reality Video

ISBN: 0-595-36633-3

59. How to Turn Poems, Lyrics, & Folklore into Salable Children's Books: Using Humor or Proverbs

ISBN: 0-595-36735-6

60. Job Coach-Life Coach-Executive Coach-Letter & Resume-Writing Service: Step-by-Step Business Startup Manual

ISBN: 0-595-37100-0

61. Where to Find Your Arab-American or Jewish Genealogy Records ♦ Also: Mediterranean, Assyrian, Iranian, Greek & Armenian

ISBN: 0-595-37325-9

To order call 1-800-AUTHORS

About the Author

Popular science journalist, **Anne Hart**, is the author of 61+ books. She writes feature articles on genealogy, ethnology, and DNA for magazines, holds a graduate degree, and is a member of Mensa, The American Medical Writers Association, and the American Society of Journalists and Authors.

Index

A

Allele 71, 72, 145, 198, 199, 201, 202
Ancestry.com 27, 110, 139, 212
AncestryByDNA 144, 145, 152
Appendix B
   Ethnic Genealogy Web Sites 209
Appendix D
   Permissions 223
Archaeogenetics 99, 122, 203, 204, 219
Aristocracy 65
Armenia 1, 10, 16, 17, 49, 51, 60, 80, 88, 90, 91, 125
Ashkenazi 5, 40, 41, 43, 45, 46, 47, 48, 49, 51, 52, 53, 54, 55, 57, 58, 59, 60, 62, 63, 64, 65, 66, 67, 68, 69, 70, 71, 72, 73, 74, 75, 77, 78, 79, 80, 82, 83, 85, 86, 88, 94, 105, 116, 117, 134, 191, 228
Ashkenazic Rabbinic Families 69

B

Babylonia 63
Barbujani, Guido 122
Bialystock 25, 46, 50, 63, 64, 81, 88
BioGeographical Ancestry 152
Bioinformatics 121, 204
Bukhara 107, 117

C

Cambridge Reference Sequence (CRS) 45, 56, 86, 94, 152
Cells 48, 120, 143, 157, 158, 202, 203
City Directories 132, 133, 138, 144, 153, 178, 191
Cohanim 62, 70, 127, 138, 140

Cohen 48, 49, 52, 56, 57, 62, 64, 76, 77, 79, 82, 97, 98, 125
Cohen Modal Haplotype 49, 52, 56, 57, 62, 76, 77, 79, 82, 97, 98, 125
Communities 3, 7, 25, 33, 36, 38, 39, 41, 42, 45, 46, 47, 48, 49, 50, 51, 52, 53, 54, 55, 57, 58, 59, 60, 61, 62, 63, 65, 66, 67, 68, 69, 70, 71, 73, 74, 75, 76, 77, 78, 80, 82, 83, 84, 85, 95, 96, 106, 107, 116, 124, 125, 126, 135, 139, 161, 228
Court Jew 63, 64, 65

D

Demography 2, 27, 110, 120, 135, 204
Dictionary of Genetic Terms 223
Diploid 157
DNA 26, 27, 28, 29, 38, 39, 40, 41, 44, 46, 50, 51, 52, 53, 54, 55, 56, 59, 60, 63, 64, 65, 66, 71, 72, 73, 74, 75, 78, 79, 82, 84, 85, 86, 87, 93, 94, 95, 96, 98, 99, 100, 101, 102, 103, 104, 105, 106, 108, 109, 110, 111, 117, 118, 119, 120, 121, 122, 123, 124, 125, 127, 128, 130, 132, 133, 134, 135, 136, 137, 138, 139, 140, 141, 143, 144, 145, 146, 147, 151, 152, 153, 155, 156, 157, 158, 159, 164, 167, 178, 179, 182, 184, 189, 190, 192, 193, 194, 195, 196, 197, 200, 201, 202, 203, 204, 205, 207, 216, 218, 219, 220, 221, 223, 225, 228, 229, 231
DNA for Family Historians 137, 219
DNA testing 73, 99, 100, 103, 104, 105, 106, 108, 118, 119, 121, 122, 127, 128, 130, 132, 133, 134, 135, 136, 137, 138, 139, 143, 144, 145, 151, 152, 155, 156, 167, 178, 179, 182, 189, 192, 193, 194, 196, 197, 204, 205, 207, 218, 219, 223

E

Ethnic Genealogy Web Sites 209

F

Family historians 15, 17, 48, 99, 117, 121, 133, 136, 137, 139, 219

Family history 1, 2, 3, 8, 16, 22, 25, 30, 38, 65, 73, 95, 96, 99, 100, 101, 103, 104, 105, 108, 109, 112, 117, 119, 121, 122, 123, 128, 132, 133, 134, 135, 136, 137, 141, 142, 143, 158, 164, 179, 180, 184, 186, 188, 192, 193, 196, 197, 205, 212, 218, 225, 228, 229

FamilyTreeDNA 194, 195

Founders 52, 53, 54, 55, 58, 70, 71, 93, 94

G

Genealogy 1, 2, 8, 11, 13, 15, 16, 17, 18, 19, 20, 22, 23, 24, 25, 26, 28, 30, 31, 33, 34, 36, 38, 40, 47, 65, 73, 81, 84, 85, 94, 98, 99, 101, 102, 103, 104, 111, 113, 116, 117, 118, 119, 120, 121, 122, 129, 133, 134, 135, 136, 137, 138, 139, 140, 141, 143, 149, 151, 153, 155, 169, 178, 179, 182, 186, 187, 189, 190, 191, 192, 193, 194, 196, 197, 198, 204, 207, 209, 210, 211, 212, 213, 215, 216, 217, 218, 225, 228, 229, 230, 231

Genes 1, 26, 27, 39, 40, 41, 42, 45, 47, 48, 49, 50, 51, 53, 57, 58, 62, 67, 71, 72, 75, 82, 83, 84, 85, 86, 88, 95, 97, 98, 99, 100, 104, 106, 107, 109, 110, 115, 119, 120, 122, 123, 132, 139, 140, 141, 144, 145, 146, 157, 158, 202, 204, 219, 220, 228, 229

Genetics Program New York University School of Medicine 134

Genome 42, 43, 47, 60, 73, 79, 82, 115, 121, 122, 123, 132, 133, 139, 145, 152, 157, 158, 201, 202, 203, 204, 223

Genomics 144, 152, 153, 219, 228

Goldstein 41, 42, 45, 55, 96, 97

Greece 1, 5, 14, 22, 23, 47, 50, 51, 64, 78, 91, 107, 126, 150, 210

H

Hammer 62, 77, 78, 94, 96, 97

Haplogroup 45, 48, 51, 52, 53, 54, 55, 60, 61, 70, 77, 82, 86, 87, 88, 89, 90, 91, 93, 99, 106, 116, 117, 140, 141, 146, 149, 150, 151, 199, 200, 201, 202

Haplotype 49, 52, 53, 55, 56, 57, 62, 70, 76, 77, 79, 82, 94, 97, 98, 125, 127, 192, 196, 199, 200, 202

High resolution 69, 92, 146, 151

Human Genome Management Information System 223

Human Genome News 223

Human Genome Program 223

Hungary 49, 66, 107, 125, 209

HVS-1 56, 87, 90, 92, 93, 140, 145, 146, 152

HVS-2 92, 93, 145, 146, 151, 152

I

Iran 1, 8, 9, 18, 19, 54, 60, 125, 204, 216, 217

Iraq 1, 6, 8, 9, 50, 51, 58, 59, 73, 90, 92, 107, 150, 204

Italy 45, 46, 47, 48, 50, 51, 61, 66, 68, 78, 88, 89, 91, 92, 96, 99, 100, 105, 107, 122, 125, 141, 146

L

Levine 39, 64, 80, 81, 84, 227

Levite 48, 58, 62, 70, 75, 79, 80, 82, 83, 84, 127

Lineages 41, 48, 54, 57, 58, 60, 75, 84, 85, 105, 106, 108, 116, 120, 132, 133, 134, 138, 139, 143, 144, 150, 157, 199, 200, 202, 203, 205

Low resolution 145, 146, 153

M

MadSci.ORG 157

Maternal 48, 53, 55, 62, 74, 93, 94, 106, 116, 118, 119, 120, 132, 138, 144, 152, 195

Matrilineal 39, 44, 48, 54, 56, 57, 71, 75, 85, 87, 96, 116, 122, 133, 134, 138, 146, 150, 199, 200

Medical history 121

Medieval 16, 44, 46, 48, 49, 50, 51, 52, 53, 55, 57, 62, 63, 64, 65, 67, 68, 70, 71, 73, 74, 78, 80, 81, 83, 84, 85, 91, 95, 101, 107, 125, 126, 226

Mitochondria 143, 157, 158, 159, 200, 203

Mizrahi 1, 2, 3, 5, 11, 38, 63, 64, 191, 228

Molecular genetics 47, 56, 73, 117, 120, 122, 135, 204

Morocco 59, 73

mtDNA 38, 39, 45, 46, 48, 49, 50, 52, 53, 54, 55, 56, 57, 58, 59, 60, 61, 62, 64, 66, 67, 70, 71, 72, 74, 75, 78, 82, 84, 85, 86, 87, 88, 89, 90, 91, 92, 93, 94, 96, 98, 99, 106, 108, 116, 117, 119, 120, 132, 133, 136, 138, 139, 140, 141, 143, 144, 145, 146, 147, 149, 150, 151, 152, 153, 155, 156, 157, 158, 199, 200, 201, 202, 203, 205

Mutations 27, 39, 45, 54, 72, 73, 78, 79, 86, 87, 88, 90, 92, 93, 94, 99, 109, 116, 117, 119, 122, 140, 146, 151, 152, 196, 200, 201, 202

N

National Center for Health Statistics in Hyattsville 153

Nature Reviews/Genetics 134

Neolithic 40, 51, 90, 150, 204

Network 175

O

Oak Ridge National Laboratory 223

Olson, Steve 103, 200, 203

Onomastics 120

Oral histories 121, 130, 134, 135, 166, 167, 169, 181, 186

Oxford Ancestors 103, 104, 141, 146, 147, 148, 151, 152

P

Paternal 28, 48, 55, 69, 70, 71, 76, 105, 106, 111, 118, 120, 125, 128, 132, 195

Patrilineal 39, 41, 44, 52, 70, 122, 127, 133, 134

Phenomics 115, 121, 143, 152, 188, 193, 204

Poland 1, 4, 25, 26, 28, 29, 30, 31, 32, 33, 36, 39, 45, 46, 48, 49, 50, 52, 57, 58, 63, 64, 66, 67, 68, 69, 70, 71, 74, 80, 81, 82, 83, 84, 88, 89, 91, 107, 111, 112, 113, 114

Polin 49

Population genetics 98, 105, 108, 115, 123, 205

Prosopography 26, 27, 109, 110, 120

R

Rabbinic Genealogy Special Interest Group 65

Renfrew, Colin 219

Richards, Martin 41, 42, 54, 55, 108, 147, 205

Roman Jews 94, 107

Rosenstein, Dr. Neil 63, 65

Russia 33, 36, 44, 48, 49, 63, 66, 67, 80

S

Savin, Alan 137

Science 43, 48, 55, 56, 60, 73, 75, 96, 98, 99, 104, 120, 121, 130, 134, 136, 137, 138, 155, 157, 158, 168, 204, 219, 221, 223, 231

Scriver, Dr. Charles 26, 28, 109, 111

Sephardim 1, 3, 10, 11, 19, 38, 39, 65, 66, 77, 105, 106

Sequences 53, 57, 58, 60, 61, 67, 78, 79, 86, 87, 88, 89, 90, 91, 92, 93, 94, 99, 116, 117, 119, 122, 123, 132, 134, 135, 136, 141, 145, 146, 147, 152, 153, 199, 200, 202

Slavs 20, 46, 51, 57, 68, 69, 70, 80, 82, 83, 84, 211

Sorb 51, 57, 62, 68, 69, 70, 81, 82, 83, 84, 107
Sorbian 68, 70, 75, 83, 84
Sykes, Bryan 103, 104, 146, 149, 151

T
Tangled Roots? Genetics Meets Genealogy 138
Torroni 105, 141
Transitions 94, 122, 152

U
U.S. Department of Energy 223

Underhill, Peter 138
US Census 133, 153, 191

V
Villems, Richard 139, 140

Y
Y-Chromosome 38, 39, 46, 50, 55, 62, 67, 71, 75, 76, 82, 85, 94, 96, 98, 105, 117, 119, 120, 123, 125, 127, 132, 144, 145, 155, 156, 201, 202
Yiddish 1, 26, 46, 47, 49, 50, 51, 53, 68, 69, 70, 75, 79, 80, 81, 82, 83, 88, 96

978-0-595-37325-
0-595-37325-9